MIND FREE

The breakthrough mindful self-hypnosis method

MARK STEPHENS

murdoch books

Sydney | London

Published in 2022 by Murdoch Books, an imprint of Allen & Unwin
Copyright © Mark Stephens 2022

Murdoch Books Australia
83 Alexander Street, Crows Nest NSW 2065
Phone: +61 (0)2 8425 0100
murdochbooks.com.au
info@murdochbooks.com.au

Murdoch Books UK
Ormond House, 26–27 Boswell Street, London WC1N 3JZ
Phone: +44 (0) 20 8785 5995
murdochbooks.co.uk
info@murdochbooks.co.uk

A catalogue record for this book is available from the National Library of Australia

A catalogue record for this book is available from the National Library of Australia
A catalogue record for this book is available from the British Library

ISBN 9 781 92261 611 1

Cover and text design by Northwood Green
Illustrations by Mark Stephens
Typeset by Midland Typesetters
Printed and bound in Australia by McPhersons Printing Group

DISCLAIMER: The content presented in this book is meant for informational and inspirational purposes only. The purchaser of this book understands that the information contained within this book is general in nature and not intended to replace specific medical advice or to be relied upon to treat, cure or prevent any disease, illness or medical condition. The author and publisher claim no responsibility to any person or entity for any liability, loss or damage caused or alleged to be caused directly or indirectly as a result of the use, application or interpretation of the material in this book.

We acknowledge that we meet and work on the traditional lands of the Cammeraygal people of the Eora Nation and pay our respects to their elders past, present and future.

10 9 8 7 6 5 4

The paper in this book is FSC® certified. FSC® promotes environmentally responsible, socially beneficial and economically viable management of the world's forests.

CONTENTS

FOREWORD

Twenty years ago, I was sent by my boss at Channel Nine to interview Mark Stephens who was conducting a free seminar to entice people to drink more water. My reaction was a lukewarm *okay*, but when I was told he would use meditation and hypnotherapy on the group ... I may have rolled my eyes.

Journalists, we are told, are a cynical bunch – and that's a healthy thing in my trade. To question what's being said or done, not just blindly accept it, enables us to present an honest and unbiased story to the public.

I sat, watched and listened on that day, and I spoke to all involved, finding many at that meeting just as cynical as me. Yet, after two hours something remarkable happened: people were drinking water, even those who had told me they never touched the stuff, and others who had gone there as a joke because it was a free session. Mark relaxed the crowd, meditated with them and led a group hypnosis. He even taught them how to self-hypnotise, to replenish their skill and maintain their newfound love of water. Every person who left that day said they felt switched on to water. I wasn't so cynical anymore.

Mark contacted me again to tell me he could stop people from smoking. We filmed chain-smoker Merv, who had been puffing for 60 years and couldn't stop. After a session with Mark, he quit, just like that. From time to time I would ring Merv and find that, yes, he was still off the fags. Coca-Cola addicts were Mark's next challenge, including a woman whose backyard was stacked with tens of thousands of Coke bottles and cans, decades' worth. Mark got her off the fizzy drink.

After our initial stories aired, *A Current Affair* started sending viewers to Mark with their array of sometimes bizarre problems, including the lady who was addicted to chewy snake lollies, consuming a dozen bags a day. A little *Mark magic* and she wanted nothing to do with those slippery snakes again. Viewers who had needle phobias were soon getting vaccinated. There were others: the life-threateningly obese; the sufferers of mental and physical injuries; and those living with chronic pain, made worse because their subconscious minds wouldn't allow them to escape their fears. Every single time, Mark transformed their lives, simply by relaxation and hypnotherapy. I would always ring these people, often years later, and ask if they had slipped back into their old ways. The answer was *never*.

Where Mark Stephens's skill is concerned, this once-cynical reporter is cynical no more. Over decades, I have seen him transform people's lives. The tears of thanks are often all he received and all he wanted. He has a good heart; he cares about people and helps people live better lives. I can honestly say he has *saved* people's lives. And the culmination of his lifetime's work is now in this book to help all.

Brady Halls
Reporter, *A Current Affair*

INTRODUCTION

Welcome to a journey of transformation to set your mind free. Within these pages you will learn how to overcome your biggest challenges and achieve lasting peace, health and happiness. The power of what you tell yourself – your story – cannot be underestimated. You now have in your hands the techniques and methods used by thousands of people who have changed their lives for the better. *Mind Free* is a step-by-step way to help you change your story and reshape every part of your life.

Imagine if school had one more topic: Mind and Emotions 101. Unfortunately, we never learn how to run our mind and emotions. We gain new knowledge on important subjects, but, really, what is more important than our own mental and emotional health? *Mind Free* provides you with techniques that will give you immediate results.

In 1998 when I first started writing this book, I never imagined it would take more than two decades to complete. My wish from day one was to provide a straightforward mind manual that would help people overcome some of life's biggest challenges. This book has grown from that initial desire to help, and encompasses all that I have learned and developed as a hypnotherapist and meditation teacher. The techniques, meditations, affirmations and self-hypnosis scripts have been created and gathered over the past five decades of my learning and teaching journey. Drawing from my own mindful self-hypnosis seminars and retreats and from my keynote speeches and private breakthrough sessions, I have done my best to translate within these pages what I do in person and what I know works. I have also taken some of the best sessions from the Mind Free app and transcribed them for this book. You'll find a number of case studies included to inspire you and show you that transformation really is possible. (In some of the case studies I have changed the names for reasons of confidentiality.)

Whenever we attempt to overcome challenges, break old patterns, or reach goals using outdated thinking and obsolete strategies, we are destined to fail time and again. Our mind and, more specifically, our beliefs, values, habits and emotions have been formed through the power of repetition, be that positive or negative.

What you have experienced and been told throughout your life has shaped your very existence and led you to where you are right now. Through the power of positive repetition this book will empower you to change for the better.

Rather than a book to simply read once, *Mind Free* is intended to be read, reread and workshopped. If you were with me at a live event or in a private session, I would give you time to actively participate in the workshop segments. When you get to these parts of the book, do your best to join in as if you and I were face to face. Some scripts and techniques will have a deeper impact on you than others. There is no right or wrong. Simply take on board what feels right to you.

In the same way you would take a medication several times a day, let yourself absorb the words within these pages several times a day. To alleviate what ails you, repeatedly meditate on those scripts throughout *Mind Free* that appeal to you the most or that are appropriate for your situation.

Over the years I have been delighted to have heard from countless retreat and seminar attendees who have shared not only their own success stories, but also how they had inspired and shared their learned techniques with their own family and friends, with life-changing results. In the same way, as you absorb the lessons in *Mind Free*, if anyone you know is suffering from any of the conditions covered within these pages, be sure to share what you learn. The lessons and techniques in *Mind Free* are not meant to be sitting in a drawer, on a bookshelf or in a box. They are meant to be used, enjoyed and shared.

Now, take a deep breath and relax – you are about to embark on a journey of transformation.

MY STORY

As a young child, I often knew that I was about to die. I would be frozen with fear that at any moment my breathing would stop and my life would be over.

I'd be sitting or walking and would start to feel a tightness in my chest. Sometimes I would start coughing and feel the beginning of a wheeze. In a matter of minutes, it would feel as though someone was sitting on my upper body while I was being strangled. It felt as if no air was able to enter my lungs. There were times when I was literally suffocating. The sound of my tiny gasps for any small amount of air was scary, for me and for those around me. My complete focus was on trying to get oxygen into my body, all the while thinking, 'I'm going to die, I can't breathe, I'm going to die.'

The asthma attacks had started when I was just a toddler. They seemed to come and go with no apparent rhyme or reason. One week I would be fine, the next week I would be sick. Anything could trigger an attack: smoke, physical exertion, cold air, pet hair or even laughing. I was allergic to almost everything: pollen, milk, peanuts, grass, dust, night air and exercise. In any given year I would have 40 or more days off school because I was sick. My Ventolin puffer saved my life on more than one occasion.

The landscape of my life was constant fear. Ever-present was that darkly foreboding creature lurking in the background, in a corner somewhere, just out of sight. At any moment an attack would come on and I wouldn't be able to breathe. Obviously, this created a lot of anxiety for both me and my mother. It was as if I were on a roller-coaster ride of fight or flight.

Even as a child, I was aware of how different I was from my father, Ronnie, who was an all-round sportsman, playing representative cricket, rugby league for St George and snooker, among other things. He had cabinets filled with trophies and piles of newspaper clippings celebrating his sporting achievements. According to everyone who knew him, he was a legend and an absolutely great guy.

Back in the day – and we're talking the 1950s – it was common for rugby league players to have a few beers after a match, to either celebrate their win or commiserate their loss. For some, like my father, training sessions were also followed by beer-drinking sessions. I'm sure he didn't plan to become an alcoholic. It must have just crept up on him, as it does for so many.

By the time he was in his late twenties, it was nothing for Ronnie to drink between 20 and 30 beers in a day. While he was never physically violent, his drinking led to huge arguments with my mother, Lynnie, who was not backward in coming forward, and was always one to say it how it was. Eventually, the drinking was something my father could not control and it led to some real doozies of yelling matches between them. Lynnie had to be strong: she had three children to raise as well as a full-time job and two part-time jobs.

Between the cooking, cleaning, helping us with our homework and her three jobs, along with having an alcoholic husband, it would have been a miracle if Lynnie was able to avoid having a nervous break-down. But there were not too many miracles around our house. At the age of 32, she had one. Three children under 12 and three jobs would be enough to tip anyone over the edge. I remember seeing her lying there in the hallway, unconscious. I was terrified. My first thought was that she was dead. Luckily, she recovered after a few days in hospital and continued to do her absolute best at raising my younger brother, Garry, my older sister, Donna, and me.

At around the age of five or six, I worked out that if I had a massive asthma attack, my parents would stop fighting, as my mother always rushed to my aid. I would force myself to start wheezing and, pretty much on command, I would have full-blown asthma. I believe my asthma was as emotional as it was physical. I was pretty clever. With every asthma attack, the fighting would stop and, if I couldn't be calmed, my parents would take me to the hospital.

This sad and dramatic pattern of events continued for years. They would start arguing and I would work myself into having an asthma attack to stop the fighting. Apart from those few times where it almost killed me, the plan seemed to work.

On one trip to the hospital, when I was around eight, the doctor told us about a meditation class that incorporated yoga exercises and breathing techniques. He said the deep breathing would strengthen my lungs and the meditation would help me cope with the anxiety and stress that I'd been experiencing. From medication to meditation sounded like an idea worth trying, even for an eight-year-old.

I learned the techniques and was instructed to practise simple yoga positions and breathing exercises daily, first thing in the morning and last thing at night. Each time the dark monster of an asthma attack rose up, my mother would guide me through the breathing exercises and meditation, and nine times out of ten the asthma attack would subside or disappear altogether. The meditation helped me develop a calm, steady mind, meaning that whatever was happening outside didn't disrupt how I was feeling inside, my inner state. Eventually, the daily routine grew into a daily ritual.

During those early years, I wasn't good at sports. I couldn't run far or fast and I was allergic to grass in the park, which excluded me from outdoor sports. I would run out of steam just looking at a set of steps. I was also uncoordinated and was happy to just sit around watching TV. I was chubby too. I wasn't morbidly obese, but I was sufficiently overweight to be nicknamed 'fat boy' at school.

Everybody knew not to get between me and a biscuit. From Iced Vovos and Tim Tams to Mint Slices and Monte Carlos ... I was my nan's 'little bickie boy'. Every afternoon on the way home from school I would stop in at my grandparents' house for a glass of Milo and some biscuits. If any of my grandmother's friends were visiting, she would proudly say, as I walked through the door, 'Here comes Nanny's little bickie boy.' I would then confidently sit down and live up to my name. Biscuits were such an addiction that I would hide them in my pockets and take them to bed with me. It would be fair to say I was an extreme sugar addict at this early age. Looking back, I can see that biscuits and sugar-filled lollies had become like a drug to me.

My father was far from always negative, but when he was drunk, he would look at me and say things like, 'You're a log, you're lazy, you're a fairy, and if you had half a brain, you'd be dangerous.'

Fortunately, Mum would counter every negative word he spoke. She would tell my father to 'shut up', and tell me not to believe a word he was saying because it was the drink talking. Then she would reinforce positive messages: 'You're clever, you're artistic, you're creative and you're funny.' Lynnie was always positive. She is definitely a glass-half-full kind of person. At the time, I didn't realise the impact of those positive words. What I did realise was that her positive reinforcement made me feel better.

My mother often sang me to sleep with the old Dean Martin classic 'A: You're Adorable' (The Alphabet Song). I would lie there, wheezing away, with Mum singing the positive, uplifting lyrics, which soothed me to sleep. I remember the song word for word to this day. I wish every child could have the Alphabet Song sung to them as they go off to sleep. It would certainly instil some wonderfully empowering beliefs.

Looking back, her positive reinforcement was like a delete button. Every time my father said something negative, she would delete and override it with something positive. Every time I made an excuse or said something negative about myself, she would instantly counter it with a positive saying. I feel blessed to have had my young mind programmed in such a powerfully positive way. Unfortunately, not everybody has a Lynnie in their corner.

On reflection, what happened all those years ago was this: I chose not to believe my father; I chose to believe something different. Today, if somebody tells me I can't do something or attempts to project negative beliefs in my direction, I think to myself, *I choose not to believe that*. Then I tell myself what I choose to believe: *I can, it's possible, I am strong, I am capable, I am good enough.*

If *your* I AM is negative and holding you back, we'll work on changing that self-talk to words that inspire and motivate you and nourish your life. Read on!

From a very early age, I understood stress and the benefits of doing meditation and deep breathing to counter anxiety and tension. I use the skills that hospital course taught me to this day to control my emotional state and switch off stress. Interestingly, after my parents divorced when I was about 11 years old, the asthma attacks stopped altogether and I've not had one since.

Despite the divorce helping my health, my teenage years weren't easy – I was overweight, lacked confidence and felt lost. But then at the age of 17, I found the Japanese martial art of jujutsu. I completely threw myself into training and became obsessed. I started teaching the beginners and found I had a passion for teaching. My dedication saw me eventually training for more than 30 hours a week and I loved every minute.

Jujutsu led to learning tai chi, qigong (chi kung), visualisation and more meditation, which I still practise every day.

Through my later teens and twenties, I continued to study different methods of meditation, guided imagery, tai chi and qigong under incredible teachers and masters from around the world. I attended every course possible and met every master possible. I was like a sponge, soaking it all up, learning all I could. I devoured every book I could find on Indian, Chinese, Tibetan, Japanese and Western meditation, and practised all the styles. Learning and teaching became my everything. Those early lessons changed my life and set me on the path I'm still travelling some 50 years later.

In 1987 my life changed forever. My younger brother, Garry, was killed in a motorcycle accident. He was just 21. It truly was a case of the good dying young. Garry was a happy-go-lucky soul loved by everybody. He was a helpful young guy who wouldn't hurt a fly. We had grown up sharing the same room for most of our lives and his death felt like my heart had been ripped out. My whole family was devastated, as were all his friends.

The grief was overwhelming. I buried myself in my work, often spending 18 to 24 hours at a time working without a break. It was nothing for me to work 100 or more hours per week.

Then, in 1990, everything changed for the better. I married Linda, the most beautiful, funny, talented woman of my dreams. She was like a cross between Miss Russia and Barbara Eden from *I Dream of Jeannie*, and was as clever as she was pretty (she still is).

A few months after our honeymoon, disaster struck again. I was 28 years old and discovered I had testicular cancer. It had already metastasised into a second-stage lymphoma near my pancreas. How the hell could I have cancer? I was the healthiest person I knew! Was it the accidental kicks, flicks and chops to the groin I endured during jujutsu training? Was it the medicinal marijuana that I'd smoked during my early teens? Was it my emotional state or overworking to avoid dealing with my emotional state?

I had ignored the initial signs of tiredness and the ache in my lower abdomen and put off going to the doctor. Eventually after ongoing discomfort I decided to get a check-up. The news wasn't good. Following the diagnosis, I was recommended for surgery for the primary cancer, along with radiotherapy and chemotherapy for the second-stage lymphoma. The second-stage tumour was 2.5 centimetres in diameter.

I was reluctant to undertake the radiotherapy and chemotherapy after the surgery. I'd beat this thing with juicing and meditation, I decided. I can be pretty stubborn, and I made up my mind I wanted to give this my best shot. Linda, the queen of all things healthy, agreed.

Meditation, tai chi and juicing would be the order of the day. I ran the idea past my oncology professor, Martin Tattersall, who was supportive and commented that he had seen some good results with similar programs, but that he had also seen some failures and suggested we regularly keep an eye on things.

When I mentioned this idea of a juicing program to the radiotherapy doctor he bluntly said, 'If you think you can go to Mexico, sit on the side of a mountain and meditate while drinking carrot juice, you'll be dead in six months.' That was harsh! Six months to live? I joked to friends that if I could see two more doctors and they each gave me the same prognosis of six months, that would give me 18 months.

I booked the first available flight to Mexico. By that time, the second-stage lymphoma had grown from 2.5 to 4 centimetres in diameter. It seemed as if this thing was on the march. For five weeks I sat on the side of a mountain meditating and drinking plenty of carrot juice, along with green juices, and I had coffee enemas, vitamin B12 shots in the backside every day and more organic salads than you could poke a stick at. I was the healthiest sick and dying person you could hope to meet. I was forced to reassess everything in my life, from what I ate and how much I was working to, most importantly, what was going on in my head, and what I was holding onto emotionally – in particular, the grief over my brother.

I combined every Eastern healing method imaginable and every emotional and mind strategy I could lay my hands on. I immersed myself completely and totally. I drank the juices and practised tai chi and meditation for ten hours every day. Linda continued to work, but we used up all of the money we'd been saving for a home deposit so that I could focus on healing. This is also when I became absorbed in hypnotherapy.

Two years passed and the tumour had shrunk from 4.5 to 2.5 centimetres in diameter. Pretty chuffed with myself, I thought I'd beaten the cancer. The professor said that it was possible the tumour was scar tissue, but it was also possible it was lying dormant and could regrow. The blood tests showed no cancer markers in my system. I was convinced I had beaten it. I felt amazing. I was jumping out of my skin and ready to get back into life after this two-year sojourn.

I returned to work and began to neglect my intense diet and hours of daily meditation. It wasn't that I was eating poorly, I just wasn't pumping my body full of copious amounts of live enzymes via those liquid vitamin pills I called juices.

The day after teaching a jujutsu seminar I felt a bit of an ache in my back. By the end of the day the pain was increasing in intensity. The following day it felt as if someone had hit me in the middle of the back with a baseball bat. I thought I had pulled a muscle, but the pain was different, like nothing I'd ever felt. By the time I realised something was wrong, the tumour had grown to 7 centimetres by 5 centimetres in diameter. The pain was excruciating. The cancer was back with a vengeance.

I hit the juices hard, went back to ten hours a day of meditation and tai chi, and began incorporating self-hypnosis, but it seemed too late. The meditation and self-hypnosis were reducing the pain but not completely and only temporarily. A few more weeks passed, and the tumour was now 11 centimetres by 7 centimetres in diameter. The pain was unbearable and I could hardly move. The professor said that, at the rate the tumour was growing, I may only have a few months to live.

This massive lump of cancer could not be differentiated from the tail of my pancreas and was causing my left kidney to dysfunction, beginning to encase the abdominal aorta below the heart, and causing unbearable spine, sacroiliac and hip pain. Surgery was out of the question. Something had to give. I needed to change my mindset. My stubbornness and procrastination surrounding chemotherapy had to give way to what was needed. I couldn't put it off any longer. But was it already too late?

Professor Tattersall said it was possible the cancer could perhaps be third or fourth stage and may have already moved into other areas of my body such as organs or bones. He gave the chemotherapy only a fifty-fifty chance of working. It was either do the chemo or die, I thought to myself. Not to be daunted, I enthusiastically asked him, 'How soon can we start the chemo?'

'That's a nice change of attitude,' he answered, smiling.

Within three days, every cell in my body was being bombarded with a cocktail of four chemotherapy drugs. Within a few days of the treatment, I wasn't feeling crash hot. I felt weak and had a tin-like metallic taste in my mouth. My energy was fading fast. The nausea kicked in, like a really bad case of food poisoning. Through some mix-up at the hospital  dispensary, I was given the wrong anti-nausea medication. For the next few days, I couldn't keep anything down, not even water, and I practically lived in the bathroom until I had nothing left. My energy – my life force – felt like it was nearing zero. I was rushed to the emergency ward at Royal Prince Alfred Hospital.

I had severe dehydration and my veins were starting to collapse. It was touch and go. Six doctors and nurses were unable to find a vein to hydrate me. For some reason, one doctor decided to shave the hair off the back of my wrist, but the skin just peeled back like damp paper. I felt like I had been run over by a steamroller. Is this how it all ends? I gave thought to my funeral. An open casket, I thought, and, yes, that fluorescent green Hawaiian shirt that everybody hates. I chuckled. One last joke.

I told the emergency doctor that I was going home, to which he replied, 'You'll be dead in six hours.'

Okay, this really is serious.

'Find me someone who can find a vein, please,' I whispered. Luckily, Captain Chemo, Keith Cox, the professor's right-hand nurse, was just starting his shift. They rushed him to Emergency where he gently lifted my arm, found a vein and the saline solution began to flow.

'You'll be fine, we're not losing you today,' he smiled. Captain Chemo saved my life that day, and I'll be forever grateful.

I maintained my juicing, tai chi, meditation and self-hypnosis program throughout the entire four rounds of chemotherapy treatment. Before each round of chemo, a blood test was performed so the oncologist could work out the dose of chemotherapy medication.

The professor commented that he'd never seen an immune system bounce back so quickly on this type of chemotherapy medication. He suggested I keep doing what I was doing with my juicing and meditation program. This was encouraging news.

I have only the most profound gratitude to Professor Martin Tattersall, Captain Chemo Keith Cox and all the wonderful staff, then and now, who do their absolute utmost to save people's lives in cancer wards and the broader health system. They definitely saved my life.

I recall seeing a poster on the hospital wall one day and it really stuck in my mind: Cancer is a word, not a sentence.

The chemo did shrink the monstrous tumour to 2.5 centimetres in diameter, which is the size it remained for almost 30 years. My last scan in 2019 couldn't find the tumour at all. But I still don't take any chances. I continue to juice and practise tai chi, meditation and self-hypnosis every day. And I'm still sitting on that mountain.

HOW TO GET THE BEST
OUT OF THIS BOOK

During seminars, retreats, conferences and private therapy, my main aim is to create a shift in a person's thinking so they can overcome a challenge they are facing, become unstuck if they are stuck, or reach a goal that may seem unattainable. Words are energy; they have power.

Throughout this book, in the same way I do when presenting or working with clients, we approach the change of thought from as many different angles as possible. I do this through positive suggestion, hypnosis, meditation, and having you write down and replace old excuses and negative thoughts with empowering thoughts. We do not just think of them and write them down, but we breathe them deeply into our being. We allow the thoughts to flow from our awareness, our conscious mind, into our unconscious mind and from there we breathe them into our body. I've seen people's lives change dramatically simply by changing one thought. Imagine how different life could be when you change many of your thoughts.

The Buddha said, 'All that we are arises with our thoughts. With our thoughts, we make the world.' But it's not just the world around us that is created with our thoughts – our own mental, emotional and physical wellbeing comes down to what we think. It's now time to set your mind free and transform your life.

This book is not meant to be simply read. If you just read it, sure you may pick up some beneficial ideas, but it will merely be some extra knowledge in the library of your mind. However, when you practise the easy exercises and meditations as instructed, and you participate in the workshop elements of the book, transformation *will* happen.

I have structured *Mind Free* into chapters that address the most common challenges my clients tell me they face, including insomnia, procrastination, stress, bad habits, overeating, negative thoughts, anxiety, phobias and chronic pain. Read the chapters consecutively or choose the one that relates best to your situation.

Please pay close attention to chapters 1 and 2 before working through your specific challenges. These first two chapters lay the foundation for what follows and will help you understand the techniques to change your thoughts, and the power of resetting your mind.

As well as specific exercises within each chapter, at the end of each chapter you'll discover a simple **Mind Free minute meditation** exercise with affirmations that you can incorporate into your daily life to help you improve your health and wellbeing, and increase your contentment and happiness.

After the minute meditation there are **three keys** to help you focus on the three most powerful steps to deal with the challenge discussed in that chapter.

At the end of each chapter, you'll also find the **three decrees**. As you read every page of this book, you'll discover we focus on three empowering ways of thinking. A decree is an instruction, an official order or a law. In this way, instead of listening to the old orders from your unconscious mind, you will, one thought at a time, replace them with a decree set by you. As you breathe each word into existence, feel it, see it, hear it and be it. As you command it, so shall it be. Each decree is directly connected to the theme of the chapter and contains the following to help change your thinking:

- **Decree 1 – Positive emotion words.** This could be any word that helps you change the way you feel. Words like *energy, strength, determination, power, laughter, love* and *joy* are all great examples of single words that can help you change your state from negative to positive.
- **Decree 2 – Short power declarations.** Using *I am* declarations about yourself, along with empowering beliefs, will support you in making the changes you want to make. Examples such as *I am strong, I am capable, I am good enough, I can do it* and *I make it happen* are all wonderful declarations that will nourish your mind and body. We breathe these thoughts into every part of our being.
- **Decree 3 – Empowering affirmation statements.** From a few words to a longer statement, these affirmations will help you overcome negative self-talk. *Today is the day, now is the time and I am a person of action. My health is my wealth, my health is number one. Every day is precious, I make time for me. I am loving, lovable and loved. I cherish each day and appreciate the small things in life. I project love and happiness to all I meet.*

Imagine the words that resonate with you the most floating from each page, and with each breath they enter your being. Every time you repeat a power word, declaration or affirmation, you'll begin to discover these new thoughts sinking into your mind and heart. From there, they will spring into the front of your mind over and over. As you begin to live these words and breathe them into existence, you will lift yourself and those around you.

We breathe words into our mind, into our heart, and they radiate from there through our body and back into the world.

While I give you plenty of ideas on positive thoughts and empowering affirmations, the magic happens when you either choose from my suggestions or make up your own list of thoughts, statements, declarations and affirmations and breathe them into your life. Step by step throughout this book you will learn exactly how to do that, and at the end of each chapter you'll find space to write your own powerful, life-changing decree.

Above all, the final chapter of *Mind Free* is the **21 States**. This vital chapter unites all the work you've done through the book. It's a holistic approach to your life, empowering you to change your state from negative to positive. The list of 21 States covers the main positive states we all want in our lives. By reading – and rereading – the 21 declaration affirmations, you will continually reinforce the positive messages to your mind and body, allowing you to change your state whenever the need arises.

At the back of the book I have included a bonus **Mind Manual**. This section includes an expanded selection of meditation and self-hypnosis scripts connected to the theme of each chapter. You can refer to this section at any time once you've read the relevant chapters.

In the Mind Manual you'll also find empowering affirmations: positive, uplifting words to help you overcome the self-sabotaging talk in your mind. Repeat them to yourself twice daily, as a morning and evening meditation. As you begin to believe what you tell yourself, you'll discover how much easier it is to overcome your challenges, and to reach for your goals.

Also, in the Mind Manual, you'll find mandalas to mindfully colour in. Colouring in can be a powerful way to stop the cycle of negative thoughts and focus on creating new empowering ones. Feel free as you colour in the mandalas to add your own pictures, power words and affirmations.

I encourage you to make this book your own – draw, write and make notes on the pages. Highlight or underline words that stand out to you, jot down thoughts that come to you while you're reading, and colour and doodle as much as you want! Make this your hands-on workbook for resetting your mind and transforming your life.

Once you've finished the exercises in the chapters, the Mind Manual library can become your daily go-to section of the book to help you create a daily routine that becomes a ritual.

A ritual, according to the *Oxford English Dictionary*, is 'a solemn ceremony consisting of a series of actions performed according to a prescribed order'. Having daily rituals gives us certainty and structure. When we have certainty, to a degree we are able to predict our future. When we turn our meditation time into an important ritual, we make it sacred, giving deep meaning to a series of steps for our own betterment.

As we move from suffering, through surviving to thriving, the repetitive nature of our rituals creates a wonderful sense of progress and becomes a positive anchor in our lives. You can start building your ritual with as little as a few minutes of meditation or mindful self-hypnosis to start and end each day.

To learn how to create your own ritual, I suggest you focus on one challenge at a time for 30 days. For 30 days, morning and night, read the three keys, your three decrees, all affirmations and all self-hypnosis sessions in both the relevant chapter and Mind Manual section. Choose one of the 21 States to read daily. Ideally, do this when you wake up and just before you go to sleep when your brainwaves are in a dreamy state and the doorway to your unconscious mind is open. After 30 days move onto your next challenge.

You may ask, can I really change my life in 30 days? Yes! The more you immerse yourself in *Mind Free* the more you will realise you have everything you need *already within you* to bring about rapid and lasting change. Create the ritual and the ritual will create your future.

MINDFUL SELF-HYPNOSIS AUDIO AND VIDEO SESSIONS

To support you in making the greatest change possible and get the best out of this book, I have recorded three mindful self-hypnosis sessions. You can listen to these sessions or watch the videos by visiting mindfreeapp.com and clicking on the image of the book cover. To access the sessions, you will need to enter the code: **mindfreebook** (all in one word and lower case).

Over the past 40 or so years, I've watched people transform themselves with positive beliefs, self-confidence and a determined energy using the techniques you'll find in *Mind Free*. I have witnessed the transformation of children, teenagers and people in their twenties all the way through to those in their nineties – people who had lifelong conditions that they had given up hope of ever changing, from severe post-traumatic stress disorder, chronic pain, insomnia and weight issues to bad habits, anxiety and overwhelming sadness. I've had the wonderful pleasure – the honour – of sharing part of their transformation journeys.

If you have hit rock bottom or are desperate for change; if you are stuck and want to be unstuck; if you know you're not reaching your potential but truly want to; if you're generally happy with your life but want more joy, more healing; if you are simply inspired to step up and make the changes to your mindset that you know you need to make, then this book will help you in doing exactly that. By the time you finish *Mind Free* you'll know how to apply mindful self-hypnosis to your everyday life. You'll have replaced negative thoughts with positive empowering thoughts. You'll have created new healthy rituals for healing.

You will have set your mind free.

CHAPTER 1
MIND FREE

How do you free your mind? Why would you want to? What does mind free mean? Negative thoughts could be likened to prison bars. They lock you into a certain way of thinking and behaving. It's as if, by repeating a thought over and over, you are focusing on, meditating on or hypnotising yourself with that thought – an imprisoning thought. None of us want to live life in a negative thought prison. To set your mind free means to live a life filled with empowering beliefs about yourself and the world that will impact every area of your life in a positive way.

In this book, I share with you techniques of meditation and self-hypnosis, along with mindfulness, to help change your mind, to move from negative thinking to positive thinking, from limiting beliefs to empowering beliefs (see p. 231 in the Mind Manual for step-by-step instructions on how to meditate and practise self-hypnosis). Before you apply the techniques, it's useful to understand more about them.

WHAT IS MEDITATION?

Meditation is many things to many people. For me, meditation is a time to slow my mind and clear the energy I may have taken on from people, places and projects. It's a time to reset and recharge. Meditation is also a wonderful way to connect my conscious mind with my unconscious, to gain a deeper understanding of myself. As I calm and slow my thoughts, it seems as if the world around me calms and slows too. Meditation helps me to be happier and more content. After 50 years of daily meditation practice, I'm not about to stop anytime soon.

Let's face it, our minds wander from thought to thought, and it can feel like we generally have no control over what we're thinking. The harder we try to stop certain thoughts, the more they seem to control our life.

For thousands of years, different religions and cultures have had their own various forms of meditation. The word meditation itself comes from the Latin word *meditari*, meaning to think or reflect upon something, to ponder or contemplate.

People constantly tell me they've tried to meditate but were unable to concentrate, so they got frustrated and gave up. Meditation is the simplest of things and yet it can be difficult if you're not guided in the right way. Meditation can be practised anytime, anywhere, either individually or in a group. In the pages that follow you will learn simple yet powerful meditation techniques, step by step, to help free your mind and achieve peace and greater happiness.

MINDFUL MEDITATION

Some years back at Little Forest Health Retreat, which my wife, Linda, and I run, we had the good fortune of being visited by a Tibetan Rinpoche lama.

A key point to the Rinpoche's message was regarding mindfulness. 'We often get caught up thinking of the past or worrying about the future and forget to be present and mindful,' he said. 'To access the present moment by cultivating our attention on what is happening in the moment is the state of being or meditation. Walking, gardening, doing the dishes, mowing a lawn or knitting gives us an opportunity to meditate on what we are doing. Become one with the task and, rather than attaching a story to it, you become mindful of what is unfolding at each moment. If a thought enters your mind, be mindful of it and let it pass.'

Wouldn't it be amazing if you could turn any activity into a meditation? The great news is, you can. It's as simple as directing your awareness from one sense to another, and focusing your attention in the present moment and on what you are doing. Take a cup of tea. From the preparing of the tea to the pouring of the tea, and then sitting mindfully as you move your arm and feel that movement, you watch the cup as you take slow sips, you feel the temperature, you taste the flavour, you smell the aroma and you feel yourself swallowing the tea. This is mindful meditation.

The key to mindfulness is each time your mind wanders, which it will, bring your attention back to whatever it is you are meditating on. If you are mindfully drinking a glass of water and your mind wanders, bring your attention back to the water. If you are mindfully walking and your mind wanders, bring your attention back to your walking. If you are mindfully eating an apple and your mind wanders, bring your attention back to the apple.

There are many different forms of meditation, including moving meditations like yoga, tai chi and qigong (pronounced chee goong). You have seated meditations where you simply sit and breathe: you might count to a certain number as you breathe in and out, or maybe you don't count. Then there are focused-attention meditations like staring at a spot, listening to a gong, listening to nature or focusing on a candle flame. Mantra meditation such as the *Om* will guide you to focus on a word or phrase, and you chant this either quietly or loudly for a set period of time. Prayer is a form of spiritual meditation, sometimes with the burning of frankincense or other essences, focusing on your own connection to your god, nature or the universe.

Transcendental Meditation (TM) is where you are given a secret mantra, a word or a series of words, to repeat in your mind. TM helps you slow your thoughts by giving you something to focus on.

Loving-kindness meditation is a Tibetan Buddhist meditation that helps you cultivate compassion and kindness to yourself and others. Zen meditation guides you to focus your attention inwards with your eyes relaxed, but not closed, and your focus is on thinking about nothing and simply being present.

Progressive muscle relaxation is a form of meditation where you focus your attention on each part of the body while thinking *relax*. Visualisation or guided imagery is another form of meditation where you picture things in your mind's eye such as a scene in nature or floating in space. There are walking meditations, guided meditations, unguided meditations, reflective meditations, chakra meditations, sound meditations and so many more.

For the past few years, mindful meditation has been all the buzz. From celebrities to high school students, everyone seems to be incorporating mindfulness into their everyday life.

The beauty of mindful meditation is that you can simply be present in the moment with whatever you are doing. If you are sitting and breathing, you simply sit and breathe. If your mind wanders, you bring it back to your breathing. If you are doing the dishes, you focus your attention in that present moment as you feel the temperature of the water, notice the bubbles and feel your movements while simply watching what is happening in front of you. Whatever you may be doing or experiencing, you can be present in that moment. When your mind wanders, you bring it back to the present moment.

For years at our seminars and retreats, I've been teaching mindful eating. You simply sit quietly with your food as you notice the colours of the food, the movement of your arm, the temperature, texture and flavours of the food, the action of swallowing and the feeling of the food moving down into your stomach. When you eat mindfully, you can eat less and feel more satisfied. When your mind wanders, you bring it back to the present moment.

In life we so often get stuck in the past or the future. Our mind spends a lot of time drifting. Meditation is a wonderful way to bring us back to being here and now, in the present moment.

Numerous research studies in recent years have irrefutably proven the benefits of meditation, which include reduced stress and anxiety, better memory, improved learning and problem-solving, improved attention and concentration, better sleep, reduced pain, lower blood pressure, more satisfying relationships, feeling more present, enhanced self-awareness, more positive thoughts and increased happiness.

Hopefully that's enough to inspire you to create a daily ritual of meditation.

In the same way you have other routines in your daily life, you have the opportunity to create a simple meditation routine. And the best part is, one minute is all it takes – mindful minutes of meditation. If you can count to ten you can meditate. Counting six breaths to ten is a minute of meditation. You can meditate in a minute and benefit. After 50 years of practising meditation, I can confidently say that 30 one-minute meditations will create a similar benefit to a single 30-minute meditation. In fact, the 30 one-minute meditations may even be more beneficial as they keep countering stress at regular intervals throughout the day.

Try one of the following one-minute meditations to see how quickly you can transform how you feel.

COUNTING MEDITATION

Sit comfortably and feel your breath flowing in and out for one minute. Begin to count each breath, one at a time, from ten down to one. Simply feel your breath as you count. On the in breath think of the number and, as you exhale, think of the word *relax*. When you get to one notice how relaxed you feel.

CALMING MEDITATION

Bring to mind a time when you felt totally calm. It may have been years ago or recently. Breathe that feeling into your heart. Think the word *calm*, feel the feelings of calm and let your mind drift to a picture – a time or a symbol in your mind that represents the feeling of calm. Continue to breathe that calm feeling into your heart. You may even like to imagine your heart as a beautiful flower opening up to the morning sun, with beams of light radiating into you. Think the thoughts, *I am calm*. Allow these healing words to overflow from your heart through your entire body. *I am calm*. Feel yourself beginning to smile as you breathe the words *I am calm* up into your mind as you inhale and all the way down through your body as you exhale.

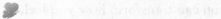

Meditation doesn't have to be difficult. I often hear people say, 'I can't focus; my mind keeps wandering; what's the point?' However, if you meditate for five minutes and your mind wanders for three minutes, you've just meditated for two minutes and that's a good thing.

Remember, the main thing with meditation is that when your mind wanders – and it will – bring your attention back to the meditation. You keep bringing your attention back to the meditation no matter how many times your mind wanders. Rather than trying to completely reject or stop your thoughts, allow them to come and go. Embrace your mind and your thoughts.

Experiment with as many different meditations as you can and discover which technique works best for you and fits into your life.

You can apply meditation to your everyday life or use it specifically to help whatever conditions you may be working on. While meditation may not be a magic bullet for all of life's issues, it certainly helps you make positive changes. When you make meditation part of your everyday life, you'll begin to notice the benefits in no time at all.

A number of years back, while in Perth, I heard there was a massage therapist nearby who had spent a decade living in a Tibetan monastery as a monk. I wasn't missing out on such an opportunity and booked in for a session.

On the way to the therapy room, I wondered if maybe I might be able to get a mantra from the monk. I'd love to have a mantra, especially from a Tibetan-trained monk. As we sat and discussed what style of massage I would like, I quietly asked, 'Would you be able to give me a mantra?' He simply smiled. I laid down and received the most wonderful massage treatment with the occasional conversation that lasted for a minute or two at a time. A few times throughout the massage I thought about my mantra request and that he hadn't given me a mantra yet. Eventually the treatment was over and I wondered if he had simply forgotten about a mantra. I returned to my room thinking about that mantra. I had really wanted a mantra. I was with a monk and I didn't get a mantra.

Some time passed, and all thoughts of my mantra request were gone. And then out of the blue a thought popped into my mind, *less is more*. The thought made me smile. I realised my massaging monk had repeated the phrase 'less is more' a number of times throughout our conversation without me realising. I was happy, I had my mantra.

Meditation can be summed up as *cultivating the mind*. By the time you finish this book, you will master meditation and it will become an essential tool for helping you overcome your challenges.

WHAT IS HYPNOSIS?

In *Mind Free*, as well as meditation methods, I introduce you to self-hypnosis techniques. Many of the world's greatest athletes, successful business entrepreneurs and most-respected leaders have used some form of self-hypnosis to achieve great success and belief in themselves. Some may not even realise that this is exactly what they are doing, but there is no doubt they are practising self-hypnosis.

Hypnosis is often described as a process of focused concentration that leads to very deep relaxation or a state of heightened awareness. Hypnosis dates back thousands of years, with almost every culture having their own form of hypnosis or trance-like state. From the Indian yogis to the Native American sweat lodges, from the tribal dances of the Africans to the Australian First Nations peoples practising deep listening and silent awareness, hypnosis has been used by humankind in one form or another to achieve a different state of being.

Three thousand years ago, the Egyptians had what they called 'sleep temples'. Greece and Rome followed suit and sleep temples flourished. A person with a problem would enter the temple and meet with the healing person or priest of the day. They would lie down and the healing person would look them in the eye and say, 'You are well, you are well, you are well' over and over. Miraculously, the person would stand up and oftentimes forget they had ever had a problem.

During the late 18th and early 19th centuries, French nobility popularised hypnosis through mesmerism. German physician Franz Anton Mesmer was in great demand, his practice growing to a size that became difficult for him to handle. It was reported almost 3000 people a day sought his healing touch.

A Scottish surgeon, James Braid, believed that mesmerism was a swindle and he set out to discredit the practice. Yet, eventually, Braid became fascinated and convinced by mesmerism. In 1842 he introduced the terms 'suggestion' and 'hypnotism' from the Greek *hypnos*, meaning sleep.

In India in the mid-19th century, an English surgeon, James Esdaile, used hypnosis in more than 3000 operations, of which 300 were major procedures. He discovered that, when his patients were in the hypnotic state, the mortality rate dropped from 50 per cent to 5 per cent. His patients also experienced greater comfort during and after surgery, and had an increased resistance to infection.

In 1892, the British Medical Association (BMA) commissioned a special committee of 11 doctors to investigate the nature of hypnotism. The report stated, 'The Committee, having completed such investigation of hypnotism as time permitted, have to report that they have satisfied themselves of the genuineness of the hypnotic state.'

In the early 1900s, a French pharmacist named Émile Coué discovered the power of autosuggestion, which he named 'waking suggestion'. Coué is credited with the famous affirmation 'Every day, in every way, I am getting better and better.' It was Coué who discovered that it was the suggestion being accepted by the mind of the subject, rather than the actual suggestion given by the hypnotist, that achieved results. Conversely, he attested that negative thinking patterns could make an illness worse.

In 1955 the BMA stated hypnosis was a valuable medical tool because as a treatment 'it has the ability to remove symptoms and to alter morbid habits of thought and behaviour'.

In 1958 the American Medical Association approved hypnosis for therapeutic use, followed by the American Psychiatric Association soon after. This was largely through the efforts of Dr Milton Erickson, who described hypnosis as 'a state of intensified attention and receptiveness to an idea or a set of ideas'.

Hypnosis could also be described as a state of relaxation that allows the unconscious mind to be directly communicated with through positive suggestion and imagination for a specific purpose.

By the standards of modern hypnosis, activities such as meditation, relaxation therapy, autosuggestion, guided imagery, visualisation and closed-eye processes are all forms of self-hypnosis.

**Every day, in every way,
I am getting better and better.**

What are you suggesting?

All hypnosis is self-hypnosis. Even when you are sitting there being hypnotised by a hypnotist, you are the one actually hypnotising yourself. As 19th-century Portuguese monk and hypnotist Abbé Faria is said to have theorised, 'Nothing comes from the magnetiser, everything comes from the subject and takes place in his or her imagination.'

Think of the hypnotist as a tour guide. In this book I am your tour guide. You are the one making the journey. You are deciding which exercises to do, what suggestions you are taking on board and what to apply. It is important to remember *you* are in control at all times. In the hypnotic state you are relaxed but focused on the suggestions, imagery or ideas put forth by the hypnotist. You then either accept or reject those suggestions. Exactly the same applies with *Mind Free*. Only take on board the suggestions that feel right to you. The positive suggestions are designed to assist you in changing those things you want to change.

Try the following exercises to discover how the power of your mind can change your experience. As you do each exercise, notice which one impacts you the most. Remember, you are in control, you are the hypnotist and you are learning how to harness the power of your imagination.

THE LEMON TREE TEST

Imagine there is a large lemon tree in front of you. You reach up and twist a lemon off the branch. Holding the lemon in your hand, you feel its cool bubbly texture. Imagine now that you are taking that lemon into a kitchen; you pick up a knife and cut the lemon into wedges on a chopping board. Imagine you are bringing that piece of lemon up towards your mouth. Maybe you can sense the smell of the lemon and, as you bring it to your lips, you can taste the sour lemony taste. Close your eyes for a moment, or leave them open if you prefer, as you imagine you are sucking on that lemon, squeezing it and tasting the lemon juice. Take a moment now to notice if you have more saliva in your mouth.

The interesting thing is, as you know, there was no lemon – it was all in your mind. Yet, intriguingly, chemical changes just took place in your body to produce saliva. You see, the body doesn't know the difference between a real experience and an imagined experience. This is why it's so important for you to take control of your mind. Your mind is powerful beyond what you know it to be. You have unlimited potential. It is time to harness the power of your mind.

FINGER MAGNET TEST

Clasp your hands together, with your palms touching and your fingers interlocked. Hold this position for a moment, and then point your two index fingers straight out (as in the picture). Stare at the space between your fingers and imagine a powerful magnet is pulling them together. The more you stare at the space between your fingers and think of a powerful magnet drawing your fingers together, the more your fingers will be drawn together, until they touch.

With this exercise, there is no magnet; however, the more you think of the word magnet, the more you feel your fingers being drawn together. This is a great example of the power of your imagination

BOOK AND BALLOON TEST

Step 1: Either sitting or standing, hold both arms directly out in front of you at shoulder level. Turn your left palm facing up and turn your right palm facing down.

Step 2: Imagine tied to your right wrist a bunch of colourful helium-filled balloons. In your left hand, imagine a pile of very heavy books.

Step 3: Think of the books getting heavier and heavier, dragging your left hand down. At the same time, imagine the balloons are lifting your right hand and arm up into the air. Your right arm is getting lighter while your left arm, holding the books, is getting heavier and heavier (as in the picture). Close your eyes and imagine this now as you feel the weight in your left hand and feel the lightness in your right hand. Focus on the arm holding the books while you think *heavy, heavy, heavy*. Bring your attention to your other arm with the balloons attached to your wrist, thinking *lighter, lighter, lighter*. Maybe you'll notice your hands drifting apart. At the very least, you should feel the difference in heaviness or lightness between your two arms.

As with the other tests, there were no books or balloons, except for those you created in your imagination. As you begin to understand how powerful your mind is, you can really start to harness your own mind power to make the positive changes in your life you wish to make.

HYPNOTHERAPY FOR STRESS AND ANXIETY

As you probably know, simply telling yourself not to feel anxious or not to let something stress you out doesn't work. Stress and anxiety are unconscious feelings and to overcome them you need to bypass the mind's conscious critical faculty and connect with your unconscious.

'Stinking thinking' (getting stuck in a cycle of toxic thoughts) and emotional overload often lurk behind the veil of stress and anxiety. Hypnotherapy helps you access your unconscious mind, enabling you to slow down and tame the thoughts and emotional triggers that bring on or increase feelings of stress and anxiety. When you enter a state of hypnosis, you gently sink into a deep relaxation with heightened awareness. In this state, you can actively reprogram the part of your unconscious mind that tells you to feel anxious or stressed; that tells you to reach for the unhealthy food, drink or cigarette; that tells you, you aren't good enough.

The fact is, you are good enough and you are far stronger than you think yourself to be.

WHY PRACTISE MINDFUL HYPNOTHERAPY?

From the time our lives begin, our minds are bombarded and programmed by family, friends, teachers, media, TV shows, music, movies and social media. When you take a minute or two here and there throughout the day to be mindful, you clear your mind of mental clutter. Think for a moment, how much *stuff* is there in the garage of your mind?

When mindfulness and hypnotic techniques are combined, the whole is greater than the sum of its parts. Being mindful enhances the effects of hypnotherapy by helping you to enter a deeper state of relaxation and lead the wandering mind back to the now. Hypnotherapy takes mindfulness to a whole new level, allowing you to focus on the challenge you wish to overcome and to achieve a specific outcome.

What does mindful self-hypnosis look like?

In the first part of a mindful hypnotherapy session, you will tune in to the present moment. Mindful awareness of your breathing helps you switch off or slow down thoughts of the past and any concerns about the future. You may still notice sounds around you, observing them without judgment and without labelling them. The same goes for any feelings or thoughts that arise, which strengthens your ability to witness and experience through non-attachment. As the hypnotherapy element is added to the session, visualisation, metaphors and positive suggestions are included to help you overcome your specific challenges.

Mindful breathing

Breathing is such an integral part of meditation and hypnotherapy – and life – yet we often don't give it the attention it deserves. Think about it for a moment: life begins with our first breath and ends with our last breath. Your breath is always with you. It's the one thing you do almost more than anything. The average person takes 16 breaths per minute. And to think you can be meditating or achieving deep relaxation by simply taking a few breaths and watching, feeling or listening to the breath flow in and out of your body.

There is only one thing we do more of than breathing: thinking. In the next chapter you will delve deep into this and, as you discover how to master this part of your existence, your life will be transformed forever.

WILL YOU MAKE ME DANCE LIKE A CHICKEN?

Unfortunately, many people confuse clinical hypnotherapy with stage hypnosis. While some of the techniques used to get a person into a trance-like state are similar, the difference is dramatic. One is for entertainment, convincing people to do silly things for a laugh and a fun night out. The other – the form I practise – is to help people overcome challenges, improve study, conquer phobias, sleep better, relieve pain, stop smoking, shed excess weight and deal with other life challenges. So, you won't be dancing like a chicken while reading this book (unless you want to).

Put simply, without knowing it you may have allowed yourself to get into a negative trance-like state through any number of life experiences and events. But it is time to break the trance and to *unhypnotise* yourself. The reality is that the *best* hypnotist in the world for you is *you*. The time for negative suggestions is over, and positive suggestions have already begun.

In the chapters that follow, you will learn how to harness your own hypnotic powers, and you'll learn how to meditate like a monk.

You're more powerful than you realise, and you will learn how to use that power.

You are the hypnotist. Are you ready?

CHAPTER 2
RESET YOUR MIND

I can't.

Imagine if you could?
How would things be different if you did?

It's too hard.

What part of it isn't hard?
How can you make it doable?

I don't have time.

What if you made the time?
And you begin to realise, you can make time
for things that are important.

Change is easy.

Everything you achieve or don't achieve comes down to the story you tell yourself. How often do you let self-defeating talk get you down? How often do you use self-talk that builds you up and gets you excited? How often do you allow excuses to control your life?

If you want to change your life, first you need to reset your mind.

Numerous studies have estimated we have between 6000 and 50,000 thoughts a day. That's a lot of thinking. Let's say you have 50,000 thoughts a day. This amounts to as many as 18 million thoughts a year, give or take. This is the one thing you do every day more than breathing. You think. The problem is many of our thoughts may be negative and a high percentage of our thoughts are repeated day in day out. And if every part of our life is controlled by our thinking, which it is, it makes good sense to change what you are thinking, if you need to.

Think about your computer for a moment. How many files, songs, pictures and videos are stored in your computer? Have you ever had a frozen screen? Has your computer ever slowed or stop working altogether, and the hard drive packed it in? What about the blue screen of death – have you had that one? What about losing your wi-fi connection? Have you ever had a file just disappear? Have you ever run out of space on your computer? What programs are you running? Do you have any outdated software or really old programs that don't provide the results you need? Have you ever had spam emails?

Let me pose some questions for you to consciously consider. How many files, songs, pictures and videos do you have stored *in your mind*? Has your mind ever felt so overloaded that it just went blank? Have you ever felt frozen or stuck emotionally? Has anything ever been said to you that you shouldn't have listened to, and you ended up replaying that thought time and again? Do you ever feel disconnected? Do you ever feel as though you know what to do but you just can't seem to develop an action plan? Have you felt as though there's just too much negative noise inside your mind? Do you sometimes feel that you have no more time, energy or space for anything? What programs are you running? Do you have any outdated thoughts or old strategies that don't seem to produce results? Have you ever had anyone spam your mind?

If you answered yes to any of the above questions then it may be time to delete some of those old thoughts and strategies. It may be time to change the programs you are running in your unconscious mind. You may need to create some more space, energy and time in your life. This might be a good time to delete some of the old files you've been storing that don't serve you well, that fail to help you reach your goals or nourish your life in any way.

Think about how poorly your computer would run if you never upgraded it, never deleted old stuff and never improved the memory.

It's time to clean up, delete old programs, upgrade and reboot your mind. It is time to set your mind free.

Before we dive deeper into resetting your mind, try this short meditation.

AFFIRMATION MEDITATION

Relax your body as you feel, think about and see the affirmation *peace release*. As you inhale, imagine or feel the words you read floating into the front of your mind. As you exhale, let the words float on your breath to the back of your mind and breathe them into your heart and every part of your body, every cell of your being. You can then breathe these words back into your mind and into the world simply by thinking them or saying them aloud.

METHOD 1: Slowly breathing in and out, let the words float on your breath. Breathe in for the first half of the affirmation and exhale the second half of the affirmation.

Breathing in, *Peace*
Breathing out, *Release*

METHOD 2: Breathe in for the entire affirmation and repeat the affirmation when you exhale.

Breathing in, *Peace release*
Breathing out, *Peace release*

Breathe new positive thoughts into yourself and breathe them back into the world.

THE POWER OF MINDFULNESS

When I first met Linda in 1989, she was an absolute vision of beauty and good health – and she still is. Her smile could, and still does, light up a room. Her breakfast back then was often a tall glass of carrot, apple, celery, beetroot, cucumber and ginger juice, and, you guessed it, still is. Our first few dates were at vegetarian restaurants.

One day, we were driving along a main road where there was a KFC and a McDonald's right next to each other.

'I wonder what the food is actually like,' Linda said.

'You've never eaten there?' I was surprised.

'No. Why would I?' she asked, matter-of-factly.

'So, no McDonald's, no Kentucky Fried Chicken, but what about Red Rooster or Pizza Hut?'

'No, never.' Linda was shaking her head.

Linda values her health – one of her favourite sayings is *only goodness enters my body* – and she deeply understands the power of mindfulness. Linda started yoga at the age of eight. Her mother, Valli, a pure angel, and also a vision of health, would let Linda have the occasional Monday off school to join her in a yoga class. From that very young age, Linda learned that movement, breathing and meditation all unite to form a sense of peace and presence. When Linda walks, she breathes in a meditative way – she makes it a meditation. When Linda is eating an apple, she's eating mindfully – it's a meditation. When Linda is washing the dishes, she is in the moment, present – it's a meditation.

I'm convinced that much of Linda's day is meditation. There is no time set aside to practise meditation. Life *is* meditation. Effortless meditation. If we are walking and I ask Linda what she's thinking, her usual response is, 'Should I be thinking of something? I'm just walking and breathing; I'm feeling my legs move.' When both preparing and eating a meal, Linda is mindful and tuned into the moment. It's *all* meditation.

While I consider myself to still be a work in progress, and likely always will be, I continue to make an effort to incorporate and schedule my meditation routines and healthy choices into parts of my day, whereas for Linda it truly is effortless. A calm presence permeates everything she does.

'Don't forget to breathe,' Linda just called from the next room. Was I holding my breath? I think I was. I *was* holding my breath. How did she know I was holding my breath?

In jujutsu, and all martial arts for that matter, one thing you learn is how to counter. Somebody attacks, you counter with a defensive move such as a throw or a strike. In life, there are a great many things we need to counter. We counter dehydration with water. We counter sitting with moving. We counter unhealthy food choices with healthy food choices. We counter negative thoughts and negative emotions with positive thoughts and positive emotions, and on it goes.

The truth is, you can achieve more than you ever thought possible. You are stronger than you think. You've already overcome many challenges, making you a survivor. *You have what it takes to move from surviving to thriving.* We so often limit ourselves and our potential with negative self-defeating talk. Often these thoughts repeat over and over like a broken record becoming a self-fulfilling prophecy. Negative thoughts continuously generate negative feelings that then lead to more negative thoughts. An awareness of when these negative thoughts are popping up allows you to transform those doubts and excuses into empowering beliefs. This is the power of mindfulness in relation to thoughts.

If you want to change a bad habit, or how you feel, or any area of your life at all, you must first change what's going on inside your mind. Think about it for a minute. You could change your hairstyle, you could change the clothes you wear, you could change your job, your relationship or where you live, but if you don't change the inside, inside your mind, nothing really changes. You drag the old story and life's baggage into the future with you. The same patterns continue to repeat themselves unless the story changes and the baggage of life is released. In the same way you would clean out a wardrobe, a drawer or your garage, you need to let go of those thoughts that are not serving you or bringing joy into your life.

Some of the most common limiting beliefs I so often hear are:

- It's too hard.
- I'm too tired.
- I have no energy.
- What's the use?
- I'll do it later.
- I don't have time.
- I'm not good enough.
- I'm a poor sleeper.
- It's impossible.
- I'll just have one.
- I have no willpower.

And on it goes. There are literally thousands of negative thoughts, excuses or limiting beliefs that can stop you from being your best self, achieving your goals and being consistently happy.

I can tell you there is one sure way to overcome this: associate every positive word you read and think with a positive feeling. One day at a time change your thoughts and change your emotional state. When you start to tell yourself, *it's possible*, then everything *is* possible. You feel the good feelings of possibility. When you start to tell yourself that you are in control or you have the power to change, then suddenly you start to feel in control and you start to make positive changes.

When you tell yourself you can't, you won't. When you tell yourself something is too hard, that negative thought generates a feeling of overwhelm and the something will feel too hard. In many instances, you won't even try because of the thought, *it's too hard*.

As you start to tell yourself that you have the power to change, you begin to realise you have a choice, and it's your prerogative to change. Changing one thought has the power to completely change your life.

Change is good.

Change is easy.

Throughout your life, you've changed many things. Oftentimes we resist change or we get stuck in a comfort zone, believing it's too hard to change, that this is the way I am. It's those thoughts that keep us stuck. Now is the time to embrace change. Change will happen with or without you, so you might as well accept and embrace change, and take control.

Think of your problem as already solved and you are halfway there. Thoughts are energy. Every thought generates a feeling. Your feelings inspire more thoughts that in turn give rise to more feelings, and those feelings continue to produce more thoughts. When a thought is negative, it generates a negative emotion. When your thought is positive, it generates a positive emotion. When your unconscious mind is overflowing with negative thoughts, a downward spiral of more negative thoughts and negative emotions follows. When your unconscious mind is overflowing with positive thoughts, it creates an upward spiral of more positive thoughts and positive emotions, as illustrated on the facing page.

CHERYL'S STORY

Cheryl's life was controlled by one overpowering limiting belief that held her back. For longer than she could remember, 49-year-old Cheryl had told herself that she had no memory. The belief of having no memory had a range of other connected negative thought habits such as *I've got a brain like a sieve*, *I can't remember anything* and *I must be stupid*. These negative thoughts in Cheryl's unconscious mind led her to leave school at 14, to not go after jobs that she wanted to go for, and to not participate in courses that she really wanted to do. The belief of having no memory also generated thoughts of *why bother* and *I'll probably fail*.

Cheryl was part of a sales team. During a company training session on presentation skills, each participant delivered their favourite three minutes of their sales pitch to the group. When it came to Cheryl's turn, she refused to stand in front of the group, claiming she couldn't remember what she was supposed to say, explaining she had no memory, and that she only ever did phone presentations where she could read the sales script. What Cheryl failed to realise was that, after working for the company for three years and speaking with ten to 15 clients a day, she had actually read the script more than 7500 times and most likely knew it better than anyone. Unfortunately, Cheryl's negative beliefs, which had been replaying in her mind most of her life, had eroded her self-confidence. These negative thoughts created feelings of low self-esteem and hopelessness.

I asked Cheryl if she would like to be a demonstration subject so we could delete the negative thoughts from her mind. She agreed. When I asked how long she'd had no memory, she answered, 'I don't know, I can't remember.' Cheryl burst into laughter, as did the rest of the group. 'They all know I have a brain like a sieve and I have no memory,' she said.

One of the group called out, 'Only because you keep telling us so.'

Cheryl claimed to have no memories at all from before the age of 14. I led Cheryl into a meditation session. After a few minutes of gentle guiding to discover the root cause event, she opened her eyes and said, 'I just had a flashback! I was about two years old and I was on the change table. My mother was telling me not to wriggle or move or I'd fall and hurt myself. I wriggled, I moved and I fell and hurt myself. I saw my mother standing there, saying, "Why don't you listen to anything I say? You don't remember anything."'

Cheryl could suddenly remember and became exhilarated. 'It's not even my belief, it was my mother's belief,' she said.

I took Cheryl deeper into a meditative state and had her imagine she was looking down at that original time again, when the belief began. This time, knowing that it wasn't her own belief, I guided her to come up with some positive beliefs of her own, while letting go of the old negative story. I told her she didn't need to think that way or feel that way anymore. And if it was okay, she could let go of all the pictures, thoughts and feelings connected to the old negative beliefs relating to her memory. Cheryl opened her eyes and smiled. 'I have a wonderful memory; I can remember anything that's important.'

I asked Cheryl to reflect on several times in the past where the beliefs *I have no memory, I have a brain like a sieve, I can't remember anything* and *I must be stupid* had held her back in life. This helped her realise that things could have been different, and how going into the future her life can and will be different. In only a short time Cheryl had deleted the old thought of having no memory and it was now gone forever.

As the seminar finished, I whispered to Cheryl that she had unknowingly practised the sales script thousands upon thousands of times. I suggested that she probably knew it better than anyone and asked whether she would be happy to present in front of the group at the next day's workshop. She agreed.

The next morning, overflowing with confidence, Cheryl rose from her seat and delivered a knockout three-minutes sales presentation – to loud cheers and a standing ovation.

Within two weeks, Cheryl was the number one performer in a sales team of 25. Three months later she was still the number one sales performer in the team, week in week out, and she had started a TAFE course that she had been putting off her entire adult life.

ARE YOU IN TWO MINDS?

Each of us has a conscious mind and an unconscious mind. Your conscious mind is everything held consciously in your mind and the mental processes you are aware of in the moment. It is the part of your mind that analyses and thinks. You may think about what is happening around you – what you are consciously aware of. While you are working or doing an activity, you are consciously aware.

Your unconscious is everything else. It is the hard drive of your brain and body, and the domain of your feelings, emotions, memories and urges. Your unconscious mind is outside your conscious awareness. Habits are unconscious, and that's why they can be hard to break with willpower alone. Your unconscious could be likened to one long-playing recorder that stores everything you see, taste, smell, feel and think. And then it replays experiences, feelings and thoughts repeatedly.

Your brain is a supercomputer, and this book is your manual on how to run your brain for your best results. Throughout *Mind Free* we will work on creating a positive connection between your conscious mind and your unconscious mind while releasing as many negative thoughts and feelings as possible. To overcome challenges and achieve goals we need a happy balance between the two parts of the mind.

When you are consciously aware of reprogramming your unconscious mind, you have a stronger recall. As your unconscious mind records the new thoughts, the positive suggestions will stay in your unconscious mind and have a profound effect on how you feel and how you behave.

Everything you read in this book will help you learn consciously and unconsciously, allowing you to make the greatest amount of change possible.

CRAPPY VERSUS HAPPY – THE POWER OF POSITIVE THINKING

Let yourself become more and more aware of the following fact: it is not the events in your life that are affecting you, it is *your reaction* to those events. Knowing that in the blink of an eye you can change your thoughts and how you feel is the key. Try the following exercise to see how your thoughts can rapidly help you change how you feel.

Sit or lie comfortably. Take a few moments to listen to your breathing. Notice your breath effortlessly, rhythmically flowing in and out of your body. Focus on the air as it moves in and out without any struggle on your part. And for another moment, bring your attention to your eyes. Notice that any second your eyes will blink. Wait for it. And even if you tried to stop them, your eyes will blink. And just like that you can change your focus. That is how long it takes to change your mind or how you feel. Thoughts come, thoughts go, feelings pass. We are in a constant state of change. Where is your attention?

Can you recall a time when you were completely happy? Remember that time now. Take a moment to feel those happy feelings.

Can you recall a time when you were so filled with laughter that you almost fell to the ground laughing? Why was it so funny? How were you standing or sitting? Go ahead and remember that time now. As you recall that time, notice how you feel now.

Just for a moment or two, remember a place that makes you feel really happy, a place where you are filled with joy. What do you feel, see and hear? What are you saying to yourself while in this happy place?

As you hold on to those good feelings, come back to your breath and the present moment. How do you feel?

And herein lies the key. If you want to feel crappy, think crappy thoughts, play old crappy movies from the past on the screen of your mind and imagine crappy things happening in the future. If you want to feel sad, keep thinking sad thoughts, playing the same old sad movies or imagining sad things happening in the future. Conversely, if you want to feel excited, think exciting thoughts, remember exciting moments from your past, imagine exciting things happening in the future. And the same applies to every negative emotion and positive emotion. If you want to feel gratitude, compassion, joy, love or any other positive emotion, think the thoughts that will generate that emotion.

In year ten at school, the first day after the summer holiday, I got in a fight with another student. He punched me from behind, in the side of the head, and I put him in a headlock before the fight was broken up. I was pretty angry that he hit me in the head for no reason. Then one of my friends said, 'Did you hear his mum died in the holidays?' In that moment everything changed, as I was filled with sympathy and compassion. How could I hold on to anger? The anger vanished in a fraction of a second. I apologised for putting him in a headlock and said I was sorry to hear about his mum. He apologised for punching me. I told him to punch me any time he wanted and we both laughed.

The important thing to remember here is that *you* are not the problem. The story you attach to the problem, what you believe and affirm, *is* the problem. Your perspective, the way you are looking at something, may be the problem. When you change the meaning you attach to your problem, then the problem changes.

When I started jujutsu at the age of 17, I wasn't very fit, flexible or strong, and I was totally uncoordinated. In those early days, I was constantly doing things the wrong way. I would throw kicks that went awry, punches would miss by a mile and my judo was dismal at best. Luckily, the fifth dan, Brian, was incredibly patient. I'm sure he was shaking his head on the inside, as he calmly demonstrated defensive moves and techniques again and again. 'When you repeat something enough times, it becomes automatic,' he said.

I heeded Brian's advice and, after every class, I would go home and practise the moves for another hour with an imaginary partner. In the morning, I would get up and, after a few stretches, I would practise the moves again. During my lunch breaks at work, I would mentally rehearse the moves, along with a meditation. Little by little, day by day, I started to make progress. As the weeks and months passed, my skill levels improved. My defensive moves began to flow, my kicks were hitting their targets, my punches were accurate and my judo, while not my strongest area, was improving.

On the day of my first grading, yellow belt, I was both excited and nervous. I'd practised the moves a thousand times. When I arrived at the dojo, self-doubt started creeping in. *What if I stuff up? What if I forget what I'm supposed to do? What if I mispronounce the Japanese name of a judo throw or, even worse, do the wrong judo throw? What if I'm the only person who doesn't get graded?* Just before the grading started, sensing my nerves, Brian came over to me, nodded, looked me straight in the eye and said, 'Just breathe, you've got this.'

Just breathe, I've got this became my mantra that day. I started meditating on that thought and affirmed it over and over again. Whenever it was my turn to be attacked, I thought to myself, *just breathe, I've got this.* That positive thought totally deleted the doubts and the nervous, negative thoughts. Nine out of ten of my defensive moves were as perfect as they could be, for my skill level. I remembered the names of the judo throws and proficiently pronounced them when called upon to do so. My punches and kicks landed exactly where they were supposed to land.

Getting my yellow belt that night had a profound impact on my life. I'd achieved the goal I set out to achieve and felt proud. Thoughts of being unfit, weak and uncoordinated were gone. My story had changed. No one could take my yellow belt away from me. I immediately set my next goal: orange belt – harder defensive moves, new strikes to learn, new judo throws to master, all ahead of me. But this was only a stepping stone towards my ultimate goal.

From the corner of my eye, when no one was watching, or so I thought, I would look at Brian's sturdy black belt with its five white stripes, each denoting another level of black belt. I would stare into space, visualising myself with my own black belt around my waist and handling the attacks a black belt could handle. I imagined myself running my own school.

'You'll have to work hard,' Brian said, expressionless.

Old program – *What if I fail?*
Upgrade – *Just breathe, I've got this.*

The good news and the bad news about beliefs is that they stick with you. More than 40 years later, the empowering belief, *just breathe, I've got this*, is still with me. By replacing negative thoughts with positive thoughts, every new moment is a new opportunity to change for the better. Be aware, though, that it may take some time to increase the moments of positive thoughts, joy and happiness. There is no need to rush things. This is not a race; this is *your life* and, as with any endeavour, with persistence you will be rewarded. Every morning is a new day, a fresh beginning. Every day is a new opportunity to start again if we need to. Only by leaving yesterday behind can we be free from the troubles of the past. Take the positive lessons with you but not the negative feelings. Yesterday's failures and mistakes are exactly that – yesterday's – they don't belong to today. Accept them, learn from them, let them go.

LET GO OF LIMITING BELIEFS

Exactly what is a limiting belief? It is a belief about us or the world that limits our ability to move forward and be the best we can be. All limiting beliefs began with a limiting decision. There was a time in your past when something happened, an event that made you decide on a limiting belief that became your view of the world. Letting go of limiting decisions and beliefs is like cleaning your computer of a virus or bug that may be slowing your computer down or stopping your system from working altogether.

Limiting beliefs are the negative self-talk patterns that repeat like a broken record over and over, stopping you from achieving your goals. You could actually describe a limiting belief as a *negative trance state*. Think about it: if you say *I don't have time* over and over, you are literally in the I-don't-have-time trance, aren't you? If you say to yourself and others continuously, *I don't have time*, you will never have time to prepare a healthy meal, or go for a walk or go to the gym. If you say to yourself, *why bother?* then why would you bother? If you say to yourself, *it's too hard*, it will be too hard. These are self-fulfilling prophecies.

A contaminated mind is a negative mind.
A free mind is a happy mind.

It is time to delete the spam and old programming in your mind. It's time to clear your mind, and set your mind free.

One of the most effective ways to change an old thought pattern is to create a new positive and empowering thought pattern. The real secret to ask yourself – to ask your unconscious mind – is, what positive learning or new belief do you need to know so the old belief no longer has any power over you? What is there to learn? What wisdom do you need? When you stay focused on negative thoughts, you will get more of the same. Instead focus on a new positive thought, a new idea and a new feeling. Make no excuses.

It's about taking baby steps and doing small things that will make a big difference. Nobody is asking you to bungee-jump off a bridge or to run a marathon in record time. When you continuously say, *having one won't hurt*, you give away your power and will continue to struggle because one often leads to two or three, or a whole packet or a whole bottle. While you focus on what is going wrong, how bad things are, how crappy you feel, that is what you will get more of … things going wrong and you having crappy feelings. You need to change your focus. You can do it! I know you can. It's also important to remember that things do go wrong and crappy things will happen, but what story are you attaching to the events and how many times will you replay the thoughts and experiences in your mind?

When we live in the past, if that past was negative or traumatic, we are weighed down. Our body keeps thinking we are experiencing the old events over and over. The mountains of negativity may seem impossible to climb, but small steps take you a long way. Post-traumatic stress disorder (PTSD) is the perfect example of the past replaying itself over and over. When it comes to the past, let it pass. Tell yourself, *that was yesterday.*

Pay attention to what you're thinking. Shoot down any negative self-talk. Replace it with something positive like, *I'm ready to change: I can, I will, I must.* Repeat it a thousand times and take one small action step, then another, and another and another. It's time to interrupt the old pattern.

CHANGE YOUR STORY

Having heard almost every possible excuse, it's clear to me that, for most people with challenges, the problems often come back to what we believe about ourselves. What's your own personal story? What limiting stories are you telling yourself? What is holding you back? What beliefs and thoughts define and drive you? What is your big WHY? How can you change your story?

Imagine if Alice in Wonderland never went down the rabbit hole, or Amelia Earhart told herself she couldn't fly solo across the Atlantic, or Elvis kept driving a truck, or the Beatles listened to the story that their music wouldn't catch on. Imagine Muhammad Ali saying 'I'm not bad' rather than 'I am the Greatest.' Imagine all the people ... who could change their lives by telling themselves a new story.

What story will lift, inspire and motivate you?

You will begin to realise that the more options you have with positive thoughts, the easier it is to keep moving towards your goal. When you are heading one way and there is a roadblock, you find a way around, an alternative route. You wouldn't be reading this right now if you hadn't hit some sort of roadblock, would you? Isn't it time for a new direction, a new story? It's time to turn things around.

Now is the time to reconsider your old beliefs. It's time to change your story. As you reconsider each old excuse or negative thought that held you back in the past, you can release it from your unconscious mind. You can delete the old thoughts.

Look at the negative thought checklist on the opposite page and mark the beliefs that are part of your story. Add others if you need to.

How many of the negative thoughts did you tick or highlight? Look at each negative thought pattern and consider whether that belief is an issue for you. Think about it. Every time you repeat a negative thought, you give it power. How many times do you use those phrases? This is the old programming. If you have said a thousand times that you are not good enough, you've been stuck in the I'm-not-good-enough trance. And there is a pretty good chance that someone else put you in that trance. Who told you that? That was their belief, not yours. What are you choosing to believe? It's okay to change your mind.

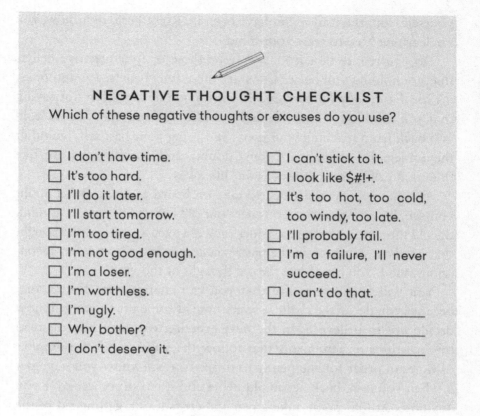

NEGATIVE THOUGHT CHECKLIST

Which of these negative thoughts or excuses do you use?

- [ ] I don't have time.
- [ ] It's too hard.
- [ ] I'll do it later.
- [ ] I'll start tomorrow.
- [ ] I'm too tired.
- [ ] I'm not good enough.
- [ ] I'm a loser.
- [ ] I'm worthless.
- [ ] I'm ugly.
- [ ] Why bother?
- [ ] I don't deserve it.

- [ ] I can't stick to it.
- [ ] I look like $#!+.
- [ ] It's too hot, too cold, too windy, too late.
- [ ] I'll probably fail.
- [ ] I'm a failure, I'll never succeed.
- [ ] I can't do that.
- [ ] _____
- [ ] _____
- [ ] _____

One thought can change your life. You have the power to change. Take a deep breath in and repeat in your mind, *I have the power to change.*

The solutions you'll discover on the next few pages are designed to guide you to a new way of thinking. Read them over as many times as necessary as you reinforce new empowering beliefs. Let's tackle some of the most common limiting beliefs, and loosen the grip you may have on these negative self-talk patterns.

You are about to retrain your brain with questions, ideas and suggestions that will challenge your old way of thinking. The following language patterns are a form of self-hypnosis that will allow you to disconnect the old patterns. These questions help you to unhypnotise yourself from the trance you have been in. Right here, right now, you are learning how to reset your mind.

Do you realise that it may only be three or four negative beliefs that are holding you back? Consider these four beliefs: *I'm too busy, it's too hard, why bother?* and *I'm not good enough*. I'm not saying that *you* think these exact thoughts, but if you did, they would hold you back from reaching your goals and being your best self, wouldn't they? Negative thoughts, beliefs, doubts and comparisons are like thieves, stealing the quality of your life away.

At some point you decided to take on board a certain belief about yourself. It's now time to reconsider your old beliefs. It's time to unthink the old thoughts. As you reconsider each old excuse or negative thought that has held you back in the past, you can let it go from your unconscious mind. You can delete the old thought or thoughts.

You will begin to realise that you can change your beliefs and, because you decided to believe something at some point, you can now decide *not* to believe it. In the next exercise, you may need to read the questions or statements that follow the limiting belief a number of times in order for the penny to drop. You will know you have got it when you look back at the old belief and it has no power over you anymore. At that point, take a pen and cross it out, getting rid of the old negative thought pattern, and deleting the old program. Upgrade your mind by repeating your new empowering beliefs.

There is power in repetition.

Old program – *I'm too busy*.
Upgrade – *I make the time*.

Everybody processes things at a different speed. You may read one of the following language patterns once and get it straight away, or you may need to read this entire section every day for 30 days. You will find it easy to leave behind the negative thoughts when you change each limiting belief in your own time.

When you get to each positive affirmation, repeat the new belief as many times as you feel you need to. As you carefully read each word that follows, you will flood your mind with positive thoughts and you won't have room for the negative ones.

Following are hypnotic language solutions to some of the most common negative beliefs. Take your time reading this section slowly either aloud or quietly in your mind as you think about the questions and contemplate the answers. When you get to each italicised affirmation – each *new belief* – at the end of the questions, take a moment to breathe in those thoughts that have meaning to you or are thoughts you would like to adopt. As you breathe the affirmation in, imagine the words floating into your conscious mind, and then breathe them into your unconscious mind and into every muscle in your body. You may like to repeat each affirmation three or more times to really lock it into your mind.

Are you ready?

I don't have time

Really? When will you have time? How can you not have time? At what time will you have time? How much time do you actually need to do what you need to do? How important is your goal? How many ways are there in which you can make the time? No time for your health? Let yourself begin to experience the power of this thought:

I make the time.

It's too hard

How is it too hard? What part of it isn't hard? What makes it hard? Imagine if everything in life was too easy. How can you make it doable? How can you update your old thinking patterns? What changes do you need to undertake to make your happiness and health uncomplicated and effortless? What would you have to think or say to yourself to make it easy? What else would you like to change?

I'll make it easy.

I'll do it later

How much later? Isn't it already later? How late do you want it to be? Would you, could you, should you do it now? Could you possibly put off putting it off? Imagine if your motto were *I can, I will, I must*. What would happen in your life if you took action? How good will you feel when you do it now? Associate the following words with a feeling of action, and begin telling yourself:

I'll do it now.

I'll start tomorrow

That's funny: I thought tomorrow never came. Isn't today the day and now the time? What is wrong with today? What is wrong with right now? Don't start today unless you want to achieve results. How good would you feel if you started today, right now? For how long do you want to put it off? How many tomorrows do you have: are they infinite? What will continue to happen if you tell yourself, I'll start tomorrow, next week, next month or next year? Rather than starting Monday, one day or someday, why not start today? You will feel so good when you start today. Imagine what would happen if you did start today. What are you waiting for?

Today is the day, now is the time.

I'm too tired

Too tired for what? What's making you tired? Did you know the more exercise you do, the more energy you have? Could you keep going until the tank is empty? Are you eating tiring foods? Imagine what you could do if you ate healthy foods that gave you lots of energy. How fresh and alive would you feel? Have you ever felt like you just wanted to get up and move? And you begin to realise, the more active you are, the more fat you burn. Increased activity equals increased energy. Increased activity equals increased health. The more active you are, the better you feel. This is a pure and simple fact.

I am fresh and alive.

I'm not good enough

Says who? Compared to who? What are you not good enough for? What if you *were* good enough? Whose standard are you trying to live up to? What have you done that is good enough? Two words to consider: stuff 'em! You damn well *are* good enough. And what if just being good enough was not good enough and you were actually more than good enough? Who decides who is good enough and who is not good enough anyway? The fact is, not only are you good enough, you are *more than* good enough. And well done on making it this far into the book. More and more, as you begin to realise you are good enough, your self-esteem will improve, and you'll feel a whole lot better.

I am more than good enough.

I'm a loser

What would you have to lose to be a winner? What thought could you delete from your mind? And even reading this now, you begin to see things differently and even feel differently, don't you? You can change overnight, and in fact you can change right now. Being a winner is easy. Ask my friend Mark Hoffman. Hoffy entered his first triathlon many years ago. The day after that first event, I asked how he did in the race. With the enthusiasm of an Olympic athlete he said, 'I AM A WINNER.'

'You won?' I asked with equal excitement.

'No, I came in last out of more than 300 people, but I crossed the finish line, so I AM A WINNER,' said Hoffy.

Who are you and what will you do?

I am a winner, I will succeed.

I'm worthless

Who put that price on you? In what currency are you worthless ... the currency of the nation of BS? How much would you have to be worth to be worth something? And now you begin to realise how much you are worth; how much would you have to be worth to be worthy? Now keep in mind the exchange rate could change at any moment, and then you would be priceless. You have nothing to lose and much to gain. You deserve success.

I am worthy, my life is priceless, I deserve success.

I'm ugly

Says who? No one else is quite like you. You are you. You are the one. The truth of the matter is that many people radiate an inner beauty. What are you projecting to the world? As the following words travel from the page into your mind, you'll begin to realise this truth:

I am loving, I am beautiful, I am me, I am free.

Why bother?

Why not bother? Imagine what you could achieve if you *did* bother. What is it you are actually bothering about anyway? What if you didn't bother about not bothering and started to bother about your health? And isn't *bother* such a funny word anyway? How will your life change when every day you take positive steps towards your goal? The effort you make will eventually become effortless as you begin to bother in a positive way. It's time to bother. Pay close attention to this suggestion:

My goal is worth it, I am worth it.

I don't deserve it

When did you decide that? Who told you that? What do you deserve? How will you know when you do deserve it? You will realise, as you let go of the past, you start to deserve it more and more. You don't need to think the old thought any more. Sooner or later, maybe straight away or in a few days from now, you will begin to realise this:

I do deserve it.

I can't stick to it

After you finish this page, the next one gets even easier. You are changing your mindset and beginning to realise that sticking to it is easy. This time things are different because you are removing the mental blocks. You feel more and more motivated to stick to it, to make it happen, to go for it, to make this the time. You can change overnight or you can change in an instant. Because when change happens, it is instant. It is up to you. Past events aren't always a precise prediction of what will happen in the future, are they? Think about the humble postage stamp. It has one job: to stick to one thing until it reaches its destination. Realise quit-ability is not for you but stick-ability is. You can easily stick with it.

I easily stick to it.

I look like $#!+

MythBusters proved you can polish a turd so what's the problem? How long will you continue to be so judgmental? I am sure you realise you are so much more than what you judge yourself to be. It is such a useless judgment anyway, isn't it? How could you start being kind to yourself and shine on, you crazy diamond?

I shine like a diamond.

It's too hot, too cold, too windy, too late

It will always be too something, when you think with a too-this or too-that mentality. It isn't the actual weather that causes the problem, but the thinking about it that creates the problem. And maybe you can put your health off for a while, but how long do you really want to put off your happiness? There are many incredible stories of people who went walking on cold, windy and even hot days. What else will you talk yourself out of? And, more importantly, what will you talk yourself into?

Any time is a good time.

I'm a failure, I'll never succeed

Your unconscious mind could be equated to that of a five-year-old. How long will you continue to put yourself down? Imagine for a moment that you are with a five-year-old, talking to them, and they are trying to achieve something. Would you tell them they are a failure and they will never succeed? I think not. Your unconscious mind needs clear instruction. It needs positive reinforcement. It's now time to let go of the old beliefs. It's time to know you are a winner, and you can achieve anything you set your mind to.

I am a winner, I'm ready to succeed.

I can't do that

Bet you can! Malala Yousafzai was shot after speaking out against the Taliban but she continued her activism and went on to win the Nobel Peace Prize at just 17. Henry Ford went broke twice before finding success, but he never gave up. Albert Einstein was labelled intellectually disabled by his teachers, and he went on to win the Nobel Prize in Physics. Oprah Winfrey ran away from home after years of abuse, but her self-belief made her one of the most successful and inspiring people on the planet. Steven Spielberg was rejected from film and TV school no less than three times. J.K. Rowling's Harry Potter manuscript was rejected 12 times before getting published. Babe Ruth, arguably the greatest player and home-run striker in the history of baseball, also held records for the most strike-outs in a season – he is famously quoted as saying, 'Every strike brings me closer to the next home run.' Be willing to *give it a go* and keep going until you succeed. Let nothing and nobody stand in your way.

I will keep going until I succeed.

You have unlimited potential.
I am capable and can make things happen.
Anything I put my mind to, I can achieve.
I have unlimited potential.

Old program – *I can't*.
Upgrade – *I can, I know I can*.

THINK FOR YOURSELF

The question to ask yourself is:

Are my beliefs supporting me, nurturing me and moving me towards my goals, or are my beliefs limiting me, hurting me and stopping me from reaching my goals?

The fact is, if you continue to do the same behaviours and get the same results – results you're not happy with – you really need to take a good look at your beliefs and the story you are telling yourself. Given that many beliefs are something somebody else said, it's time to stop thinking other people's thoughts. It's time to think for yourself. It's time to choose not to believe the old negative thoughts and choose to believe a new set of thoughts.

Imagine how you would feel if every time somebody projected a negative thought in your direction you gently smiled and thought to yourself, *I choose not to believe that*. Imagine if every time a negative thought popped up from your unconscious mind you quietly whispered to yourself, *I choose not to believe that*. Imagine for a moment that you could delete every negative bit of programming, every doubt, every useless belief, every piece of rubbish someone else said to you or about you simply by telling yourself, *I choose not to believe that*. Well, you can. Think it, whisper it, speak it or stand on top of a mountain and scream it out as loud as you can.

I choose not to believe that.

Remembering that your thoughts generate feelings, and the way you feel determines how you act and behave, what positive empowering beliefs can you come up with about yourself?

Create new beliefs

Read through the examples of negative beliefs and empowering beliefs listed below. Then, in the space provided, list your most common excuses or negative thoughts in the left column. Look at each one you've written and ask yourself what you need to think instead. While telling yourself either aloud or in your mind *I choose not to believe that*, cross out the negative belief and then write as many new empowering thoughts on the right as you can think of. The aim is to outweigh the negative thought with as many positive thoughts as you can.

Ask your unconscious mind for a lesson in wisdom and truth. It may also help to think of the opposite thought to the negative thought. State what you need to know in the positive. You will quickly get the idea of how this exercise works.

NEGATIVE BELIEFS	EMPOWERING BELIEFS
I don't have time	I make the time
It's too hard	I make it easy
I can't	I can
I'll do it later	I'll do it now
I'm always hungry	I'm satisfied
My work is more/too important	My health is number one
I'll start tomorrow	I'll start today
I have no energy	I have an abundance of energy
I'm not good enough	I am good enough
I'm a loser	I am a winner
I'm worthless	I am worthy

NEGATIVE BELIEFS

POSITIVE BELIEFS

1 _____

_____

_____

_____

_____

2 _____

_____

_____

_____

_____

3 _____

_____

_____

_____

_____

1 _____

2 _____

3 _____

4 _____

5 _____

1 _____

2 _____

3 _____

4 _____

5 _____

1 _____

2 _____

3 _____

4 _____

5 _____

MIND FREE MINUTE MEDITATION

Take one minute to immerse yourself in the following power statements and affirmations as a mindful self-hypnosis practice. As you read, think about and feel each word that follows, imagine these words floating off the page while flowing into your mind and heart when you breathe in. As you exhale, breathe each word into every muscle and every cell of your body. Begin to think these words and speak them either aloud or whispering as you breathe them into the world. You'll start to notice these affirmations will float with you each and every day as you change how you feel and act – as you change your life.

Breathe in, *just breathe, I've got this*
Breathe out, *just breathe, I've got this*

Breathe in, *I am good enough*
Breathe out, *I am good enough*

Breathe in, *I can do it*
Breathe out, *I can do it*

Breathe in, *I have an abundance of energy*
Breathe out, *I have an abundance of energy*

Breathe in, *I can, I know I can*
Breathe out, *I can, I know I can*

Breathe in, *I have unlimited potential*
Breathe out, *I have unlimited potential*

THREE KEYS TO CHANGE YOUR LIFE
WITH POSITIVE THINKING

LESSON 1: If you want to change your life, you first need to change your mind. Thoughts generate feelings. Feelings create thoughts that can manifest as actions. In other words, our actions, thoughts and feelings are all interrelated – they are connected. Change your thoughts and you'll change how you feel and act.

LESSON 2: Breathe each positive word you read that reso- nates with you into your mind and exhale it into your body. Then breathe the word or words from the back of your mind to the front of your mind and back into the world, into existence and into your life.

LESSON 3: You are the master of your own thoughts. Choose not to believe negative thoughts by telling yourself, *I choose not to believe that.* Discover your own new story as you take time out to read, recite and practise the 21 States and scripts found in *Mind Free.*

DISCOVER MORE MIND FREE

For more mindful self-hypnosis to help you reset your mind, go to p. 243 of the Mind Manual. You can also listen to recorded sessions on resetting your mind via the Mind Free app and website mindfreeapp.com.

The three decrees

I hereby decree that my day will be filled with strength, energy, determination, confidence, compassion and belief. I command, my body follows. I am deserving, I am authentic, I am courageous, I am learning, I am growing, I am transforming, I am positive, I am thankful. I start and end each day with gratitude. I can do it, so I do. My health is my wealth. I treat myself with love and respect as I make time for me. I am good enough and I am worthy.

On the following scroll, copy the above in full or part, and combine with your own statements. Or, if you prefer, select your own positive emotion words, short power statements and empowering affirmations. Combine them to form your own personal decree by you, to you, for you.

Official Decree

_____

_____

_____

_____

_____

_____

_____

_____

_____

_____

_____

_____

_____

_____

_____

Signed

CHAPTER 3
STRESS LESS

Everything stresses me out.

What doesn't stress you out?
How would you feel if you could take a deep breath
and blow stress away?

I can't cope.

Can you recall times you have coped?
Imagine you *could* cope with challenges and handle
whatever life throws your way.
And as you begin to tell yourself, *I easily cope*,
you will cope.

I can cope and it's easy to relax.

Is stress really such a bad thing?

The simple answer is: No! Our inability to unwind and let go of stress is where the problems arise. How you look at stress will determine whether or not you are positively or negatively impacted by it.

A stress-free world is unrealistic. The effects of stress on our well-being are determined by how we cope with each situation.

So, why do some people cope while others are affected so intensely? It boils down to our reaction and our thought process before, during and after we experience a stressful event. We hear of increasing incidents of car rage, phone rage, computer rage and even shopping trolley rage. With more people becoming more stressed, it's up to each one of us to increase the calm in our life and to create some harmony for ourselves and those around us.

Not all stress is bad. The stress associated with watching your favourite sporting team can be a good kind of stress. The excitement and the rush are all a part of enjoying sport. The stress or pressure of a timeframe to complete a task can be a good stress: we are motivated and work faster to finish on time. The event doesn't determine the impact as much as the actual story we attach to it. Riding the dodgem cars at the local carnival can be a good stress. Going on a date, getting a new job and the anticipation of reaching a goal are all examples of good stress. Let's face it, if we don't have some degree of stress, life would be pretty dull. It's often these moments of excitement that add colour to our life. We simply need to look at stress differently.

FIGHT OR FLIGHT

The fight-or-flight response has been with us since prehistoric days. When faced with danger, our cave-dwelling ancestors were often saved by the dramatic changes that took place in their bodies when they were confronted.

If this was you, your heart would start to pump faster, supplying your muscles with the much-needed energy for running or fighting. The hypothalamus area of your brain would trigger the release of adrenaline and cortisol into your bloodstream. Your breathing rate would quicken, and your capillaries – the tiny blood vessels under the surface of your skin – would temporarily shut down to reduce the chance of bleeding to death if injured. Your digestion and sexual functions would be turned off. You would see better, your reactions would be faster; everything around you would become a possible threat as you view the world from a position of fear. You would be in a state of heightened alert.

This state of heightened alert – being in the red zone – is fine when we are in danger. But when everything starts to stress us out, from minor everyday events to major events, the prolonged stress takes a heavy toll.

These days, there is very little chance that a sabre-toothed tiger or other wild animal will attack us on the way home from work. However, the modern-day equivalent of our furry, fanged foe is very real. The threat could be an angry boss, running late for an appointment, too many bills, an angry partner, children swinging from the rafters or a dentist appointment. While not life-threatening, most of these modern-day pressures are very real. The problem is, we can't run away every time there is a problem. Mostly, we just have to sit there and deal with it. These problems continue to pile up, one on top of the other.

The way you think about or look at stress will determine how your body responds to it. If you think of stress as a negative, your body will be impacted negatively, and your health affected. If you think of a stressful event as a positive challenge, then your body will be impacted positively.

Old program – *Everything stresses me out.*
Upgrade – *I stay calm and happy.*

DENISE'S STORY

Denise was a single mum with three children under the age of eight plus a 14-year-old daughter. Denise worked a full-time job and two part-time jobs just to make ends meet. She had been separated for a little over a year.

Denise's mother had organised for her to attend one of my Inner-makeover weekend retreats.

'Everything stresses me out. The children stress me out, work stresses me out, I'm not sleeping well and that stresses me out, my ex stresses me out, and I just have no time for me, and that stresses me out,' explained Denise, as she shared her story with the group.

'I eat when I'm stressed, I eat when I'm tired, I eat when I'm feeling emotional, I eat at night out of habit and to comfort myself.'

Obviously, Denise had a lot on. I empathised with her, but also knew it was important to help her look at stress in a different way, along with practising some stress-busting techniques. We needed to activate Denise's pressure-cooker release valve and wake her up from the stress trance.

Over the next two days, Denise learned a variety of techniques to help her think and feel differently. We practised a number of one-minute meditations that weekend, meaning Denise and the group had simple techniques that they could apply at almost any time of the day or night, should the need arise. One of the techniques Denise really liked was the one-minute meditation, *I feel at peace.*

This is a great meditation that you can practise anywhere, anytime. Simply take a slow deep breath in while thinking the thought, *I feel at peace*, and as you exhale you think the thought, *I am at peace.* You let the words flow in on your breath, *I feel at peace*, and as you breathe out you feel the thought, *I am at peace*, flowing through your entire body.

After two days of nonstop meditation and hypnosis, Denise floated out of the seminar.

Two weeks later, I had a call from Denise's elder daughter. 'What have you done with my mum? She attended your seminar two weekends ago,' she said.

Holy guacamole, I thought to myself, her mum's gone missing, this is terrible. 'How long has she been missing?' I asked.

Her daughter laughed and explained that the woman who came home after the weekend retreat was not her mother. This woman looked like her mother and sounded like her mother, but was definitely not her mother. She went on to thank me because her mum was no longer stressing out at every little thing in life, and she seemed so much happier.

A few months later, I heard from Denise herself, who didn't know her daughter had called, and we had a good laugh. Denise was now setting aside time every morning and every night to practise a short mindful self-hypnosis session, and when she needs to throughout the day, she breathes in, *I feel at peace*, and breathes out, *I am at peace*.

When you think of stress as beneficial or as a positive experience, it can reduce the feelings of overwhelm. The most powerful thing you can do in regard to stress is to have a positive attitude. In this chapter I'll help you learn how to identify what stresses you out, how to handle stress and how to recover from stress. I also include simple strategies to change your inner-dialogue when it comes to stress, plus some easy and effective stress-busting meditation and self-hypnosis techniques to try.

UNDERSTANDING YOUR STRESSORS

Physical stress, such as when we are in danger, is the easiest type of stress to identify. Mental and emotional stress can be much harder to pinpoint and may be caused by events or changes at work, at home or in our relationships. It is when we resist change that we are affected. Stress can increase when we feel helpless, such as if you lose your job or don't have job security. When there are no rewards or recognition for the work we do, it can affect us mentally too.

Stress can be ongoing, such as when either you or a close family member is suffering from a serious illness or you are going through challenging times in your relationship. We also experience stress when we feel as though we are not achieving our goals or fulfilling our own needs. If there is a problem and we bury our head in the sand rather than facing the problem, the stress can increase because the problem remains.

Liken yourself to a pressure cooker. Sitting on top of the pressure cooker there is a steam-pressure release valve. As each minor event throughout the day continues to pile up on top of major life challenges or significant events, it's like steam building up inside the pressure cooker.

If the release valve is not working, then the pressure simply continues to build up, which can eventually affect our health. The ultimate pressure-cooker release valve is meditation. Later on in this chapter, you'll find a simple meditation technique to help you release stress.

Prolonged stress – when the pressure-cooker release valve isn't working – can lead to burnout. If you constantly feel mentally depleted, physically exhausted or emotionally drained, and you find you aren't your normal energetic or happy self, emotional burnout may be just around the corner. When the emotional tank is empty, feelings of helplessness, hopelessness and loss of motivation become all too common.

Burnout doesn't just happen after a single event, however, unless that event was the straw that broke the camel's back. When the ability to handle stress is overtaken by the increasing demands of a job, combined with other challenges such as poor sleep, relationship issues, family health problems, personal medical conditions or significant life changes, the constant build-up of stress can be all too much.

Overload of work with unreasonable deadlines is one of the main causes of emotional burnout. The constant and seemingly never-ending stress makes your body produce excessive amounts of the stress hormone cortisol. When we end up in a constant state of fight or flight, these higher levels of cortisol wreak havoc on both our body and mind. Often, people will reach for alcohol, drugs or food as an anaesthetic, but unfortunately this is only a short-term distraction that ends up adding to the problem.

Most people make more of an effort looking after their mobile phone, checking its power and keeping it safe than they do of themselves. Why wait to have a heart attack, a stroke, chronic fatigue or a complete breakdown until you do something? Why can't you at least treat yourself as well as you treat your phone? You recharge your phone. It's time to recharge yourself or pay the price.

TYPES OF STRESS

The following twelve areas are the dirty dozen of stressors – common triggers for stress that should be considered as you develop the newer calmer you. Next to each is a simple solution for you to consider – and the more you practise countering stress the better you will become at feeling relaxed.

1. **Negative thoughts:** Change one thought at a time.
2. **Negative emotions:** What baggage are you carrying? Let it go.
3. **Negative input:** Avoid negative people, the news and negative self-talk.
4. **No release valve:** This book is full of release valves; find the ones that best suit you.
5. **Unhealthy environment:** Avoid places you feel are not healthy for you.
6. **Overcommitment:** How, when and why do you overcommit? Learn to say no.
7. **Overwork:** Reduce your workload, delegate and cut back on time wasting.
8. **Poor diet:** How can you improve your diet? Make healthy choices.
9. **No support:** Build up a support network that will help you rise above it all.
10. **No goals:** Set goals so you have something positive to focus on.
11. **Lack of control:** Take responsibility and control – *it's your life.*
12. **Lack of exercise:** Develop a simple routine. Walk for 30 minutes a day.

HANDLING STRESS

How many times have you imagined something bad was going to happen and it never did? A loved one is running late and you imagine the worst, making yourself sick in the process. The boss calls you to their office and you immediately think the worst: I wonder what I did wrong, I'll probably get the sack, how will I support my family? You receive a letter that looks official and before you even open it, you start to panic. Nine times out of ten, it's nothing. Your loved one was caught up or simply got lost, the boss was just letting you know that the company is implementing a new system and the letter was junk mail. Even when the situation is grim, it doesn't help if we make ourselves sick with worry.

Knowing how to identify and cope with negative stress and turn it into a positive is the key.

Be aware of what stresses you.
Take action to counter the effects of stress.
Take three deep breaths and let it go.

The power of exercise

Let's think of our prehistoric ancestors again for a moment. We now know about the changes that have taken place in the body during the fight or flight response. What else happened? When the threat was on, our ancestors either ran, or stayed and fought. In both cases there was physical exertion. The muscles were used, energy was expended, and hopefully by being able to react faster, leap further and run with greater speed, they survived. After a short period of time everything returned to normal.

Unfortunately, today when we are under stress, there is very little likelihood that we have exerted ourselves as our ancestors did, and we have not therefore cleared the toxic chemicals from our system. This is where the danger lies. These days, the adrenaline and cortisol may still run, our heart may still beat faster, and many of the other changes may still take place. We just don't have the chance to let it go. If stress hormones are constantly released into our body, even if in smaller amounts, and nothing is done to counter them, the cumulative effect can have devastating side effects. How often do we hear of people off work on stress leave? How many different stress-related illnesses are there? How many people use substances to reduce stress?

When you exert yourself physically through exercise, your breathing becomes more rapid, your heart rate increases, more blood flows to the brain, making you more alert. As your heart pumps more blood to your muscles, it takes blood away from your digestive system.

This is the same thing that happens when we are under extreme stress. Therefore, the more you exercise, the more you are conditioning yourself to handle stress. You are training your body to cope, as well as activating your pressure-cooker release valve. Get moving.

Zen and the art of living in the now

Have you ever met somebody who is constantly living in the past? Or have you met someone who is always worried about what might go wrong in the future?

To a degree, we are all probably guilty of daydreaming into the past or the future. Living in the now doesn't mean forgetting our past or ignoring the future. When living a NOW life, we are aware of both the past and the future, but we don't dwell there.

Becoming one with whatever it is you are doing and being fully in the moment is what *living in the now* really means. When you live fully in the day you are in, you experience the experience. When you completely accept who you are, where you are and what you are doing, you are living in the now. Being present is a great way to destress and to handle stress. Mindfulness helps you be more Zen and live in the now.

Learning to say NO

Overcommitment is a sure-fire way to create more stress. When we take on too many responsibilities and make promises that are hard to keep, we really put the pressure on ourselves. During my twenties, I would often agree automatically to things that I really didn't want to do. I was the classic *yes person*. Nothing was too much trouble. The problem was I always had so much on my plate – too much – and it almost killed me.

When we are in conflict with ourselves in this way, it's not healthy. If we say yes to doing something that will keep the other person happy but at the same time cause our own unhappiness, where is the sense? Some people are masters at getting others to do things for them. Unless you want to be a sucker forever, and suffer for it, sometimes you have to say no.

It's not wrong to help people. So, if it makes you feel good and you have the time, go for it. But remember … it's your time. If you don't want to do something, just say so.

Old program – *I can't say no.*
Upgrade – *Saying no is easy.*

RECOVERING FROM STRESS

Bouncing back from or preventing prolonged stress and emotional burnout is possible by breaking the patterns that deplete you. Following these six steps will create new healthy rituals in your life that will nourish and nurture you. Read through these steps and repeat the positive upgrade affirmations at the end of each step to help reprogram the way your mind deals with stress.

It's time to show yourself the respect and self-love you deserve. Let the healing begin.

Step 1: Time out

Ensure you take time out for yourself. This can be as simple as taking a warm bath, reading a book, listening to music, gardening, catching up with friends or family, creating a gratitude journal, sitting in the sun, unleashing your creativity with arts and crafts or colouring in (which is a great meditation). When it comes to managing your stress levels, *me time* is essential. It's like a pressure-cooker release valve that helps you let go of stress. The key is to find what works for you – your own personal release valve. Once you find it, incorporate it into your daily life. For me, meditation, stretching, yoga, qigong, tai chi, surfing and walking help me achieve me-time balance.

When you take time out for yourself, you are saying, *I'm important*. The fact is, *you* are the most important person in the world.

Old program – *I don't have time, my work is more important,*
I don't deserve it.*
Upgrade – *I make time for me because I'm important and*
I deserve it.

Step 2: One-minute meditation ritual

Upon waking and just before going to sleep, your mind is in the ideal relaxed state for a few minutes of meditation or self-hypnosis.

While there are literally thousands of ways to meditate, the easiest place to start is by simply slowing your breathing down and using an affirmation to help you focus. As you slowly breathe in, think the thought *I feel at peace* and, as you exhale, relax your body while thinking, *I am at peace*. Repeat this ten times for a deep feeling of relaxation. At any time of day or night use this simple technique and, with three slow deep breaths, you will be activating your own pressure-cooker release valve.

If three minutes feels like too long for you right at this moment, then remember your breath is always with you and it takes just one minute to do this simple exercise:

1. Allow the thought *in* to flow into your mind as you inhale.
2. As you exhale think the thought *out*.
3. Slowly breathe in thinking *in*.
4. Slowly exhale as you think *out*.
5. Take five more slow breaths thinking *in* and *out* with each breath.

Remember, at any time you can take note of whether you are breathing in or out and take a few slow breaths to slow your mind down. You may like to imagine you are blowing stress or negative energy away as you relax more deeply with every breath.

Many people think they don't have time to meditate or it's too hard. Simple meditations can be done in as little as a minute, anytime, anywhere. And you can turn anything into a meditation, even doing the dishes or sweeping the floor. It's as simple as this: be present, be in the moment with what you are doing and keep breathing. When your mind wanders (and it will), bring it back. This is mindfulness, and it's one of the best ways to manage stress.

Old program – *It's too hard, I can't cope, everything stresses me out.*

Step 3: Get moving

Movement is critical in preventing and recovering from extreme stress and emotional burnout. Yoga, tai chi, stretching, strength training, riding a bike, power walking, boxing, martial arts and dancing are all great ways to counter the stress hormones and increase the feel-good hormones of serotonin, dopamine and endorphins. You want to feel good? Get moving. It's time to recharge yourself physically.

Old program – I don't have the energy, I can't be bothered.
Upgrade – I run my own race at my pace, I love to move and I am worth it.

Step 4: Eat right

The ultimate diet is a real food diet. You know what that is. Do your best to eat what nature intended: food from the land, from the sea, from the ground, from a tree. Your body craves water all the time, so make sure you stay hydrated with your eight to ten glasses of water every day. Do your best to reduce or eliminate alcohol and sugar-filled drinks. Eat more raw foods and eat lightly at night. It's time to recharge yourself nutritionally.

Old program – I'll just have one, I've worked hard, I deserve it.
Upgrade – I choose health, only goodness enters my body.

Step 5: Emotional reconnection

Are you ready for an emotional recharge? How are you feeding yourself emotionally? Where can you find your joy? What did you do when you were younger that was fun or brought joy into your life? What story are you telling yourself that will lift and nourish you? Going for a walk in nature is a wonderful way to reconnect. Spending time with people who are positive can aid your recovery. The fact is, you are a survivor and so much stronger than you think yourself to be.

Practise self-compassion and compassion to all others. By reading this you are practising self-compassion. Know too that others are suffering, and ask that they too may find peace and, as you do that, you may just find that your own problems disappear.

Old program – *I feel powerless, there's no hope.*
Upgrade – *I am here, I am me, I am free. I am strong.*
There is always hope.

Step 6: Breathe mindfully

Breathing is the most important function we perform. Our nose acts as a filter, as well as warning us when the air is not safe to breathe. Breathing through the mouth is like a fish out of water gasping for air. Our mouths are meant for eating, drinking and making sounds. When speaking and singing, we obviously breathe through the mouth. At other times, we should make a conscious effort to breathe through our nose.

When first practising conscious breathing, concentrate on breathing naturally via the nose. The nose's most important function beyond smell is the absorption of fresh oxygen, or chi (energy). Next time you are on a beach or in a garden or park after rain, take a deep breath through the nose and let yourself feel the invigorating lift. Then take a deep breath through the mouth and feel the difference. We naturally take a few deep breaths through the nose when we are in a natural environment and the chi is in abundance.

Once you've practised conscious breathing through your nose, move your focus to abdominal breathing, which also massages your internal organs. The more we breathe correctly and oxygenate the body, the more refreshed we feel.

Shallow chest-breathing may only take in approximately one third of your potential lung capacity. When you let the lower abdomen expand naturally as you inhale, the diaphragm is drawn down a little. This allows more air to enter the lungs from the bottom up, in the same way liquid fills a bottle.

You don't need a specific time of day to practise abdominal breathing; make it a part of your everyday life while walking, sitting, talking and playing sport. Allow yourself to feel your abdomen rise and fall with every breath. Your chest and shoulders remain completely relaxed throughout. It may be difficult at first not to move the chest and shoulders, but perseverance will pay off and you will reap the rewards. From the navel up, everything should be completely relaxed as you focus on the lower abdomen. Constantly let your shoulders relax throughout your breathing practice.

MIND FREE MINUTE MEDITATION

Take one minute to immerse yourself in the following power statements and affirmations as a mindful self-hypnosis practice.

Breathe in, *I am calm and in control*
Breathe out, *I am calm and in control*

Breathe in, *I feel at peace, I am at peace*
Breathe out, *I feel at peace, I am at peace*

Breathe in, *I let it go*
Breathe out, *I let it go*

Breathe in, *all is well, I am well*
Breathe out, *all is well, I am well*

Breathe in, *I am the most important person in the world*
Breathe out, *I am the most important person in the world*

Breathe in, *my mind is calm, I am calm*
Breathe out, *my mind is calm, I am calm*

THREE KEYS TO RELEASE STRESS

LESSON 1: Rather than thinking of stress as bad and negative, think of stress as positive and a challenge. When you have a positive outlook, you reduce the release of cortisol and increase the release of natural feel-good chemicals.

LESSON 2: Take time to switch stress off. Know what triggers your stress and keep releasing the build-up of stress with breathing, meditations and mindful self-hypnosis. Release the pressure-cooker valve of life with mini-meditations. Breathe mindfully.

LESSON 3: When you tell yourself to be calm, you will feel calm. Breathe the stress away as you continue to delete the old programs and upgrade the software of your brain.

DISCOVER MORE MIND FREE

For more mindful self-hypnosis to help you stress less, go to p. 250 of the Mind Manual. You can also listen to recorded sessions on stress via the Mind Free app and website mindfreeapp.com.

The three decrees

I hereby decree that peace, control and calm flow through me this day. I am peaceful, I am centred, I am in control and I am relaxed. I stop and breathe. I easily and naturally release stress. I let it go. Deep breathing is my superpower. I am the most important person in the world and I take time for me.

On the following scroll, copy the above in full or part, and combine with your own statements. Or, if you prefer, select your own positive emotion words, short power statements and empowering affirmations. Combine them to form your own personal decree by you, to you, for you.

Official Decree

_____

_____

_____

_____

_____

_____

_____

_____

_____

_____

_____

_____

_____

_____

_____

_____

Signed

CHAPTER 4
STOP PROCRASTINATING

I'll do it later.

Isn't it already later?
How will life change when you become
a do-it-now person?

I'll start tomorrow.

How about starting next week, next month
or next year?
Imagine what you'll achieve when you start today.
What would happen in your life if you took action?

I can, I will, I must – do it now!

How many times have you told yourself you will start a new project first thing on Monday, or build something, or clean something over the weekend, only to find that life simply got in the way?

Have you ever had everything ready to start a project, only to say to yourself, *I'll just do this or do that first*, then find that hours or days have passed, and you haven't even begun? How many times do you actually say that you are going to start something and then you get distracted?

What have you been putting off?

Nobody is immune to procrastination, but why? Well, it's so much more pleasurable to get instant gratification from doing something easier first, rather than starting something that we've been systematically putting off. In some cases, we attach so much pain to doing a project that it becomes easier to simply not do it at all. But here is the question you need to consider: how many times have you completed something that you had been putting off, only to realise it wasn't that hard after all? Most of the time we make the problem or the pain out to be much worse than it actually is.

Ask yourself this: what value am I getting from all the distractions that are stopping me from taking action on my goals? Because if you think about it, you are swapping your future, your health and your results for all these distractions. Are they really worth that much? As we all know, 'If you always do what you've always done, you'll always get what you've always got.' It's so true, isn't it?

The problems occur when we continually put off those things that we really want to do, or we avoid doing things that are very important. Think: making that doctor's appointment, starting an exercise routine, quitting smoking or signing up for that course that could lead to the career we've always dreamed of. Procrastination can lead to massive amounts of unnecessary stress, as well as eroding our self-esteem as we look back and think to ourselves, *I've got no willpower* or *why didn't I do that?* And on top of the procrastination, we end up feeling guilty, sad or embarrassed, because we haven't done what we said we were going to do.

CHANGE YOUR INNER CONVERSATION

The chant rings out through houses and offices around the world: *I'm too busy, I don't have time, I'll start later.* The *I'll start Monday, someday, one day* is the ultimate delay excuse and a destroyer of dreams, goals and your ability to get things done.

What you need to start to tell yourself is *I get it started, I get into it, I get it done.* And the more you repeat *get it started, get into it, get it done*, the more you will motivate yourself to take action. The more you tell yourself motivating thoughts, the more you'll feel motivated. Motivating thoughts and feelings of motivation are always followed by action.

Old program – *I'll start Monday, someday, one day.*
Upgrade – *I get it started, I get into it, I get it done.*

WHY DO WE PROCRASTINATE?

For some people, procrastination is about perfectionism. If it's not going to be 100 per cent fault-free, they don't want to do it. The reality is, something is better than nothing. Remind yourself of that: *something is better than nothing.* The fact is, we do not have an unlimited bank account of time, even though we often spend our time as if we do. Each of us gets exactly the same 1440 minutes every day. Whether you are running a country, running a household or running to catch the school bus, we are all given the same precious minutes each day. And yet the same person who is too busy and has no time will often find themselves spending hours on social media, surfing the net, watching TV or participating in other distracting activities while having no time to do the things they know they should do and want to do.

Procrastination is not always about what you want to start and are putting off, but also specific things that you'd like to stop. In some cases, procrastination can be tied to wanting to stay in your comfort zone. Many people put off improving their health or changing bad habits such as smoking, excessive drinking, too much coffee, sugar addiction or eating junk food.

Take a moment to assess what you've been putting off. Think about all areas of your life, including health and fitness, relationships, family, career, community, home, study, personal development, arts and crafts, and anything else you've been procrastinating about. Now, right now, make a list of ten things that you have been putting off that you would like to achieve.

1 _____

2 _____

3 _____

4 _____

5 _____

6 _____

7 _____

8 _____

9 _____

10 _____

As you look at your list, consider how great you would feel if you took action on each of these things. Consider for a moment how long it would actually take you to take action on what you've been putting off.

Am I just lazy?

No. Being a procrastinator doesn't necessarily mean that you're lazy or unsuccessful, even though you may convince yourself of this. There are often unconscious blocks getting in the way of you achieving what you want, and we'll explore these in a moment.

Some procrastinators live by the deadline. Their excuse is: *I work well under pressure*. Unfortunately, they're just creating a whole extra layer of unnecessary stress. Leaving things to the last minute can put you into a state of fight or flight, which can put stress on your body and lead to a whole host of health issues. Other procrastinators achieve a hell of a lot but avoid important personal things that actually need to be done. Procrastination is not laziness; it's a matter of mindset. To put it simply, if something is not important enough to you, you will either put it off or not do it. When you truly focus on what's important, you can get things done. Can you guess what happens when you create a mindset of *get things done*? You stop putting it off, and you get things done.

Pleasure or pain

The cleaning, the assignment, the dentist and all those tasks we have to do usually only get done when the thought of not doing them is more painful than the thought of doing them. In essence, we get the energy to do these tasks by avoiding the pain. So, when the deadline to achieve a task is getting so close that we can't bear the pain of not doing it anymore, our motivation level skyrockets from zero to 100. We make the time, we prioritise and we get things done. We stop wasting time and we get stuck into it. Imagine if you could tap into this level of motivation on any given day every time you look at your to-do list. When you focus on what's important, you will get things done.

Procrastination often comes down to the story that we attach to the project or task. Rather than telling yourself you'll do it later, say to yourself: *do it now, do it now, do it now*. Rather than saying you'll start on Monday or next week, tell yourself: *do it now, do it now, do it now*.

If you're able to start something right now, take that first step. An action plan without a clear goal in mind and a timeframe or schedule is really nothing more than scribblings on a piece of paper or an idea. Creating a timeline to work towards will help you stay on track.

OVERCOMING THE MIND BLOCKS STOPPING YOU

When working with people who want to give up smoking or quit drinking, the first question I ask them is this: on a scale of one to 100, what is your motivation level to change this behaviour? If they say anything less than 100, we need to work on their motivation levels before we start.

You may think that all you need to do is be motivated to complete an important task, but the fact is, anyone who is a serial procrastinator will have a range of unconscious blocks that need to be worked on first. These blocks may have started early on in life and could have begun by simply hearing a family member say, 'I just don't have time' or 'There's too much to do'. At some point the thought may have embedded itself in your mind and eventually became part of your story. It's possible that you've been overwhelmed at times and ended up feeling stuck, or you've had a fear of failing so you keep putting tasks off. The thoughts and feelings sit there in your unconscious waiting to rear their ugly head when least expected.

These unconscious blocks are generally the long list of excuses, old unhelpful beliefs and negative thoughts that pop up in our mind. When you change your thinking from, *I'll start tomorrow*, *next week* or *next month* to *get it started, get into it, get it done*, all of a sudden you begin to build momentum. By thinking these thoughts, you feel more motivated. You have the positive feelings and the energy to tackle any project. Before you know it the tasks you've been putting off excite you and you move from achieving one goal to another.

Self-esteem

The better we feel about ourselves, the more energy we have and the happier we are. When we feel energetic and happy, we feel as though we can achieve anything. Self-esteem is basically the story you tell yourself about yourself. So where do these stories come from?

If you have been constantly told that you are not good enough or you cannot do something, some of these negative comments from others are going to get stuck inside your head. Once you start repeating these negative comments in your mind, they become beliefs about yourself, and these beliefs control your actions. These are the unconscious blocks stopping you from taking action and achieving your dreams. So, inside of your mind, instead of saying *get it done* you think or say to yourself *I'll do it later* or *I can't do it*. The great news is, you can change your mindset to focus on what's important and reprogram your mind to say, *do it now* or *I get it done*.

When should I do it?

The *I'll-do-it-later* syndrome is responsible for so many unfulfilled dreams. But, as we know, later never really eventuates. Replace the whole concept of doing it later with the do-it-now strategy. Every time you are about to put something off, say to yourself three times, *do it now*. Rather than telling yourself you'll do it later, tell yourself, *now is the time and today is the day*. You are reading this now, therefore you are not procrastinating.

Old program – *I'll do it later*.
Upgrade – *I do it now*.

ADRIAN'S STORY

Adrian was a self-professed master procrastinator. He had a long list of things that he'd been putting off for years, including clearing out his garage, getting on top of his mounting debts, going to the dentist and getting fit. As a self-employed tradesman, he explained that there was always so much to do and that he never had enough time for those things he'd been putting off. He kept telling himself he would do tasks at the weekend or next week or when he was on holidays; however, with a young family, there was always so much to do and so little time. And having put on around 20 kilograms over the previous few years, he just didn't have the energy to face the list of things that needed doing.

I explained to Adrian that while he continued to use the self-defeating talk of *I'll start next week*, next week would never come. Whenever he told himself he had no time, he would have no time, and when he told himself that he had no energy, he would have no energy. Adrian said that between his workload and his family responsibilities, anything beyond that was overwhelming.

I told Adrian that he had two choices. Choice one was to continue doing what he was doing and keep getting the same results. Choice two was to make a decision, get organised and get things done.

Once we determined that Adrian had the desire to stop procrastinating and to achieve his goals, the next step was the how. I explained to Adrian that he needed a clear plan to feel more motivated and that, by breaking everything down into small doable steps, each task would be a whole lot easier. Rather than having all these extra things to do bouncing around in Adrian's head, we came up with a step-by-step action plan in order of priority.

Adrian gave himself 24 hours to ring the dentist with the aim of getting an appointment in the next 14 days. He had four weeks to clear out the garage, six months to reach his goal weight of 80 kilograms and 12 months to reduce his debt by $13,000.

The next thing was to help Adrian change his identity from being the master procrastinator to being the person of action. This was partly done by guiding Adrian to change the story he had been telling himself. Below is a copy of Adrian's limiting beliefs and excuses in the left-hand column and the new beliefs he came up with in the right-hand column.

OLD BELIEFS AND EXCUSES	NEW BELIEFS
I don't have time I'm too busy	I make the time My goals are important
I'll start next week	I'll do it now
There is too much to do	I'll make a plan and stick to it I get things done
It doesn't matter	Everything matters
I have no energy I'm too tired	I have an abundance of energy I just do it
I am a master procrastinator	I am a person of action

Because Adrian had developed a number of bad habits such as staying up late watching TV, having too many coffees, buying lunch every day, eating takeaway dinners and enjoying a few too many beers, we not only needed to replace the thought of doing these things, but also replace the image in his mind. After I guided Adrian into a meditative state by having him focus on his breathing and progressively relax each part of his body, I had him bring to mind one time-wasting or money-wasting habit at a time and, as he considered this problem and visualised the trigger of himself about to tackle the problem, I had him think: *I don't need it, I don't want it, I won't have it* or *I don't need it, I don't want it, I won't do it*. I then had him imagine he was throwing that old picture out into the distance, with the image shrinking away to nothing.

At the same time, I had him picture the new Adrian flying in over the top of the old picture. We made the new picture of the positive behaviour or state big and bright, as Adrian was doing the new behaviour. This effectively took the old picture out of his mind. I had him throw it away while thinking, *I don't need it, I don't want it, I won't have it*, and at the same time swapping in the new picture as he felt himself being drawn towards his objectives. We did this with each problem until the only image in Adrian's mind was that of him taking action on his goals.

To help reinforce Adrian's motivation, I recorded a short mindful self-hypnosis session for him to listen to upon waking every morning.

The good news is that Adrian did get to the dentist, he took six weeks to clear out the garage and three months to reach his goal weight, and he is consistently moving towards reducing his debt.

Change your mind and you'll change your life.

THE POWER OF MOTIVATION

If the projects or activities you want to achieve are not important enough or not a priority, then you'll simply keep putting them off. If you don't feel motivated, you won't have the energy to do them. The funny thing is, people will think or say that they are not motivated, but from the moment they wake up to the moment they go to sleep, they'll do 101 things outside their goals. If this is you, it shows you that you are motivated, but the real problem is that your motivation is towards the wrong things. Attach motivation to your goals and you *will* get things done.

I'd like you, just for a moment, to remember a time when you were really motivated. Maybe you were motivated to finish a project, to clean the house, to get creative or something else. It could have been recently or maybe it was years ago. Bring to mind that time, and imagine the good feelings of being motivated and getting things done. As you reflect on that time, bring to mind the thoughts you were thinking. What were you telling yourself that was helping you feel motivated to finish what you started? Were you telling yourself thoughts like: *This feels good, I can do it, I've got this, I can't wait to finish, I have plenty of energy, I'll keep going until it's done*?

If you had any other thoughts at all that motivated you, write them down in the space below. Or bring to mind any other thoughts that will motivate you to get things done. Or write down the thoughts from above that motivate you. What could you tell yourself to feel really motivated?

MOTIVATING THOUGHTS

_____

_____

_____

_____

_____

When you can attach the state of motivation to each of the projects or tasks you have been procrastinating over, all of a sudden you will begin to feel and think differently about getting them done. Make things important.

Bring to mind something that is really important in your life. Maybe it's your family, friends, a pet, your career, arts and crafts, music, hiking or something else. It could even be the intangibles you value in your life such as honesty, love, respect, achievement, fairness, enthusiasm, learning, the environment or anything else at all.

Take a moment to write down what is important to you – in other words, what you truly value.

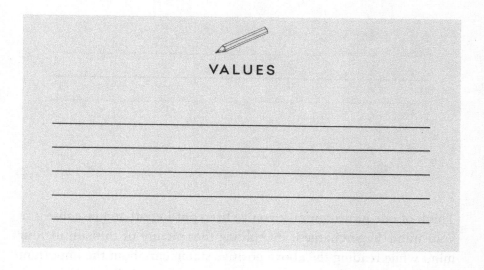

VALUES

Now ask yourself, what do you think when you look at the above values list? What is the story you attach to these important areas of your life? Why are these values so important? What do they mean to you?

Do a quick brain dump of anything that comes to your mind that is a positive statement relating to what you value in your life and what is important to you. For example:

I aim to finish what I start. I value achievement. I am a person of action and get things done. I make the time. I make a plan and enthusiastically stick to the plan. I have plenty of energy and I just do it. I enjoy the great feeling of looking back at my completed goals.

How could you attach a similar story to the projects or tasks you've been putting off? Write your own new positive statement in the space below.

MY POSITIVE STATEMENT

_____

_____

_____

_____

_____

Think of one project or task you've been putting off and visualise it in your mind. Supercharge it by holding that picture or thought in your mind while reading the above positive statement about the important things in your life. Do your best to attach those feelings to this one project or task you've been putting off.

HOW TO GET THINGS DONE

You have just focused on what motivates you and what is truly important in your life. Reminding yourself of your values and thoughts that motivate you is a major step to overcoming procrastination. Now, here are more solutions to help you stop putting things off and, instead, help you to *do it now*.

Building momentum

For some people, tackling the hard things first might be the best way to go. If that works for you, great. It's easy to see the psychology behind this. If you can complete a large, hard-to-do task first, you can surely tackle the smaller parts of your project. On the other hand, you could start with small tasks and quickly achieve them, giving you momentum to keep going. Do whatever works best for you.

Visualisation

When you mentally rehearse reaching a goal or completing a task, the likelihood of achieving that task is greatly increased. This has been proven by basketballers who have imagined themselves shooting a basket, Olympic athletes who have visualised themselves winning, and even you and me when we have planned a project in our heads before starting it.

When you start to think about your goal and visualise or imagine you are completing whatever it is you've been putting off, you create a blueprint for success. When you take a moment to step into that vision of you achieving your goal, then anything is possible. When you have a plan to follow and you start to take action, you will achieve what it is you set out to achieve. No one else is going to do this for you. It is up to you.

A powerful procrastination affirmation is: *If it is to be, it is up to me.* You can tell yourself this over and over again. Breathe it into your being. *If it is to be, it is up to me.* You realise it is up to you – it *has* to be you – because no one else will do this for you. You are the one, there is no one else. It would be great to think there is someone out there taking action on our goals for us, but unfortunately, they are not. It's up to you!

**Old program – *I'll do it later, I don't have time.*
Upgrade – *If it is to be, it is up to me.***

Picture your future self

This is a simple visualisation exercise that will help you create a blueprint for success by picturing your future self. Simply insert your goal or the task that you wish to achieve. For the best results, make sure your goal is more pleasurable than painful, that you are fully motivated to achieve your goal and that you have released any limiting beliefs. Before starting, quieten your mind so you can really tune into the visualisation.

Take a few slow breaths as you think about your final moment of success in reaching your goal or completing the task you want to complete. Create a picture in your mind. What can you see? Think about your goal as you imagine or look at this representation in your mind's eye. See yourself in the picture. Feel yourself being drawn towards the happy, confident you, completing tasks, reaching goals and achieving whatever it is you put your mind to.

I'd like you to step inside that image or goal and notice your feelings. Take a step right into yourself, at your goal. Imagine you are looking through your own eyes. Go right into the picture, feel the feelings, see it, smell it, taste the sweet success of achieving your outcome. What do you feel? What can you hear internally and around you? What are you thinking to yourself? As you are there in that image, take a mental note of how you are breathing. Are you sitting or standing? How does it make you feel, as you see all the things associated with your final moment of success?

In the same way you would adjust the sound or colour on a TV, adjust the picture, the colours, the brightness, the feelings, the sounds. Make the image as real as possible. You may even like to make the picture bigger, make it huge or make it lifelike.

Think of yourself having reached your final outcome. What do you see, what are you feeling, as you are looking through your own eyes inside that picture? Think to yourself, *yes, I did it and it was easy!* Think to yourself, *how great is this? I've done it.* When you achieve your goals, you feel amazing. And the fact is, you *are* amazing. Sometimes we just need a little reminder.

Action plans

Your action plan is the daily fuel that drives you towards achieving your goals. Your action plan is a reminder that helps keep you on track. Your action plan is your list of what needs to be done and when you will do it. By keeping the plan simple you have a greater chance of succeeding. Include your outcome, steps to be taken and how long you will give yourself to achieve your outcomes. You could also incorporate your action plan into a calendar, diary or timeline to work from.

Meditation

To eliminate procrastination in your life, you need to free your mind of unnecessary clutter so that you can zoom in on what really matters: this is what meditation achieves. Practise the meditation exercises throughout this book to connect with the moment you are in, and clear your mind of distractions. This will refocus you on your goals and values and help you stop procrastinating. A few minutes of meditation several times a day is worth incorporating into your daily action plan and as you persevere you will reap the rewards of a calm yet focused mind.

Remember: when you focus on what's important to you, you get things done.

Set your mind free

Another way of decluttering your mind to help you focus on your goals is to become aware of, and then delete, the negative thoughts and excuses that you've used in the past to justify your procrastination.

This quick exercise will help you set your mind free from unnecessary clutter. In the following table, do a quick brain-dump. On the left-hand side, note the top three beliefs or excuses you make relating to procrastination. On the right-hand side write down as many new empowering beliefs as you can that will help you delete the old thoughts and take action.

OLD PROGRAM	UPGRADE
1 _____	1 _____
_____	2 _____
_____	3 _____
_____	4 _____
_____	5 _____
2 _____	1 _____
_____	2 _____
_____	3 _____
_____	4 _____
_____	5 _____
3 _____	1 _____
_____	2 _____
_____	3 _____
_____	4 _____
_____	5 _____

As soon as you have completed the above exercise, cross out the 'old program' so those excuses are gone forever. Review your upgraded empowering thoughts by repeatedly reading them aloud or quietly in your mind until you feel the new thoughts are fully installed in your unconscious mind.

I get it started, get into it, get it done.
Today is the day and now is the time.

MIND FREE MINUTE MEDITATION

Take one minute to immerse yourself in the following power statements and affirmations as a mindful self-hypnosis practice.

Breathe in, *I get it started*
Breathe out, *get into it, get it done*

Breathe in, *today is the day*
Breathe out, *now is the time*

Breathe in, *3, 2, 1*
Breathe out, *get it done*

Breathe in, *I make the time*
Breathe out, *my goals are important*

Breathe in, *if it is to be*
Breathe out, *it is up to me*

THREE KEYS TO BEATING PROCRASTINATION

LESSON 1: Repeatedly tell yourself, today is the day and now is the time to take action. Pay no attention to the old excuses. Replace the old outdated thinking as you continue to motivate yourself with positive uplifting thoughts.

LESSON 2: Specifically think of your goal, take action on your goal and avoid time-wasting and unnecessary distractions. Make a plan and do something every day to work towards your goal.

LESSON 3: Visualise yourself achieving your goals and completing your projects. Picture yourself doing what needs to be done to achieve your results. Tell yourself that *you* are the one to get things done.

DISCOVER MORE MIND FREE

For more mindful self-hypnosis to help you stop procrastinating, go to p. 257 of the Mind Manual. You can also listen to recorded sessions on beating procrastination via the Mind Free app and website mindfreeapp.com.

The three decrees

I hereby decree that today I immerse myself in motivation, action and determination. I am a doer. I am capable. I am energised. I am driven. I am an achiever. I make every minute count because today is the day and now is the time. As I get it started, I get into it, I get it done. I am the one, there is no one else. I feel a sense of accomplishment as I finish each project. I am making progress as a do-it-now person. Time is precious and I value every minute. My goals are important and I am important. I now know, if it is to be, it is up to me.

On the following scroll, copy the above in full or part and combine with your own statements. Or, if you prefer, select your own positive emotion words, short power statements and empowering affirmations. Combine them to form your own personal decree by you, to you, for you.

Official Decree

_____

_____

_____

_____

_____

_____

_____

_____

_____

_____

_____

_____

_____

Signed

CHAPTER 5
BREAK YOUR BAD HABITS

I have no control.

What do you have control over?
How many times have you had control?

I can't stop.

**Imagine you were able to stop, by starting
something new.**
**How will your life change when you replace bad
habits with good habits?**

I am in control.

We all have at least one – if not ten – bad habits. Think about it for a moment. From the moment we wake up to the moment we go to sleep, our entire day is driven by habits. That habit may be switching on the TV the moment you get up and putting the kettle on for your morning cup of coffee. Some people are in the habit of skipping breakfast and grabbing something on the way to work or school. Other people are in the habit of staying up late and then not being able to sleep properly.

When you think about it, our habits make up a big part of our life. Good habits developed over time help you achieve all sorts of goals and improve your health and happiness. And on the flip side, bad habits can hold you back. The impact habits have in our lives cannot be underestimated.

While often starting as something occasional, a habit develops as an action that is repeated over and over again. Trying to break a habit with willpower can seem almost impossible. It's important to remember you are not your habits. Habits are something you do but they are *not* you. And yet we can identify ourselves by our habits: I am a smoker, I am an alcoholic, I am always late, I love fast food, I am not a morning person ... and on it goes. Part of the difficulty is that, in the case of some habits, we identify as the problems. But you are not the problem, and you are not the habit. *You are the solution.*

Breaking bad habits has been something I've specialised in over the years as a hypnotherapist. From nail biting and extreme junk-food addictions to smoking and sugar addiction, when approached with the right attitude, breaking habits is easier than you may think.

MERV'S STORY

'Hi, my name's Merv. Can you help me stop smoking?' said the gravelly voice on the end of the line.

'Sure, Merv. Why do you want to stop smoking?'

'My doctor told me that, because I'm in my seventies, it's about time I stopped smoking. Plus, I've noticed it's starting to affect my eyesight and my stamina,' Merv continued. 'I've been smoking two packs a day, you know, since World War II.'

'Well, that's a long time to be smoking, Merv, and good on you for making the decision to be smoke free.'

But Merv had some concerns. 'I've tried patches, gum, cold turkey. I read a stop-smoking book and even went to a hypnotherapist, but none of it worked.'

'Maybe you just weren't ready to stop, Merv,' I said. 'Are you ready to stop now? Are you 100 per cent ready, because if you're not, nothing will work.'

Merv was 100 per cent ready. He said he'd had enough.

I invited Merv to join a lunchtime stop-smoking seminar I was running the following week. I assured Merv there would be no pressure, and that he would only stop if he truly wanted to stop, and that he would do fine. I explained that once you get your mindset right, breaking any bad habit is easy.

In the seminar we covered the most common smoking triggers, replacement strategies such as meditation to destress, and breathing exercises. Through a guided hypnosis session participants were able to change their belief of being a smoker to that of being a non-smoker and to visualise themselves in the future being smoke free with no desire for a cigarette whatsoever. Merv left feeling inspired but unsure as to whether or not the hypnosis had worked.

Twelve months later I had a phone call from Merv. 'Hi Mark. I just want to let you know today is the one-year anniversary since I stopped smoking. And I feel really good, so thank you.'

We had a good chat and I asked Merv if he ever felt the urge to have a cigarette.

'I have no wish whatsoever to smoke again. Strongly entrenched in my mind is the belief that there is nothing good in a cigarette, so there is no reason to want to try one. And I'll never put that cocktail of toxic poisons in my body ever again.'

Every 12 months for the next five or six years, Merv would call on the anniversary of the day he stopped smoking. I would always ask him if he ever felt like a cigarette and he would answer the same way, explaining that he would never put that cocktail of toxic poisons in his body ever again.

Then for five or six years I didn't hear from Merv. A few times I thought to myself that Merv would've been in his late eighties by now. He was a great guy and I really enjoyed our little chats, along with his positive attitude and gratitude. It was coming up to World No Tobacco Day. I fondly remembered Merv and our chats, and thought of how well he had done and what an inspiration he was. The next day the phone rang.

'Hi Mark, it's Merv. Sorry I haven't called, but I lost your phone number,' he said apologetically.

I was so excited. 'Great to hear from you, Merv. It's been a while.'

'You didn't think I was dead, did you?' he joked.

I laughed and asked him what he was doing that day.

'I'm just in the garden, planting some new vegetables and getting all the weeds out.'

'Why don't I come over, and we'll have a cuppa?' I said. Merv only lived 30 minutes away, so I jumped in the car, headed over and hung out with one of the nicest of blokes you could ever meet. Merv reflected on what had changed in his life since he had given up smoking more than a decade ago. His eyesight and stamina improved, along with his overall health. Moneywise, he was able to save up and buy a new car. He eats healthy foods, many from his garden, and exercises regularly. Again, I asked Merv if he ever feels like having a cigarette.

'That cocktail of toxic poisons? I have no desire whatsoever.' Merv said that a major driving force to stop smoking, besides his health, was that as a long-time smoker he felt he owed it to other long-time smokers to encourage them – if he could do it, so could they.

Good on you, Merv, you are an inspiration to anyone wanting to break a bad habit.

WHAT ARE YOUR BAD HABITS?

Bad habits are a pretty serious matter. They can ruin our love life, affect our work and study, impact our health, reduce our self-esteem and, in some cases, such as the habits of smoking, drinking or drugs, cut our life short.

Following is the big A to Z list of the most common bad habits I have heard of, based on workshops and seminars I've held over the years. Have a look through this list and either highlight or tick the habits that apply to you:

- ☐ alcohol
- ☐ always saying sorry
- ☐ being judgmental of self or others
- ☐ biting nails
- ☐ bragging
- ☐ bullying
- ☐ buying lunch every day
- ☐ being overly affectionate in public
- ☐ checking emails too often
- ☐ chewing gum
- ☐ chewing on a pencil or pen
- ☐ chocolate
- ☐ coffee
- ☐ comparing yourself to others
- ☐ complaining
- ☐ cracking knuckles
- ☐ eating dinner late
- ☐ eating fast
- ☐ energy drinks
- ☐ falling asleep while watching TV
- ☐ fast food
- ☐ fidgeting
- ☐ finishing other people's sentences
- ☐ gambling
- ☐ gossiping
- ☐ grinding teeth
- ☐ hair pulling
- ☐ hoarding
- ☐ ice cream
- ☐ late-night snacking
- ☐ leaving the toilet seat up

- [ ] lip biting
- [ ] lying
- [ ] nicotine gum
- [ ] not listening
- [ ] not showering
- [ ] not washing hands
- [ ] not doing homework
- [ ] online shopping
- [ ] overusing medicines
- [ ] picking skin
- [ ] procrastinating
- [ ] public pimple popping
- [ ] running late
- [ ] saying yes to everything
- [ ] scratching
- [ ] shoplifting
- [ ] shopping
- [ ] sitting too much
- [ ] skipping breakfast
- [ ] sleeping in
- [ ] smoking/vaping
- [ ] snacking
- [ ] snacking while cooking
- [ ] social media
- [ ] speeding
- [ ] spitting in public
- [ ] starchy carbohydrates
- [ ] staying up late
- [ ] sugar drinks
- [ ] surfing the net
- [ ] swearing
- [ ] talking constantly about an ex in a new relationship
- [ ] talking too much
- [ ] talking with a full mouth
- [ ] throat clearing
- [ ] too much salt

- [ ] too much time online
- [ ] too much TV
- [ ] using phone in bed
- [ ] video games
- [ ] watching porn
- [ ] working all the time
- [ ] worrying.

THE BAD HABIT SOLUTION

How many of those bad habits did you circle or highlight? Don't feel overwhelmed – there is a solution, a process, to breaking bad habits:

- List your bad habits.
- List your triggers.
- Select a substitute (what can you do instead?).
- Use the habit-swap visualisation technique.
- Practise mindful hypnotherapy techniques.

I'll break these into two major steps so that you can work through the process.

Step 1: Write it all down

Select your bad habits from the previous list and write them out in the first column on the next page. If you have a bad habit not included on the previous list, include that in the space provided as well.

A short pencil is better than a long memory. By writing your habit down, you take the first step towards overcoming the habit. By writing your habit down, you take the habit from the thought realm into the action realm and this shows commitment.

The key to overcoming bad habits is not to simply stop doing what you are doing. Just stopping something you may have done thousands of times takes a lot of willpower. Take smoking for example. If someone has smoked 20 cigarettes a day for 30 years, this adds up to 219,000 cigarettes. With the average smoker taking at least ten drags on every cigarette, this adds up to 2,190,000 drags.

The key to success is to replace the unwanted behaviour or state (the bad habit) with a new behaviour or state (the new healthy habit). To do this, we need to know what triggers your bad habit.

In the middle column write down your triggers for each habit – for example, perhaps coffee is your trigger for having a cigarette, or you always have chocolate or watch TV after dinner, or you bite your nails when nervous, or once you go to bed you get out your phone.

In the right-hand column, write down what new positive or healthy habit you could replace the unwanted habit with. For example, if you drink soft drinks, diet drinks, milkshakes or too much alcohol, you could replace the unhealthy drink with a new healthy alternative such as herbal tea, green tea, water, sparkling water with a twist of lime or lemon, or a fresh fruit and veggie juice. You'll see an example of this process already in the table below.

Put pen or pencil to paper and make your list. Change one habit at a time. Make drinking water a habit. Make drinking herbal or green tea a habit. Make going for a walk a habit. This is the start of your habit-busting journey.

OLD BAD HABITS	TRIGGERS	NEW HEALTHY HABIT
Energy drink	When tired	Sparkling water

Step 2: Use the habit-swap visualisation technique

Once you know the bad habit that you'd like to change, what your triggers are and how you would like to be or act instead, you're ready to take the next step, the habit-swap visualisation technique. Choose one bad habit at a time. It's an exercise worth setting aside time for and will work best if you can practise it in a quiet place. The technique works by helping you bring your unconscious habit into your conscious awareness and throwing it away, while simultaneously replacing the bad habit with what you want to do or how you would like to be instead.

For extra strong habits, you may need to repeat the process several times, and that's okay. Once you've gone through this exercise, try out other habit-busting mindful hypnotherapy techniques (you'll find some on p. 264).

Sit comfortably or lie down. Start by thinking of the old habit and telling yourself, *I don't need it, I don't want it, I won't do it.* If your habit involves food, drink or other substance, such as smoking, tell yourself, *I don't need it, I don't want it, I won't have it.*

Bring to mind the picture of the old you about to do the unwanted habit or behaviour. Imagine you are looking through your own eyes at what you would like to change. You realise you don't need to do this habit or be this way anymore. Think of **the new you**, the you who you would be without this problem.

On the count of three, have the old you go flying off into the distance out to the horizon and shrink to nothing. At the same time, **the new you** zooms in over the top, big and bright ... 1, 2, 3, WOOSH.

Picture the person you want to become. Feel yourself being drawn towards that picture. Make it brighter and more colourful. Close your eyes for a few seconds and imagine the new you, the you that you desire to be, making healthy choices.

Clear the screen of your mind.

Bring up the old out-of-date picture again, the old you, about to do the bad habit. Every time you repeat this technique, imagine the old picture becoming dimmer and darker.

See the new you out at the horizon and swap the two pictures ... 1, 2, 3, WOOSH.

Make the picture of the new you big and bright. Feel yourself being drawn towards this picture. How good does it feel to have new choices? Close your eyes for a few seconds as you see **the new you**, happy and content with new options and choices.

Clear the screen of your mind.

Bring up the old picture. See the new you out at the horizon.

Feel yourself being drawn towards **the new you** picture. Make it brighter and more colourful. Close your eyes for a few moments as you see the new you with new options.

Clear the screen of your mind.

Bring up the bad habit, and think to yourself, *I don't need it, I don't want it, I won't have it* or *do it.*

Imagine you are throwing the old picture away as it goes shooting off into the distance. At the same time, the new picture zooms in big and bright over the top ... 1, 2, 3, WOOSH. Swap the two pictures.

Feel yourself being drawn towards the new you.

Close your eyes for a moment as you see **the new you** happy and content.

Clear the screen of your mind and open your eyes.

Repeat swapping the pictures several more times. Instead of THIS, the old picture goes flying off into the distance – WOOSH – THIS! The new picture comes zooming in over the top big and bright.

See and think about, or imagine, the new you with your new choices.

Clear the screen of your mind.

Bring up the old picture and let it go flying off into the distance – WOOSH – the new picture comes zooming in over the top big and bright.

See and think about, or imagine the new you with new choices. Think to yourself, *I am in control.*

Clear the screen of your mind.

Bring up the old picture as it becomes dimmer and darker and let it go flying off into the distance ... 1, 2, 3, WOOSH. The new picture comes zooming in over the top, big and bright.

See and think about, or imagine the new you with new choices. Think to yourself, *I am in control. I don't need it, I don't want it, I won't do it* or *have it.*

Clear the screen of your mind.

Bring your attention back to your breath and slowly start to move your body.

One habit at a time you can change your life. Congratulations on taking another step towards the new you.

MIND FREE MINUTE MEDITATION

Take one minute to immerse yourself in the following power statements and affirmations as a mindful self-hypnosis practice.

Breathe in, *I don't need it, I don't want it, I won't do it*
Breathe out, *I don't need it, I don't want it, I won't have it*

Breathe in, *I am in control*
Breathe out, *I am in control*

Breathe in, *there's always something better to do*
Breathe out, *there's always something better to do*

Breathe in, *I make healthy choices*
Breathe out, *I make healthy choices*

Breathe in, *I develop new healthy habits*
Breathe out, *I develop new healthy habits*

THREE KEYS TO BREAKING BAD HABITS

LESSON 1: Identify your bad habits, your triggers and what you would like to do instead. Remember, we don't just stop a bad habit, we replace the bad habit with a good healthy habit. What are you going to do instead?

LESSON 2: Replace one habit at a time. Your habits have likely taken years to develop. Be patient as you develop a variety of new healthy habits and remember there's always something better to do.

LESSON 3: Remind yourself, you don't need it, you don't want it, you won't do it as you throw away the old habit. See the future you, the *you* you choose to be. This is the in-control happy you, with unlimited choices.

DISCOVER MORE MIND FREE

For more mindful self-hypnosis to help you break bad habits, go to p. 264 of the Mind Manual. You can also listen to recorded sessions on changing habits via the Mind Free app and website mindfreeapp.com.

The three decrees

I hereby decree that today control, achievement and focus fill my day with an abundance of energy. I am in control, I am persistent, I am determined. I embrace change and welcome new experiences because change is good. I am what I do repeatedly; therefore, I create positive rituals and routines to improve my health and life. I have discovered there is always something better to do. I am happy and content as I make healthy choices.

On the following scroll, copy the above in full or part, and combine with your own statements. Or, if you prefer, select your own positive emotion words, short power statements and empowering affirmations. Combine them to form your own personal decree by you, to you, for you.

Official Decree

_____

_____

_____

_____

_____

_____

_____

_____

_____

_____

_____

_____

_____

_____

_____

Signed

CHAPTER 6
SLEEP DEEPLY

I'm an insomniac.

Imagine for a moment you weren't an insomniac. How would life be different if you trained yourself to be a good sleeper?

I just can't switch off my mind.

**What if switching off your mind was easier than you thought?
And how many ways do you already know that help you relax?**

I am becoming good at switching off my mind and easily falling asleep.

What's keeping you awake?

Stress, anxiety, medications, restless leg syndrome and chronic pain are just some of the triggers that can stop you from getting the good night's sleep your body needs.

For some people, an overactive mind is the major contributing factor to a poor sleep. As they lie in bed, they find themselves thinking about things that happened during the day, as well as worrying about what might happen tomorrow, pondering life's big issues and replaying events that happened years or even decades ago.

For others, the stress connected to the whole idea of going to bed and not being able to sleep creates additional stress that actually stops them from falling asleep.

If you consider yourself to be an insomniac, there is a good chance you work yourself into such a state of stress before going to bed that, even though you want to sleep, your body releases excessive amounts of stress hormones such as adrenaline and cortisol that put you into a state of fight or flight. The stress creates a vicious circle that then inhibits your ability to sleep, which in turn creates more stress that reinforces the whole idea that you are a poor sleeper. Not exactly relaxing, is it?

Sometimes, the bedroom itself carries such negative associations that even the thought of going to bed brings on a stream of negative thoughts, which then releases even more stress hormones that keep you awake.

Your evening ritual is another factor that determines whether you will get a good night's sleep or not. What is your routine in the last hour before going to bed? Do you dim the lights and have a warm bath or a shower while listening to slow classical music? Do you practise tai chi, yoga or meditation? Do you read a book or write in a journal? Or do you surf the net, check social media or watch violent TV shows, churning up your mind, to try to prepare for a deep peaceful sleep? It doesn't really make sense, does it?

Many people I've worked with over the years admit to watching crime shows filled with autopsies and murders, scary thrillers or adrenaline-fuelled, action-packed chase movies right before going to bed. Not a great way to prepare your mind for a wonderful, healing sleep. Other people I've worked with admit to overloading their bodies with refined starchy carbohydrates, alcohol or toxic, sugary products throughout the evening.

Then we have the group of people who are nodding off at 8.30 pm or 9.30 pm, and yet push through the sleepiness to finish whatever it is they're doing on the computer, scrolling through on social media or watching on TV. And then there are the screens themselves. The production of melatonin – the brain's sleep chemical – can be impacted by the blue light emitted from your TV, mobile phone or tablet, which affects your sleep cycle.

Whatever it is that's keeping you awake, rather than your brain and body being flooded with relaxing feel-good chemicals, they are flooded with stress chemicals that keep you alert and aroused, even though you may feel exhausted. Once you do get into bed, if you are in this hyper-alert state, the slightest sound or discomfort can feel greatly magnified, which further adds to the problem of relaxing into a deep, natural sleep.

THE DANGERS OF POOR SLEEP

You cannot underestimate the importance of good-quality, regular sleep. The inability to fall asleep or go back to sleep if you wake up can wreak havoc on your body, which can negatively affect you mentally, emotionally and socially.

If the quality of your sleep is poor, there are obvious long-term health consequences, including decreased productivity, drowsiness that can lead to accidents, forgetfulness, a decrease in energy levels, irritability, mood changes, inability to focus, confusion, exhaustion, lack of motivation and increased alcohol or drug use.

Other serious side effects of insomnia or poor sleep patterns include burnout, depression, mood disorders, hypertension, weight gain, a weakened immune system, gastrointestinal disorders, heart disease, stroke and an increased risk of cancer.

Knowing how important sleep is to your health and happiness, you need to ask yourself: *what's keeping me awake?* Acknowledging what might be causing your sleep issues is one of the first steps to overcoming your insomnia. These are some of the most common causes:

- an overactive mind
- physical stress
- mental stress
- TV
- computer time
- social media
- anxiety
- depression
- pain
- late-night snacking
- overeating
- coffee
- energy drinks
- alcohol
- drug use
- restless leg syndrome
- sleep apnoea
- lack of exercise
- noise
- shift work
- medication.

OLIVER'S STORY

Oliver hadn't slept for more than five years. He told me that he had been in a car accident that changed his life forever. The accident caused multiple injuries and he was put into an induced coma for two weeks. While his body began to heal over the following months in hospital, his mind continued to race. He said that he was so wound up physically that his mind would bounce from one thought to another, often replaying the accident over and over.

After five years of not sleeping, Oliver had the biggest bags you could imagine hanging below his red, bloodshot eyes. He had been unable to work because of the injuries and lack of sleep, and had been diagnosed with depression. Unsurprisingly, all of this was affecting his relationship.

During our first sit-down chat, Oliver kept referring to the accident. It seemed to me that along with his depression he was suffering from post-traumatic stress disorder. He was reliving the event and the hospital time over and over. He was angry that this had happened to him, he was sad that he wasn't able to live his normal life and he was overcome with fear about the future. He was also bombarding himself with negative self-talk.

Once we deleted all that negative self-talk and cleared away Oliver's negative emotions, we were then able to create a plan he could easily follow. We practised some progressive muscle relaxation techniques that involved flexing and relaxing each body part, one at a time. We started with flexing and tightening the feet and then relaxing the feet, followed by tightening the calves and thighs and then relaxing them and so on all the way up through the body, finishing at the head. We also practised a progressive muscle relaxation that involved instructing each part of the body to relax: head relax, eyes relax, jaw relax, neck relax, shoulders relax and so on, all the way down through the body.

Once we had finished relaxing the body physically, it was time to relax the mind. I created a hypnosis session, later titled Deep Sleep Phenomena, and it worked a treat. Oliver listened to the hypnosis during our session and started nodding off. He took the recording home with him so he could listen at night before going to sleep. I received a call from Oliver late the next morning. He had fallen asleep that night at 9 pm while listening to the recorded session. He woke up at 5 am after a solid eight hours' sleep, listened to the recorded session again and went back to sleep for another four hours. He told me he felt like a brand-new person.

After some months, Oliver continued to report that every night he was getting a solid eight hours' sleep. His life was getting back on track too: his relationship was great and he had started working part-time.

PROGRAM YOUR BRAIN TO SLEEP

When your mind is racing, it's hard to get to sleep. When you are physically wound up and unable to relax, it's hard to get to sleep. Two of the most important things you can do to help yourself get a great night's sleep is to slow down your mind and physically relax your body.

Consider how you spend the last hour or two before you go to bed. Do you spend the time doing things that are conducive to sleep or activities that churn you up?

If excessive amounts of adrenaline and cortisol prevent sleep or reduce your ability to have a good sleep, then reducing adrenaline and cortisol will improve your ability to sleep.

Self-hypnosis and meditation are excellent for helping with insomnia, as is paying attention to your natural sleep cycles. It's time to change your patterns and create a wonderful evening ritual that will set you up for a great night's sleep. Here are some techniques to calm your body and mind and reduce stress hormones so you can fall into the deep, restful slumber your body needs.

Step 1: Hop on the sleep train

Have you ever been sitting at the computer screen or in front of the TV and started to nod off? Your body knows when it's supposed to go to sleep, so become aware of your natural sleep cycles. If your 'sleep train' pulls in at a specific time and you don't jump on it, and then you miss the next sleep train, and possibly a third sleep train, you are setting yourself up to stay awake for hours.

It's so important to be prepared for the sleep train before it pulls in. Once the sleep train pulls in, you are then in the right state of mind and your body is relaxed enough to fall asleep.

First, you need to know what time your sleep train pulls in. For some people that may be 8.30 pm, 9.30 pm or 10.30 pm. Be aware of what time you would normally start to nod off and feel sleepy. Rather than pushing yourself through to finish watching that show or that Instagram story, or scrolling through your Facebook feed, hop into bed five minutes before your sleep train pulls in and go through the pre-sleep routine that follows.

Step 2: Write it all down

If you are a worrier and keep replaying things over and over in your mind, get everything out of your head and into a worry journal before you hop into bed. Do a brain dump or create a to-do list or action plan so you do not have to lie there thinking about those things.

Step 3: Appreciation

As you lie in bed and get comfortable, run through in your mind the things you appreciate and what you are grateful for. You can start with ideas as far-reaching as the universe, the sun, the moon, the stars, the clouds and rain, and then slowly bring your appreciation awareness back, closer to home: perhaps family, friends, water to drink, food to eat and anything else in your more immediate environment and life. Then list in your mind what else you appreciate, such as the roof over your head, the walls protecting you from the cold, your bed, your blanket, your sheets and your pillow. You could also go on to list other things such as appreciating your eyes, your hands, your legs, your heart, your lungs and anything else you wish to add to your appreciation list.

Simply run through your list in this way: *I appreciate the stars, the sun and the moon. I appreciate the mountains, the trees, rivers and the ocean. I appreciate my family and I appreciate my friends. I appreciate this roof over my head, I appreciate the walls around me, I appreciate my bed and my pillow.*

This helps because getting yourself into a state of appreciation transforms any negative state you may be feeling. You are unable to experience two opposing states at the same time, meaning if you are focused on appreciation, you are no longer focused on frustration, disappointment, sadness, anger or whatever it might be that's keeping you awake.

Step 4: Body and mind together as one

Practise this short relaxation technique once you are in bed to help bring you into the present moment and calm your mind and body as one.

Lying back comfortably, focus your attention on your legs. As you feel the feelings of your legs relaxing, quietly repeat in your mind, *legs in legs*. Shift your awareness over to your back and feel all the muscles in your back as you think, *back in back*. Bring your awareness over to your arms and feel the feelings in your arms as they completely and totally relax. As you let go of any and all tension or stress in your arms, quietly think to yourself, *arms in arms*.

Next, shift your awareness and your attention up to your head as you feel all the muscles in your face and your scalp relaxing. Quietly repeat in your mind, *head in head*. As you slowly breathe in and out, you relax even more deeply.

With the in-breath, quietly repeat in your mind, *body and mind* ... and, as you exhale, think, *together as one*. Continue slowly breathing in and out as you repeat *body and mind* with each in-breath and *together as one* with each out-breath. You may even find that the thought *body and mind together as one* gently pops into your mind at any time of day or night, as you slowly breathe in and out.

Body and mind together as one.

MIND FREE MINUTE MEDITATION

Take one minute to immerse yourself in the following power statements and affirmations as a mindful self-hypnosis practice.

Breathe in, *I release the day*
Breathe out, *I release the day*

Breathe in, *I let all tension drift away*
Breathe out, *I let all tension drift away*

Breathe in, *my sleep is peaceful*
Breathe out, *my sleep is peaceful*

Breathe in, *I am ready to sleep*
Breathe out, *I am ready to sleep*

Breathe in, *I am thankful for today*
Breathe out, *I am thankful for today*

THREE KEYS TO A GOOD NIGHT'S SLEEP

LESSON 1: Avoid the blue light from TV and technology before bed and stop watching anything that generates stress, such as violent crime shows. Create a pre-bed ritual that helps you relax and prepare for a good night's sleep.

LESSON 2: Change the story you are telling yourself. Rather than, I'm an insomniac, I'm a poor sleeper, I never sleep, start telling yourself: I am a good sleeper, I am thankful for today, I am happy to be able to sleep.

LESSON 3: Jump on board the sleep train. Be ready to go to bed before the train pulls in. As the train is pulling in, run through your appreciation meditation, body and mind meditation and whichever mindful self-hypnosis scripts give you the best result.

DISCOVER MORE MIND FREE

For more mindful self-hypnosis to help you get a good night's sleep, go to p. 269 of the Mind Manual. You can also listen to recorded sessions on sleep via the Mind Free app and website mindfreeapp.com.

The three decrees

I hereby decree that I am bathed in feelings of calm, appreciation and being present as I prepare for bed. I am thankful, I am relaxed, I am ready, I am safe, I am happy. My body and mind are together as one as I sink into a deep restful sleep. I am in control of my sleeping patterns and I choose to sleep through the night. I hold on to positive feelings from today. I am calming my body as I think about nothing and worry about nothing.

On the following scroll, copy the above in full or part, and combine with your own statements. Or, if you prefer, select your own positive emotion words, short power statements and empowering affirmations. Combine them to form your own personal decree by you, to you, for you.

Official Decree

_____

_____

_____

_____

_____

_____

_____

_____

_____

_____

_____

_____

Signed

CHAPTER 7
LIVE PAIN FREE

There's no relief.

What if accepting and becoming one with the pain could bring some relief?
Could you begin to realise you are so much more than your pain?

Nothing works.

How many self-hypnosis techniques have you tried to release the pain?
What if simply breathing into your feeling and blowing it away brought relief?

My body has an amazing ability to heal.

Several years ago, while in Melbourne preparing for an Innermake-over weekend retreat, I was walking along Bourke Street Mall and was stopped in my tracks by a rather unique street performer. Sitting at her 1970s red typewriter was the Bourke Street Poet, Angelina Stanton. Next to her a sign read, 'I will write you a poem, any topic you choose.' Having an appreciation for the power of poetry, I asked if it was possible to write a poem about pain. After I explained I would be working over the weekend with a group of people with both emotional and physical pain, using meditation and self-hypnosis, Angelina asked for 15 minutes to come up with something. When I returned this is what I was presented with.

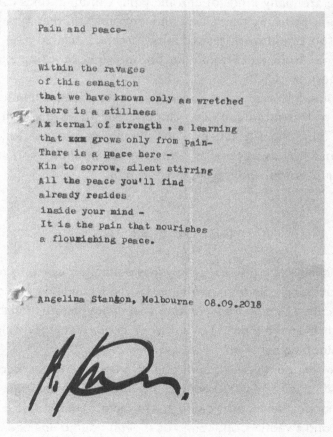

Pain and peace—

Within the ravages
of this sensation
that we have known only as wretched
there is a stillness
Ax kernal of strength , a learning
that xxx grows only from pain—
There is a peace here –
Kin to sorrow, silent stirring
All the peace you'll find
already resides
inside your mind –
It is the pain that nourishes
a flourishing peace.

Angelina Stanton, Melbourne 08.09.2018

Every attendee at the seminar received a copy.

One in five Australians suffers chronic pain. We're talking constant, relentless pain that affects every part of their lives and stops them from being able to fully enjoy the things they once loved – day in and day out.

More often than not, people living with chronic pain have tried everything to relieve it. Pain meds often don't work, pain-relief exercises barely make a difference. They can't sleep, they can't fully engage at work or with their loved ones – just getting through the day can be a challenge. As anyone who has suffered with chronic pain knows, it's a tough gig, and often it feels like there's no end and no solution.

There are many kinds of chronic pain. Common ones can include back pain, arthritis, headaches and migraines. Other types of pain include sports and work-related injuries, cancer-related pain, and pain that comes from conditions like fibromyalgia or complex regional pain syndrome (CRPS).

Ongoing physical pain can cause mental anguish and lead to feelings of frustration, anxiety, sadness, fear and depression. You are not the only one affected by your pain; it can take a toll on your family and friends as they sit helplessly by, watching you suffer. But there is a solution, and it is all in your mind!

CHLOE'S STORY

Chloe Davenport, a 14-year-old Sydney schoolgirl, came to me suffering excruciating pain from a rare neurological condition. Her daily pain was described by a pain specialist to be more agonising than the pain of childbirth. Even the touch of a feather on her arm or legs would feel like a knife stabbing her skin.

Chloe has complex regional pain syndrome (CRPS), which affects around 20 in every 100,000 people. In sufferers, the messages from the brain change the blood flow in the affected limb, causing swelling, redness and sweating, appearing as though trauma has been suffered. There is no medical cure to relieve the symptoms.

Knowing how hypnosis and meditation work, I was confident we could get a good result and, at the very least, help reduce the intensity of Chloe's pain.

On the day I arrived to see her, Chloe was limping, with agonising pain in her right leg and her arm was red and swollen, her hand clawed. In only a couple of hours, with meditation and hypnosis, Chloe's pain level went from a ten out of ten on the pain scale to a zero. The results were astonishing. Chloe's parents, Grant and Mandy, couldn't believe their eyes. By the time we finished the sessions, Chloe was walking, smiling, pain free and crying with joy for the first time in 12 months.

Chloe learned meditative exercises and self-hypnosis to train her unconscious mind, helping her to relax and de-stress. Three years later Chloe is still free of pain.

The scripts in this chapter (and in the Mind Manual on p. 277) are the ones I used to decrease Chloe's pain levels from a ten to a zero. These are techniques that you too can use to alleviate chronic pain today.

MEDICATION TO MEDITATION

Your brain is the most powerful tool in your arsenal for dealing with chronic pain. I'm not saying that pain is all in your mind, because from the hundreds of sufferers I've worked with I know it's not. However, genuine healing can occur when you harness the power of your mind. Thoughts can be a powerful medicine. With every thought you have, chemical changes take place in your body. Through meditation and self-hypnosis, you can flip the pain switch off and decrease the pain, or even eliminate it altogether.

While the pain red alert in your brain is *on*, you're in a constant state of fight or flight. This sends the stress hormone cortisol coursing through your system, which wreaks havoc on your mind and body and may even increase your pain levels.

Self-hypnosis is a natural state of relaxation that has no adverse side effects. Clinical trials have shown that it is an effective tool for reducing chronic pain levels. You can use hypnotherapy to change your perception of pain, and your response to it.

Whenever I am working with a chronic pain sufferer, I use a combination of pain hypnosis techniques and meditation to retrain the brain to reduce pain. The techniques teach you how to release and increase the body's natural feel-good chemicals and natural painkillers. You can use these techniques in conjunction with your current pain management medications, but you should always speak to your doctor first. The types of pain these techniques can help with include headaches and migraine, back, neck and shoulder pain, CRPS, post-operative pain, arthritis, sports injuries, dental pain and fibromyalgia.

If you have been suffering from chronic pain, I encourage you to give the following techniques a go. Even if you get some relief or reduction in your pain, it's worth it.

Deliberate breathing

Where the mind goes, the energy flows. A simple pain-reducing technique that works with this is deliberate breathing. It's an ancient Indian breathing meditation designed to reduce pain by breathing *into* the area of pain. As you breathe into an area where you are feeling pain, you not only reduce stress, which in itself can reduce pain, but you also direct the flow of energy within the body into the part of the body that's causing pain. There are three simple steps to this technique. Repeat them several times until the pain reduces or disappears altogether. In this exercise I've used the word *feeling* instead of the word *pain*.

Sit or lie down in a comfortable position for you, and relax. Feel your breath flowing in and out of your body. Using your mind, direct the feeling of each breath towards the area of what you are feeling. Notice on a scale of zero to ten, with ten being extreme sensation, how you rate the feeling at this moment.

As you breathe in and out, allow your entire body to completely relax like a rag doll. Allow your jaw to relax. Breathing in and out, soften the muscles of your neck. Let your shoulders flop. Continue to slowly breathe in and out, letting your arms relax. Allow all the muscles in your back to go loose and soft. Let your chest relax. As you feel your breath falling in and out of your body, relax your abdomen. Let your buttock muscles go soft and loose. Feel your hips relaxing as your breath continues falling in and out of your body. Allow your legs to completely relax. You could even picture your legs as a big bag full of loose rubber bands. Take several slow, effortless deep breaths as you bring all your awareness to the breath flowing in and out of your body. Pause for a moment as you watch your breath flow in and out. Breathing in and out, and relaxing even more, do the following steps.

AWARENESS BREATH: On the next breath, think the thought *awareness* as you direct the awareness thought to the feeling you feel. As you exhale, let your body relax even more.

ACCEPTANCE BREATH: The second breath is the breath of *acceptance*. Take a slow, deep breath in as you think the thought *acceptance*. As you exhale, let everything relax.

RELEASE BREATH: The third breath is the breath of *release*. Take a slow deep breath in as you think the thought *release* and feel the feeling of release. As you exhale, let your entire body relax, and release the sensation you've been feeling.

Take a moment to simply let your breath fall in and out of your body several times without effort. As the breath falls in and out of your body, notice on a scale of ten to zero, with zero being no feeling at all, what level is the feeling now? When you're ready, repeat the three breaths as follows.

AWARENESS BREATH: Take a slow, deep breath in, imagining your breath is flowing through to the area where you have been experiencing the feeling, and simply be aware of the feeling and your breath flowing into the area. As you exhale, let your entire body relax and let go.

ACCEPTANCE BREATH: Take a slow deep breath in, imagine your breath is flowing through to the area where you have been experiencing those old feelings. Simply think the thought *acceptance* and accept how you are feeling as you direct your breath towards that area. As you exhale, let your entire body relax and let go.

RELEASE BREATH: Take a slow deep breath all the way in and direct your breath to the area of the old feeling. Think the thought *release* and feel the feeling of release as you breathe into that area. As you exhale, let your entire body relax and let go.

Take a moment as you allow your breath to fall in and out of your body several times. Simply focus on your breathing as your body relaxes more and more with each and every breath. As the breath falls in and out of your body, notice on a scale of ten down to zero, with zero being no feeling at all, where the feeling is now.

You can repeat this deliberate breathing practice as many times as you need, to help you reduce or eliminate what you've been feeling.

Meditations to relieve pain

LOVING COMPASSION MEDITATION

Slowly breathe in and out as you think thoughts of love and compassion. As you think these thoughts feel love and compassion for the part of your body where you are experiencing that feeling. With your eyes open or closed, think to yourself, *I love my leg, shoulder, back* ... or whichever part of you is experiencing the feeling.

As you slowly breathe in and out, direct the energy of loving compassion to flow through to that part of you, and notice what's happening to the feeling.

Allow the words *loving compassion* to flow. Use all your senses. See the words, feel the words and think about, **loving compassion**.

BLOW AWAY PAIN

Notice where the feeling of discomfort is in your body right now. Imagine the feeling as a small cloud, a ball of light or a puff of mist. As you breathe in, draw the feeling up into either your right or your left shoulder like a vacuum. As you exhale, direct the feeling down your arm and into your hand making a fist. Take another slow deep breath in and, as you exhale, open your hand and blow the stress or pain away. You might even like to throw it away. Keep repeating this exercise by breathing the feeling up into your shoulder and exhaling it down your arm into your hand. Then, as you breathe in, make the fist and, as you exhale, open your hand and blow away or throw away the stress.

LEONIE'S STORY

Imagine how bad life would be if you had a headache every single day for 59 years. Leonie was born with Chiari malformation, a rare and serious neurological disorder, where the cerebellum protrudes through the base of the malformed skull, crowding the spinal cord, and putting intense pressure on both the brain and spine. It leads to a constant and extreme headache at the base of the skull.

The condition is incredibly debilitating. Leonie explained, 'Every day I suffer from severe headaches, pressure, dizziness, choking, disorientation, loss of balance, loss of memory, neck and spinal pain, nausea, vomiting, diarrhoea … and that's on a good day. On a bad day, my headache can be a 20 out of ten on the pain scale and I just want to end it all. I'm a walking pill bottle, and I've lost count of how many times I've blacked out and crashed to the ground.'

Over the years, there had been countless visits to pain clinics and specialists, and surgery that had delivered short-term relief only. Because of the pain intensity, Leonie had attempted suicide several times.

'The best way I can describe it,' said Leonie, 'it's as if a monster is trying to tear its way out the back of your head or as if a javelin is being thrown through the back of your skull from the inside.'

I was deeply moved by Leonie's situation. Both Leonie and her husband Ian confirmed that I was their last hope. If the hypnosis didn't work, Leonie was prepared to end her life, with Ian's help. 'No pressure,' I half joked to them, to bring a little ease to the moment. But this was deadly serious.

Through welling eyes Leonie said, 'If you can take the pain level down from its current nine out of ten to a five out of ten, I'll be the happiest person in the world. I'm scared that I'm never going to get any better. I'm even trialling CBD oil at $450 a month to try to get some relief. I'm 59 years old but I feel 95.'

Headaches is an area where I have had some great results, and I was ready to do my absolute best. But there was more. On top of the Chiari malformation, Leonie also went through a list of her other conditions including degenerative disc disease, sleep apnoea, type 2 diabetes, irritable bowel syndrome, diverticulitis, scoliosis, fibromyalgia, polymyalgia, recurring glandular fever, widespread osteoarthritis, bursitis in her shoulders, hips and thumbs, panic attacks, anxiety and suicidal depression. 'Other than that, you're fine?' I asked her, with a cheeky grin. Leonie explained that, to make matters worse, both her daughter and granddaughter had been diagnosed with Chiari malformation, even though it's not supposed to be genetic. Leonie's stress level was enormous.

I explained that what I wanted to do first was to bring down her stress levels and anxiety. We sat together on the couch and I ran through several relaxation and meditation techniques to help Leonie release the tension she was holding onto. I could see her stress melting away. I watched as Leonie's shoulders dropped by at least five centimetres. When I checked with her, Leonie nodded and said, 'The pain level has gone from a nine out of ten to an eight out of ten.'

Over the next two hours, I taught Leonie every meditation and pain self-hypnosis technique I knew. Each technique took the pain down by either a one or a half. Eventually, we had the pain down to less than one out of ten. Through tears, Leonie sobbed, 'These are tears of joy. I don't know this feeling; it feels so strange.'

Knowing that pain causes stress, sleeplessness, anxiety and depression, I emphasised how important it was to create a daily morning mindfulness self-hypnosis ritual and an evening self-hypnosis session. I advised Leonie to talk to her doctors and, as her relief continued, she could discuss decreasing the dosage of some of her medications.

It is now six months on and Leonie has maintained a pain level between zero and two out of ten.

MIND FREE MINUTE MEDITATION

Take one minute to immerse yourself in the following power statements and affirmations as a mindful self-hypnosis practice.

Breathe in, *I breathe energy into my body*
Breathe out, *I breathe energy into my body*

Breathe in, *my body is healing, I am healing*
Breathe out, *my body is healing, I am healing*

Breathe in, *my body is strong, I am strong*
Breathe out, *my body is strong, I am strong*

Breathe in, *I have the power to heal*
Breathe out, *I have the power to heal*

Breathe in, *my mind is calm, I am calm*
Breathe out, *my mind is calm, I am calm*

THREE KEYS TO PAIN CONTROL

LESSON 1: Stress increases pain, so it's critical to reduce stress. Practise the mindful self-hypnosis scripts in this chapter and the Mind Manual and keep turning the pain dial down.

LESSON 2: Retrain your brain to reduce pain by breathing into the feeling as you tune into awareness, acceptance and release. Direct your body's healing energy to any area of your body where it is needed.

LESSON 3: Become one with the feeling as you focus on where the feeling is from the surface of the skin, the shape, the texture and the colour. Remember to acknowledge your emotions too.

DISCOVER MORE MIND FREE

For more mindful self-hypnosis to help you manage pain, go to p. 277 of the Mind Manual. You can also listen to recorded sessions on pain management via the Mind Free app and website mindfreeapp.com.

The three decrees

I hereby decree that my day will be filled with acceptance, peace and strength. I am calm, I am healing, I am breathing, I am optimistic and I am strong. I release all tension as I increase the feeling of calm within me. Any sensations I am feeling will pass. My body is healing, I am healing. I feel at peace, I am at peace.

On the following scroll, copy the above in full or part, and combine with your own statements. Or, if you prefer, select your own positive emotion words, short power statements and empowering affirmations. Combine them to form your own personal decree by you, to you, for you.

Official Decree

_____

_____

_____

_____

_____

_____

_____

_____

_____

_____

_____

_____

_____

_____

_____

_____

_____
Signed

CHAPTER 8

RELEASE EXCESS WEIGHT

I can't stop eating.

What would happen to your weight if you listened to the message that you are satisfied?
How healthy will you be when you realise you know when to stop?

I come from a fat family.

What would happen if you ate small healthy meals and started exercising?
Could you learn to love to move?

I hate my body.

How would you feel if you loved yourself a little bit at a time?
What can you like about yourself? Maybe your ears, your eyes or your smile?

I love making healthy choices, I love to move, I love me.

Diets don't work. We live in hope that some new diet, app, juice cleanse, vitamin or gym equipment will be the answer. Often, the repeated attempts, failures and partial successes only serve to reinforce the belief that diets are hard to stick to. The reason most people fail is because their weight struggles relate to a complex range of psychological and emotional issues, including beliefs, emotions, values, motivations, stress, habits, triggers and responses to their internal and external environment. *These* are the real challenges. And these are the psychological components to losing weight that are left out of almost every diet or weight-loss program.

There *is* another way: address the specific *causes* of your weight issues by targeting those parts of your unconscious where memories, fears, food associations, self-esteem issues and negative self-talk lie. Change those limiting beliefs and replace them with positive, empowering beliefs, and you'll start the journey to a healthier, happier life.

CJ'S STORY

When CJ attended an Innermakeover weekend retreat, she weighed 103 kilograms.

'I've struggled with my weight for about 20 years. My problem was the three Cs: chocolate, Coke, chips – when I was stressed, after work, sitting in front of the TV. I always finish the day with chocolate and now I'm in the habit of having some before breakfast. I eat potato chips every afternoon and sometimes I have them for dinner if I can't be bothered cooking. I drink 1.5 litres of Coca-Cola every day. I'm addicted to it all.'

Over the years, CJ had tried many diets, from Jenny Craig to Lite n' Easy. 'I'm an emotional eater and it affects my life in two main areas. First, I can't fit into any of my clothes. The second thing is finding a life partner. I lost my thirties caring for my sick parents for over ten years. It would be nice to feel confident in clothes again and find that right partner.'

Through a combination of self-hypnosis and meditations (including some of the scripts you'll find in this book), we worked on changing the negative internal conversations CJ had been having with herself for all those years. This allowed CJ to empower herself from the inside out, to change her eating habits and, ultimately, her future.

Twelve months later CJ reported in. 'I have surpassed my goal by 5 kilograms and now weigh 68 kilograms. For the first time in my life the weight is staying off and it's easy. I can actually fit into my nurse's uniform from when I was 18 years old – that's almost 40 years ago. All my girl-friends are saying I'm getting younger. I'm completely in control of my health now that I am in control of my mind. Oh, and I've got a new man, and couldn't be happier.'

CJ had made her health important. She created a daily ritual of listening to the Mind Free meditation and self-hypnosis sessions every morning and every night. CJ's advice: 'This has helped me master my mind. You have to start your day with your mind and you have to end your day with your mind.'

We know that the best way to change your life is to change your lifestyle. Yet, many diets or weight-loss programs only address what to eat and what not to eat, and how to exercise. Every single person who has struggled with their weight knows what to eat and what not to eat. Everybody knows that to be fit and healthy you need to move your body and exercise. The problem is *staying motivated to accompany the knowledge*. Staying motivated depends entirely on the story you are attaching to food and exercise.

Why do so many people overeat? Why do so many people find it practically impossible to stick to a healthy diet? Why do people lack motivation to be healthier?

Are you overweight because you lack motivation or do you lack motivation because you are overweight?

Your brain is a supercomputer. The main reason for diets failing is that most people do nothing to deal with or replace the outdated software and programs running in their mind.

When it comes to overcoming the struggles associated with being overweight, the main areas most people need help with are:

• bad habits
• negative self-talk

- portions and food choices
- movement.

The techniques you'll discover in this chapter are not short-term solutions or a fad diet attempting to solve what is clearly a long-term issue or lifestyle problem. It is not a quick fix. It's about changing your thinking around fundamental beliefs that in turn will result in a healthier, happier and slimmer you.

You will discover how to turn negative thought patterns into positive empowering ones as you change your relationship with food.

You will learn how to transform your old, unhealthy habits into new healthy ones.

You will learn how to control portions by eating mindfully.

Your body has within it a blueprint for your ideal weight and size. Every day, people make positive changes in their lives. Every day, thousands of people stop smoking. Every day, thousands of people change careers. Thousands more make positive changes daily to their health and fitness. Now it's your turn.

CHANGE YOUR MIND FIRST

The most powerful way to change your mind and your internal dialogue is to use mindful self-hypnosis daily. As you read the following scripts each day, all your problems will, before you know it, seem like a distant memory. You'll be replacing negative, self-defeating, self-sabotaging thoughts with empowering positive ones. To help you do that, I have included several affirmations and positive beliefs written in the first person so that you can start to tell yourself a new story.

The fact is, thoughts are a powerful medicine and these empowering beliefs or positive thoughts are a form of self-hypnosis. Think about it: if you say repeatedly, *I can't stop eating chocolate*, you are in the I-can't-stop-eating-chocolate trance. In many cases, your negative thinking is like being under a spell. It's time to break the trance and wake up. As you delete the old thoughts and replace them with new positive thoughts, you are taking control of your life.

Whenever you see an *italicised* empowering statement like the one below, take a moment to let it sink in. You may like to quietly think about the new belief in your mind, you may want to whisper it, you may want to open a window and yell it out to the world. You may want to say it once or a hundred times. Breathe these words into your life.

Now it's my turn.

Overcoming your overweight mind

The overweight body is a by-product of an overweight mind. The problem starts in the mind, exists in the mind and needs to be addressed in the mind. You can read a hundred recipe books or a thousand diet and exercise books and yet still fail if you have not overcome the underlying mental and emotional issues holding you back. It's time for a new start. It's time for a new mindset.

Today is the beginning of my new life.

Stop your mental spam

How often do you let your own self-defeating attitude get you down? How often do you use self-talk that builds you up and gets you excited?

Here are some of the most common negative statements and self-talk that I hear at seminars, at retreats and with clients in private breakthrough sessions. How many of them sound familiar to you? *It's too hard, I'm too tired, I can't, I have no energy, I'll always be fat, I don't have time, I'm too busy, I'm not good enough, it's hard to stick to a diet, diets don't work, compared with others I'm hopeless, I'll probably put the weight back on, it's impossible, I'll start tomorrow, I don't deserve it* and *I'm not good enough.*

Following are some simple solutions to negative thinking and negative self-talk, and an alternative positive thought for you to consider. These will help you change your internal dialogue around food. Remember, when you read the *italicised* empowering statements, take a moment to let them sink in. Breathe these words into your life.

I'm always hungry

Even when you're asleep? Even while you're having a shower? Are you hungry physically or emotionally? Does being hungry mean you have to stuff yourself? And you do realise that fattening, unhealthy, dead, devitalised food makes you hungry, don't you? Is hunger the enemy? Isn't hunger just a feeling? Isn't being in charge of your life more important than being controlled by food? What would you have to eat to not be hungry?

I only eat when physically hungry.

I'm just too tired

Get to bed early. Eat clean foods. Avoid junk food. Move more. Before you know it, you will have boundless energy and be full of life. Looking after your health is the greatest expression of self-love. It's time to look after you.

I am full of life.

I'll probably put the weight back on

You set yourself up to fail before you start with statements like this. When you make healthy eating and fitness part of your everyday life, there is no going back to the old ways. A person can, you know, just stay healthy forever. The secret is to not be on a diet but to change your lifestyle.

My lifestyle is healthy.

I can't stop snacking

Find healthy substitutes. Make a smoothie. Have a cup of tea. Drink more water. Do an activity. Override the hunger feeling.

Between main meals I stay snack free.

Between main meals I drink water or tea.

I don't deserve it

Delete that thought from your mind. You absolutely do deserve it. With each passing day you appreciate your life more and more. You realise you do deserve good things. Your life *is* worthwhile. You do deserve to be healthy and fit, to be loved and to live the life you want. If that old thought pops up again either delete it or tell it to *shut up* or *go away*. You could make fun of the self-defeating hogwash by repeating it in a funny accent. You deserve health and happiness. Do you deserve it? Yes, you do.

I deserve health and happiness.

Emotional eating

As well as the mental aspect, there is the emotional aspect of eating, which also influences your ability to stick to a healthy eating plan. The emotions that trigger unhealthy eating or overeating may also affect other parts of your life. You probably realise that if you eat when feeling sad the sadness is not helped by eating. No amount of eating ever fixes an emotional problem. You may find it hard to incorporate physical activity into your everyday life because you just don't feel up to it. Feelings of anger, sadness, fear, hurt or guilt often lead to overeating and unhealthy food choices. Negative emotions can also lead to feelings of depression or a sense of being overwhelmed, and reduce the drive or desire to do anything, especially to move and exercise. Mindless eating is usually a symptom of emotional eating. Mindful eating is one of the best ways to control emotional eating. As you learn to change your state from negative to positive you will find it easier to control emotional eating. The 21 States in Chapter 11 will guide you day by day to feel better about yourself and transform yourself one thought and one day at a time. If you feel emotionally bankrupt, you need Chapter 11. With the simple meditations and self-hypnosis scripts in *Mind Free* you have a wide variety of techniques that will help you feel better. As you feel better you will make healthier choices.

STOP MAKING EXCUSES

Let's face it, everyone has distractions and problems. We all have obstacles and challenges throughout our lives, and that will not change. However, what will change is how you cope with these challenges and how you look at or think about the problems.

We can all create reasons and excuses as to why we didn't stick to the plan this week, couldn't walk around the block, didn't drink eight glasses of water, had an unhealthy snack or had a massive portion.

At the end of the day, these are all convenient excuses. If you are 100 per cent honest with yourself, you are most likely sick of making excuses, aren't you? It would be too easy to keep putting success off. It would be too easy to sit there and watch TV for endless hours. You don't need any help doing what you've been doing, but it is time for a change. The time for excuses has passed and the time for action is now.

It's my time to change.

Change your script

What excuses are you using? What challenges have been holding you back? Here are some strategies to help you overcome some of the most common challenges people face when trying to shed the excess kilos and achieve vibrant health.

I can't get organised

Create a daily schedule. Make sure that *you* are on your schedule or to-do list. Cut back on anything that wastes your time. Make your health a priority. This is *your* life – fit *you* into it.

I make the time.

It's all too overwhelming

Get underwhelmed. Break everything down. Get it out of your head and make a list of all the things you have to do. Get regimented if you need to. Delegate as much as possible. My mum raised three kids on her own and worked a full-time job and two part-time jobs to make ends meet. She trained us to iron, cook and clean. Get the monkey off your back. Delegate, delegate, delegate.

Small steps will get me there.

I don't have any willpower

Rather than giving up before you start because you keep telling yourself you have no willpower, focus on developing new healthy habits. Get excited about your health. Be passionate. Practise saying *no*.

My health is my wealth.

I keep thinking negative thoughts

Stomp on them, crush them and turn them into positives. *I can't* becomes *I can*. *I'll do it later* becomes *I'll do it now*. Go ahead and knock those suckers out of the park! Remember, when you change your mindset, anything is possible.

It's possible.

I always make excuses

When you live on the excuses side of life and have all the reasons ready about why you fail, why you can't stop snacking and you play the blame game, you will continue to spin your wheels and get nowhere. The time for justifying and explaining away poor health or your condition has to stop somewhere. Make that somewhere here and now.

Today is the day and now is the time.

I'm full of self-doubt

It's time to doubt the doubt. You have the ability. You have so much ability and now you will start to use that ability. You have a power within you that you are only just beginning to tap into. It's time to start believing in the most important person in the world: you.

I am the one.

I'm bored

If you are getting bored, add variety to your meals and activity. Boredom is a mindset. Bring as much variety into your cooking and training as you can. Think of junk food as totally boring. Think of TV as boring and a waste of time. Change your mind. By one thought at a time, you will continue to change your life.

Life is what I make it; I choose to be healthy.

I eat when I'm bored

There is always something better to do. Think of all the things you can do instead of reaching for fattening food. There is *always* something better to do. Memorise these words and repeat them whenever the need arises.

There is always something better to do.

I'm stuck in my bad habits

The key to breaking bad habits is to replace them with good habits. It's time to make healthy choices. Imagine what would happen if you replaced sugary drinks with water, replaced coffee with tea, replaced sweet treats with nuts or fruit. Coke becomes sparkling water with a slice of lemon. Sleeping-in becomes early-to-bed, early-to-rise. Watching TV becomes exercising or meditating. Reinforce the new habits by repeating them over and over until they become part of your everyday life. Realise you are capable of making healthy choices.

I make healthy choices.

THE POWER OF GOOD HABITS

Habits and unconscious food associations can make people eat even when they're not hungry. Food may have been offered to you as a child when you were good or did something well, and it's possible you still associate food as a reward. For many people, those sweets and treats become an addiction as powerful as any drug. Understanding how to run your brain is absolutely crucial to successful slimming.

How many times do you make excuses? *I'll do it later, I'm too busy now* or *I'm too tired, I'll get serious tomorrow. This little bit won't hurt. I don't have the energy.* Or *it's too hard* … and the list goes on and on, doesn't it? And even though we may really want to stick to a healthy eating plan or be active, we often justify the reasons why we don't. You want to do something, but the old negative pattern and excuses pop up, keeping you from your health goals. Sound familiar?

Now go ahead and think about something you want to do to help yourself. It might be sticking to a healthy eating plan, going for a daily walk, going to the gym or joining a fitness class. Choose something that will not only improve your health and fitness, but is also something you really want to do. The moment you think of the activity or the positive action, notice what negative self-defeating thoughts or excuses pop up in your mind that stop you from taking action. What are you saying to yourself? *The gym is too expensive. I have to pick up the kids in the afternoon. I don't have time for such a long walk, it might wear me out.* These are negative conditioned responses that are keeping you from enjoying a healthier, happier life. Want to be slimmer and healthier? Keep changing your story.

Overcoming the biggest poor-eating habits

Stress eating

Dehydration often leads to feelings of stress, so drink up. Drink more water, drink more water, drink more water. Find alternatives to stress eating, such as doing breathing exercises, walking, yoga, boxing classes or martial arts. Swap junk food for a piece of fruit. The list is endless: find what works best for you and make that part of your daily life.

I stay calm, I am calm.

Self-sabotage

There may be any number of unconscious or conscious reasons for self-sabotage. Your desire to succeed and be healthy has to be stronger than your desire to eat dead, devitalised, toxic, unhealthy, fattening rubbish. The more you read the 21 States in Chapter 11 along with the scripts in the Mind Manual, the more you will overcome self-sabotage. Change your relationship to food and remind yourself that food is for nutrition and energy.

Be aware of the triggers that lead to self-sabotage. Stop believing the old stinking thinking. It's time to step outside the prison bars of negative self-talk and move into freedom. Rather than thinking of yourself as imprisoned by eating healthily, change your perception to one of freedom and loving yourself, loving your health. Never again will you be on a restrictive diet. Make the last diet you were on the last diet you ever go on and make a healthy lifestyle your mission. Make your life one of health and happiness.

My food is my fuel, my food is nutrition.

Sugar addiction

Generally, when sugar hits the taste buds, all self-control goes out the window: gimme more, gimme more. When you balance out your blood sugar levels with healthy, nutritious meals, there is no need for sugar. There are so many ways to get your sugar fix naturally: oranges, apples, berries. And so many other fruits are full of fibre, minerals and vitamins, plus they have natural sugar and are delicious. Kick the habit and get healthy.

I make natural healthy choices.

Chocolate addiction

Chocolate addiction is not something to be laughed at, with severe addicts even unable to survive a day without their favourite sugar hit. You might reach for chocolate when you're feeling stressed, tired, lonely, sad or bored, or when you're happy and want a reward. Eating chocolate produces the same endorphins you get during sex, so for some people eating chocolate is very sensual. Chocolate also contains tryptophan, which is soothing and leaves the chocolate addict feeling calm. Drink plenty of water, start meals with protein, eat more raw foods, eat small, healthy meals frequently, and remind yourself: I don't need it, I don't want it, I won't have it.

I am addicted to health.

Food and drink as rewards

Create a list of as many non-food rewards as you can and put it up on the fridge. Treat yourself to health. Pamper yourself. Buy a new book or outfit. Have a warm bath and listen to relaxing music. Reward yourself with a massage or facial. Save the money you would have spent on junk food and reward yourself with something else.

I reward myself in healthy ways.

Alcohol after a hard day

Avoid treating alcohol as a reward. For Patsy, it was. She drank a dozen or more beers a night. It was having such a negative effect on her life, health and relationships that she made the decision to stop drinking. She was 100 per cent committed. Through habit-busting techniques that created an aversion to alcohol, along with meditation and hypnosis, Patsy replaced her addiction to alcohol with a new addiction for herbal teas. Lesson learned? Find alternative rewards at the end of a hard day. Save the money you would have spent on alcohol to buy yourself a gift or treat at the end of the week.

My reward is good health.

Sugar-filled fizzy drinks

Two women attended the retreat. One was drinking five to ten litres of diet cola a day. Yech! The other was drinking between a dozen and 24 cans of full-sugar soft drink a day. That's a lot of sugar – talk about a serious addiction. The retreat taught them you can replace fizzy sugar-filled or artificially sweetened drinks with healthy drinks like water, freshly squeezed juices, herbal teas and sparkling water with a twist of lemon. Months on, I heard back from both women. The great result: they were both making healthy drinking choices.

I stay hydrated in a healthy way.

Excuses not to exercise

Stop making excuses and just get into it. Pick an activity you enjoy and make it a daily ritual. Take one step and one day at a time. While you continue to make excuses, you will continue to get little to no results. Living on the excuses side of life means you give up your power – the power to live the life you want to live. It is time to take your life back, and one of the first things you can do is refuse to give power to excuses.

My made-up mind is my personal superpower.

Pain or injuries

Work out what you *can* do. Do your best to move in ways that don't aggravate your pain or injuries. Do more incidental activity. See a physiotherapist or other health professional and work out ways to reduce your pain.

I love to move in small ways.

Not enough time

When you make time, you find you have more time. If you are 100 per cent honest with yourself, how much wasted time did you experience today? If you did not waste any time, what do you have to do to make time to fit *yourself* into *your* schedule? If you do not make the time now, you will have no choice if your health suffers. Make the time now.

I make time for my health.

Too busy to exercise

How did you get so busy? Have you thought of doing a quick power walk during your lunch break? Find minutes in the day when you can do mini-activities or incidental exercise. If an hour or half an hour isn't going to happen, do your best to do mini-activities for a few minutes. Just keep moving.

My body is meant to move.

Too busy to cook healthy meals

Healthy meals are actually really quick and simple to make. In less than 40 seconds, I can make a smoothie. In one minute, I can be boiling eggs or be cooking oats while doing something else. It takes only a few minutes to prepare a simple healthy salad. I can heat soup in less than one minute and leave it cooking while I am doing other things. Or I can live a life of excuses and walk around saying, 'I don't have enough time to cook a healthy meal.'

I make time to prepare healthy meals.

Too many things going on

Get your priorities right. How important is your health?

My health is number one.

Set goals to create a healthy future

Do you know what your future holds? Is it full of good and healthy habits? The best way for you to predict your future is to create it. The best way to create your future is to plan it. The best way to plan your future is to think about it or visualise it and write down what you want – what are your goals? From there, think about your action steps and write them down. Create an action list. What action steps are necessary to reach your goal? You then go about following those action steps. How often you revisit your goal is crucial. Could you change the wording to make it a more positive statement? What action steps could you add to boost your chances of success?

Goal setting is a powerful way to make positive changes for your health and wellbeing.

Determination

Choosing to be determined is vital when you want to create good habits in your life. Can you recall a time when you decided that you just had to do something? You were highly motivated and nothing was going to stop you. Determination coursed through your veins. It could have been anything: studying for an exam, leaving an old job and finding a new one, finishing an important task, quitting smoking, stopping drinking, saving for a holiday – anything at all. Recall that time now. In a moment you will relive the event and the good feelings of having so much determination. You will look through your own eyes as you see what you saw, hear what you heard and feel the feelings of total determination. While reliving the positive event, allow yourself to feel the good feelings associated with that memory.

Do the exercise now. Close your eyes and relive that moment of motivation and determination as you see what you saw, hear what you heard, and feel the good feelings of your being determined and making a strong and positive decision. While holding on to that feeling, read the following affirmation three times and breathe these words into your life:

My health is number one, my health is my life, my health is my wealth.

To supercharge your determination read p. 211 in the 21 States on determination.

MINDFUL EATING

How would you like to eat half the amount of food and feel twice as satisfied? Unfortunately, with all of life's distractions, eating has become a mindless practice. We often eat while watching TV, or on the computer or phone. This leads to overeating, often unhealthy foods, as we miss the signals from our body to our brain that we are filling up.

Mindful eating is an active meditation that helps you stay aware and present while you eat. This simple meditation will help you feel more satisfied as you eat slowly, without distraction. When you appreciate the wonderful colours, smells, textures and flavours of what you eat, you can turn a simple meal into a wonderful meditation. Mindful eating also aids digestion and improves your relationship with food. As you are aware of what you are putting into your body, you'll be more inclined to make healthy choices.

For the best results with mindful eating, stay present while eating and, when your mind wanders, bring it back to the eating. While you eat, focus on the colour, taste, temperature and texture of the food, and the movement of your body as you bring the food towards your mouth. As you swallow, repeat in your mind this affirmation:

Only goodness enters my body.

A SIMPLE MINDFUL EATING SCRIPT

Find a comfortable spot to sit back or lie down and relax. As you feel each breath flow in and out of your body, you become more and more relaxed.

Count down from five to zero.

Five, let all tension drift away from your body.

Four, feel your breath flowing in and out effortlessly.

Three, letting go, letting go as you completely relax.

Two, allow your body to sink or flop into a really comfortable position.

One, as your body completely relaxes, your mind is open to positive suggestions.

Zero, you now realise you can simply and easily turn eating or drinking anything at all into a simple yet wonderful meditation.

Imagine that your favourite piece of fruit is in front of you. You can imagine the feeling of the fruit in your hand by simply being aware of the texture and the weight of the fruit. If the fruit needs to be peeled, then you do this mindfully, with awareness, as you simply focus on the action of peeling.

Feel your breath flow in and out easily and effortlessly.

As you imagine lifting the piece of fruit towards your mouth, you feel your arm moving. As you take a bite or put the food into your mouth, you are aware of your jaw and mouth moving.

As you begin to chew slowly and mindfully, notice the temperature, texture and wonderful flavours of the food you are eating.

As you begin to swallow the food, notice the feeling of the food going down your throat. You may even like to repeat the following thought to yourself:

Only goodness enters my body.

If your mind is distracted at any point, simply bring your awareness back to the food in front of you. Focus your attention on actions. And as you swallow, you think the following thought:

Only goodness enters my body.

You realise you can now make healthy choices.

Only goodness enters my body.

You eat for nutrition and fuel.

Only goodness enters my body.

Your health is your wealth.

Only goodness enters my body.

And as you feel the food settling in your stomach, you feel a sense of appreciation for everything that went into creating what you are eating. From the sun that shone down and the rain that watered the plant, to the farmers who grew this beautiful piece of fruit, you are grateful.

Only goodness enters my body.

As you continue to eat, your stomach turns the food into a liquefied paste so it can make its way down through your large and small intestine where all the goodness, nutrients, vitamins, minerals and water will be absorbed into your body and distributed for good health.

Only goodness enters my body.

Now, slowly bring your attention to your breath and the space you are in. Come back to the present with full awareness.

DITCH THE NEGATIVE THINKING

Self-talk can be a culmination of things you have heard throughout your life from parents, teachers, siblings, schoolyard bullies, lovers and others. You have internalised these comments over your lifetime and now believe them to be true. These repeated negative thoughts are incredibly powerful and do a lot of damage to your self-esteem and how you value your health. This negative talk is always buzzing in our heads and, after years of this steady stream of painful self-criticism bombarding our psyche, we believe it and live our lives as if it were all true. Someone puts a label on us and then we live up to it. The old programming must change.

Negative self-talk makes you feel unworthy and hampers your efforts to release weight and to get healthy. No matter how much you want to eat right, to exercise or to improve your quality of life, you will feel held back, and maybe even afraid of the change. Patterns can be difficult to break when using willpower alone. Leaving the comfort of those patterns can produce significant anxiety and stress, which in turn may be a trigger for overeating.

Your first step to understanding and beating your negative self-talk is to listen to it. Listen to your self-talk and discover where it really came from. Who really said those things and labelled you as hopeless, slow or fat anyway? Realise that it is *not* your voice. You didn't think that about yourself, someone else did. It's time to leave behind those old imprisoning thoughts and *upgrade your brain.*

In the table below, take a minute or two to do a brain dump of all the negative excuses, doubts and limiting beliefs you have used in relation to food and exercise. Write them in the left column. They are your old program. Then on the right, fill the space up with as many empowering beliefs as you can. Repeat the upgraded empowering beliefs to yourself as often as it takes until the new beliefs become your dominant thoughts.

OLD PROGRAM	UPGRADE

To complete this process of leaving behind those old, imprisoning thoughts, do this positive anchoring exercise (read more about how to create a positive anchor on p. 196).

Think of one thing that really motivates you. Remember and enjoy the good feelings that accompany being motivated and, as you do, recall the event and make a fist with your non-dominant hand. So, if you are right-handed use your left hand, and vice versa. Keep your fist held for five to 15 seconds. The moment your memory or the feeling begins to fade away, release your fist. Repeat the process for four more events or situations where you felt really motivated.

Once you have repeated the exercise five times and recall five things that motivate you, think about your exercise and healthy eating. As you do, pump your fist and say to yourself: *my health is number one.* You could also include: *do it now.* Repeat this over and over, speaking the affirmation with conviction and pumping your fist at the same time, until you feel excited about your health. Then take action.

My health is number one. Do it now.

MIND FREE MINUTE MEDITATION

Take one minute to immerse yourself in the following power statements and affirmations as a mindful self-hypnosis practice.

Breathe in, *my health is my wealth*
Breathe out, *my health is my wealth*

Breathe in, *only goodness enters my body*
Breathe out, *only goodness enters my body*

Breathe in, *I make time for my health*
Breathe out, *I make time for my health*

Breathe in, *my body is meant to move*
Breathe out, *my body is meant to move*

Breathe in, *my food is my fuel, my food is nutrition*
Breathe out, *my food is my fuel, my food is nutrition*

Breathe in, *life is what I make it, I choose to be healthy*
Breathe out, *life is what I make it, I choose to be healthy*

THREE KEYS TO RELEASE EXCESS WEIGHT

LESSON 1: Change your relationship with food. Remember food is fuel. Change the story you tell yourself about food and eating as you delete the old thoughts that kept you stuck in the old patterns.

LESSON 2: Make healthy choices as you tell yourself, *only goodness enters my body.* Eat half the amount and feel twice as satisfied by eating mindfully.

LESSON 3: Move it. Avoid sitting around for extended periods. Incidental activity, walking or going to the gym are all great ways to burn the fat. Get up and move. Your body is meant to move.

DISCOVER MORE MIND FREE

For more mindful self-hypnosis to help you with your weight, go to p. 285 of the Mind Manual. You can also listen to recorded sessions on weight loss via the Mind Free app and website mindfreeapp.com.

The three decrees

I hereby decree that I am focused on health, energy and self-love. I am good enough, I am active, I am responsible, I am happy, I am strong. I say NO to dead, fattening foods and YES to health. I make time to move every day. I love to move. I eat light at night and make healthy choices. I eat what nature intended: from the land, from the sea, from the ground, from a tree. I eat mindfully as I tune into what my body needs and always remember, only goodness enters my body. I only eat when physically hungry and I control what I eat. I eat to live. My health is my wealth. I am number one.

On the following scroll, copy the above in full or part, and combine with your own statements. Or, if you prefer, select your own positive emotion words, short power statements and empowering affirmations. Combine them to form your own personal decree by you, to you, for you.

Official Decree

_____

_____

_____

_____

_____

_____

_____

_____

_____

_____

_____

Signed _____

CHAPTER 9
LIVE PHOBIA FREE

Before reading this chapter, please ensure you have read chapters 1, 2 and 3 as they will help prepare you for the information here and lay the foundation for you to overcome your phobia.

I'm too scared, I can't do it.

What would happen if you learned to release your fears and stay calm?
Did you know that slow, deep breathing helps you stay in control?

What if I die?

What if you knew you were safe and strong?
How good will you feel when you train your mind to be calm, in control and confident?

I breathe deeply and stay calm.

Spiders, flying, heights, even chickens: phobias come in many different forms. A phobia is your brain's way of telling you that a situation or object presents extreme danger, even though that fear might be completely irrational and unfounded. Phobias can develop at any time of your life, but often start when you're a child. They are twice as common among women than men.

These overwhelming fears can be debilitating, causing you stress and often affecting your ability to perform everyday tasks. Some will impact major life decisions, such as which job to take, where you live and who you surround yourself with. Others, such as agoraphobia and social phobia, can be extremely isolating, as they stop people from socialising or putting themselves in new situations. Being controlled by phobias means living your life in a constant or near-constant state of fear. And nobody deserves to live that way.

WHAT IS A PHOBIA?

A phobia shouldn't be confused with a fear; they are two different things. Fear is a normal emotional and physical response to dangerous things or situations. Fear protects us from harmful situations and gives us a clear message: it's time to get away. A phobia, on the other hand, is excessive anxiety related to certain objects or situations that is out of proportion to the actual danger presented. A phobia twists our natural fear response into something persistent and seemingly impossible to control.

You *know* the object of your phobia might not be life-threatening or especially dangerous, but that doesn't stop you from going into full-scale flight-or-fight mode at the mere thought of it. As a result, you'll do everything you can to avoid it.

How do phobias start?

For many people, a phobia starts from a single traumatic event. For example, if you were bitten by a dog as a child, you may have developed an all-pervading terror of dogs. Some people will take on board another person's fear and associate it with their own. How many people developed a fear of sharks after watching *Jaws*? For others, the anxiety builds up slowly over time. For example, several rough plane trips may have seen you go from having a minor fear of flying to a crippling, full-blown phobia.

So, what happens inside your body and brain?

Everyone reacts differently to phobias. Some people will experience a tightening of the throat and feel as though they can't breathe, others will develop a rapid heartbeat or they might feel as if they've totally lost control over their situation. Some people have panicky feelings, others visualise or imagine things not going the way they expected them to or going very badly. Some people repeat negative thoughts in their mind over and over again. Others have sweaty hands, dry mouths and shaking knees. Some people feel dizzy, while others are convinced that they're going to die.

JIMENA'S STORY

Probably the most severe phobia case I've ever worked with was a woman who came up to me during a break in a training seminar and said, 'I've got a severe phobia of public speaking and I'm extremely claustrophobic. I can't go into small spaces.' Jimena told me the problem started when she was in a car accident at the age of 23, a crash that almost killed her. She was in a coma for several weeks and, when she awoke, she was in plaster from head to toe and a breathing machine was keeping her alive. When she first opened her eyes, Jimena was surrounded by doctors and nurses, and that was the traumatic moment for her, because she couldn't remember the crash at all.

Waking up in that hospital surrounded by people was the root cause of Jimena's problems with speaking to more than two or three people at a time. Every time she had to speak in front of people, she said it felt like her throat was locking up, her chest was being crushed and she'd start to tremble and sweat. Overcome and frozen with fear, Jimena would have to leave the room because she couldn't even talk. Her experience also meant that she had panic attacks every time she had to get in a car.

I told Jimena we could treat her phobias in ten to 15 minutes as a demonstration during the seminar. She said, 'Well, let's give it a go.'

When everybody came back from the break, I explained Jimena's situation and how I would be reprogramming events from her past so they no longer affected her present and her future.

During the demonstration, I used a number of different techniques including releasing fear, changing the negative thoughts, mindful hypnosis and laughing at the problem. By the end of the session, Jimena was smiling.

I said, 'So how are you feeling?'

She replied, 'About what?'

'Well, is there a problem?'

'A problem with what?' she asked.

We had removed the problem in 15 minutes to the point where she'd totally forgotten that she'd ever had claustrophobia and a fear of public speaking. Jimena couldn't even remember why she was sitting up there on the stage. Everyone in the room was laughing supportively and she was laughing too.

Some months later, I phoned Jimena to check on how everything was going. She said, 'Everything's great!'

'So, no problems?' I asked.

'Problems with what?' she replied.

Because we had reprogrammed her brain, she had totally forgotten about her phobias. I said, 'Well, you used to have that old problem in the past with the–'

She stopped me. 'Oh, you know, Mark, I've never even given it a second thought.'

Understanding different types of phobias

Phobias are a type of anxiety disorder and fall broadly into three categories: social phobias are a fear of social situations, such as being around people; agoraphobia is the fear of being trapped alone in an inescapable space or a public place; and then there are specific phobias, which are a fear of a specific object, such as snakes, spiders and needles.

Specific phobias are the most common type of phobia, and include natural environment fears such as fear of lightning, thunder, water and storms. Animal fears include fear of snakes, rodents, spiders, dogs and the like. Medical phobias include fear of seeing blood, receiving injections and visiting a doctor. Then you have situational phobias including fear of bridges, flying, heights, driving and many more.

Some of the most common phobias people experience include fear of:

- public speaking (glossophobia)
- flying (aviophobia)
- heights (altophobia)
- small spaces (claustrophobia)
- snakes (ophidiophobia)
- spiders (arachnophobia)
- dentists (odontophobia)
- needles and injections (trypanophobia)
- dogs (cynophobia).

There are some more unusual phobias too, such as paraskavedekatriaphobia, a fear of Friday the 13th; hippopotomonstrosesquipedaliophobia, a fear of long words; pteronophobia, the fear of being tickled by feathers; pantophobia, a fear of everything; bibliophobia, the fear of books; coulrophobia, a fear of clowns; and ablutophobia, the fear of washing or bathing.

GLENDA'S STORY

Glenda had a longstanding phobia of snakes, spiders and rats, but especially snakes. The phobia was so extreme that if Glenda even saw a snake on TV, she would close her eyes or leave the room. In the hope of overcoming her crippling fear, Glenda volunteered to participate in a morning TV show with me.

The snake handler arrived with a three-metre python in a sealed crate. Glenda jumped out of her waiting-room chair and ran screaming from the room. After assurances that the snake was no longer in the room, Glenda agreed to return so we could get on with the therapy.

Step one was to teach Glenda a simple breathing exercise so she could stay calm and relaxed. Step two was to have Glenda recalling times when she felt calm, happy and in control. As she remembered those times, she formed a fist with her non-dominant hand. This was to create the positive anchor technique whereby Glenda could pump her fist if she was feeling fear, which would help her change her state to one of calmness, happiness and control. Step three was exposure therapy. Glenda was shown pictures of snakes. The first was of a pink fluffy toy snake. The next was two cartoon snakes forming a heart shape. This was followed by a picture of a calm-looking yellow snake.

Gradually, Glenda was introduced to photos of real snakes, then an image of the humorous character of Mr Bean with a large black and green snake slithering around his shoulders. This was followed by several other images of real snakes. Eventually, I took a large, plush, black and green toy snake from my bag, which Glenda happily played with and wrapped over her shoulders like a shawl. She then played with several rubber toy snakes. I explained to Glenda how snakes are similar to people and they really just want to be loved. To help her relate to the snake, we came up with a funny name for it. Glenda invented the name Flipner. In case Glenda needed distracting, we practised singing Elvis's *Love Me Tender* to the tune of the national anthem.

We then began the hypnosis session. During this, Glenda was able to release her fear and visualise that Flipner was a friend she loved. As we made our way onto the set, Glenda was feeling calm, happy and in control. Once we were seated and the cameras began to roll, David Campbell, the show's host, asked Glenda how she was feeling about snakes. Glenda exclaimed, 'I love snakes!'

David commented that only an hour earlier he had watched her in hair and makeup freaking out when they showed a picture of a snake on TV. He then asked Glenda if she was happy for the snake handler to bring a snake out. Glenda said she was.

Dan from the Australian Reptile Park came onto the set carrying the python. He sat next to Glenda, who showed zero fear. Glenda patted the python and, at my suggestion, placed the snake over her shoulders and around her neck like a shawl, just as we had practised. Glenda was all smiles while continuing to pat the snake, commenting how beautiful Flipner was, before singing the snake to sleep with the words from *Love Me Tender*. Glenda remained cool and calm while Flipner fell asleep in her arms.

A few weeks later I received a message from Glenda saying that not only had her fear of snakes disappeared, but she no longer worried about spiders or rats, and she was feeling more confident and in control of all areas of her life.

THE SOLUTION? RETRAIN YOUR BRAIN

The good news is, whatever your phobia – sharks, dogs, flying, small spaces or the bogeyman – with positive reconditioning, it can be overcome.

You were not born with your phobia. A phobia is a learned experience: perhaps a traumatic event or a series of events has brought on this phobic feeling for you. Because it's a learned experience, you can unlearn it. With the right training, you can reprogram your brain and remove the old beliefs, fears and conditioning, and instil new beliefs and new behaviours. From there, you can get on with your life, free of fear.

I have worked with numerous people who have experienced a wide range of phobias and *every single time* their phobia has completely disappeared. For many of them, following treatment they've never thought again about the phobias that once ruled their lives.

Maybe I've mentioned your fear in this chapter, maybe I haven't. But whatever your fear, I'm going to teach you how to disconnect the root cause – that is, what triggered the fear in the first place. I'll also give you resources, tools and strategies to help you shift to a positive state, free of fear and able to take control of your emotional state and life. By the time you finish the following exercises – retraining your brain – you will be more in control of your thinking and how you're feeling. You will have moved from fear and panic to a place of peace.

ALEX'S STORY

For almost 50 years it was impossible for Alex to get an injection because of his extreme needle phobia. No blood tests, no dentists, no vaccines. Desperate to get his COVID jab, he thought hypnosis might help him overcome his fear.

Trypanophobia, the extreme fear of having injections or undergoing medical procedures, is estimated to affect one in ten adults. The symptoms range from a racing heart and dizziness to breathlessness and nausea.

'I tried to get the COVID vaccine,' Alex told me, 'but as soon as I felt the needle touch my skin I became highly anxious and felt like I was going to be sick. My body locked up, my stomach was in a knot and then I went into flight mode. I got out of there as fast as I could.'

Fear of needles often stems from a childhood traumatic experience of getting an injection at the dentist or doctor. For Alex Rosales, this was not the case.

Alex grew up in Argentina during the 1970s. The country was overrun with crime and violence. Kidnappings were common practice. Alex left for school one day and never made it home. He was just 11 years old. During the 1976 military coup, both Alex and his father were abducted. Alex was cruelly poked on his arms and legs with syringes, screaming until a ransom was paid. He was released in the early hours of the next morning. The family were given refugee status and fled to Australia.

I knew hypnosis could help Alex overcome his extreme fear of needles. I began by helping him relax, guiding him through slow, deep breathing while counting back from ten to one. We also used the mantra *calm* on the inhale and *control* on the exhale for even deeper relaxation.

I then taught Alex how to create a positive anchor by making a fist while recalling the happiest moments in his life, which included the moment his son was born. (A positive anchor acts as a distraction while also helping you maintain a positive state.)

Following these techniques, we did the main mindful self-hypnosis session. With Alex in a deep state of relaxation, I used positive suggestions such as:

Getting an injection is easy.
Injections keep me healthy.
I stay calm when getting an injection.
I am calm, I am strong, I am safe.
I am calm, I am in control.

I showed him the peace release meditation: breathing in *peace*, breathing out *release*. In *peace*, out *release*.

Then, while he was still deeply relaxed, I took him through the experience itself with this description: before you realise it, the injection is over. It happens so quickly, you hardly notice it. You hardly feel a thing. A little pinch at most and then it's all over. You realise you had nothing to fear. You feel really proud of yourself. You've taken this step forward in your life and you realise that you are in control.

After this two-hour session, Alex was ready to get his jab. He went to the clinic feeling calm and in control. When the time came for his injection, he pumped his fist to create a positive anchor and looked the other way. Alex was given the injection without him even realising it had been administered – he couldn't believe it was all over. His phobia of needles was gone.

Next up for Alex: the blood test his doctor has been wanting him to get for years.

No-fear physiology

The fact is, fear, anxiety, panic attacks and phobias have two very important determining factors: your focus and your physiology. What are you focusing on? What are you thinking? What are you saying to yourself and what is your physiology? What's your posture? How are you breathing? What emotional state are you getting stuck in?

Sit down and take on the posture and physiology of being anxious or frightened. How would you feel and what would you say to yourself? Would your chest tighten? Would your shoulders be rolling forward? Would your breathing become more rapid? Notice how you feel as you do that. My guess is that you'll feel pretty dreadful.

Let's totally change your state by taking on a strong, confident physiology. Stand up, take a deep breath in, roll your shoulders back, smile, look up towards the ceiling. How do you feel now? My guess is you feel pretty differently from how you did when you had the physiology of fear. So, what does that tell you? What it means is that, by changing your physiology, you can affect what you're thinking and feeling. Just doing that may not completely get rid of your fear, but it will go some way towards making you feel better and more confident.

How would you be breathing if you were confident? If you felt strong, how would you be standing? Always remember that your physiology will affect how you're feeling.

Relaxing your body is a powerful way to positively change your physiology. Let's do a breathing exercise to help you relax.

Sit down, get really comfortable and let your eyes close. There's nowhere to go and nothing to do right now, except relax. Watch your breath moving slowly in and out. With every outward breath, quietly repeat in your mind the word *relax*, and let all your muscles become soft and loose.

Now we are going to count backwards all the way from ten down to one. And with each breath, you will become twice as relaxed as you were in the breath before.

Take a slow, deep breath all the way in.

Ten, hold for a moment and then exhale all the way out as you become twice as relaxed. Take another slow deep breath all the way in.

Nine, hold for a moment and then exhale all the way out, letting go. Take another deep breath all the way in.

Eight, twice as relaxed. Hold for a moment. Exhale. Letting go, letting go. Breathing all the way in.

Seven, hold. Double the relaxation as you exhale all the way out. Slowly breathing all the way in deeply.

Six, hold your breath for a moment, and then exhale slowly. Doubling your relaxation. Twice as relaxed. Slow deep breath all the way in.

Five, hold. Letting go all the way out. Feel your entire body relaxing. Take another slow deep breath all the way in.

Four, hold. Exhale. Relaxing more deeply. Slowly breathing in.

Three, hold. Let it go, just exhale slowly. Twice as relaxed. Take a slow deep breath all the way in.

Two, hold. Let the breath flow slowly out as you relax, letting go. Breathe slowly and deeply all the way in.

One, hold your breath for just a moment and, exhaling slowly, feel your body completely relaxing.

Now, from this relaxed state, seal inside you that feeling of being completely relaxed. Imagine sealing that feeling inside as though you're closing a Tupperware container. Just snap it shut. And notice how good it feels to be completely relaxed.

Now who did that? You did. You took the breaths. You told yourself to relax as I suggested, but it was you who actually did it. And you can do that anytime you're starting to feel anxiety, panic or stressed. You can take ten slow deep breaths and count backwards. Counting backwards from ten down to one.

Fear release

There's one thing I know about you. Inside you, in your wonderful unconscious mind, you have all the wisdom, all the knowledge and all the answers. The fact is, you already know what to think so you can let go of the fear.

Would you like to let go of fear, or shrink it down so that it no longer overwhelms you? Is it all right for your unconscious mind to release this negative emotion today and for you to be aware of letting go of that fear?

Trust your unconscious mind because it has all the answers.

Ask your unconscious mind what it needs to learn from the event, a learning that allows you to let go of the emotions easily and effortlessly.

Ask your unconscious mind: *What do I need to know here? What is a positive lesson that will help me let go of the old fear?*

Think about those thoughts floating from the back to the front of your mind. Breathe any positive thoughts that come to you along with the following thoughts into your mind and exhale them into every part of your being.

I am stronger than the fear
I am in control
I am powerful

I am doing my best
I am determined
I release all fear
I feel at peace, I am at peace
I am strong
I am safe

Think to yourself, *I now release all pictures, thoughts and feelings connected to the old fear.*

Imagine all the old pictures, thoughts and feelings connected to the old fear drifting away. Imagine them dissolving and disappearing.

Now go out into the future and imagine an event that, in the past, may have made you feel that old negative emotion. Go ahead and float out into that future event, and notice if you can feel that old emotion. Maybe you'll find that you can't. Then come back to now.

If you still feel the old emotion, you may need to repeat the exercise. When you float back ensure the positive lessons are stated in the positive and come up with as many empowering thoughts as you can.

Remember, the more you tell yourself a positive story, the more positive you will feel.

Clowning around

Now it's time to be a little bit silly. Problems can only be problems when we give them power. But when we can laugh at a problem or poke fun at it, it ceases to have the same control over us.

These next few techniques are aimed at loosening the grip you have on the problem or the grip the problem has on you. You may even find that by the time you finish this section, you no longer have any concern about your phobia, and that your fear or your phobia has completely disappeared.

First, imagine you're an inventor of wacky, crazy toys. You work at a big toy factory, and you're the person who invents and names the toys. You could even picture yourself in a white coat with a silly hat on and a pair of zany glasses. Remember, these are silly, crazy toys.

Now, consider your problem, whether it's fear of flying, planes, cars, trains, heights, spiders or snakes. It doesn't matter. Whatever your phobia or fear is, consider that fear or that phobia and, rather than calling a plane a plane or a snake a snake, give it a silly name. Come up with the most outrageous gobbity-goockity-type name you can, and just think about it for a moment.

From this moment onwards, you will no longer refer to the fear as a fear or a phobia, you will now refer to it as the whatsamathingy, the zoobidy-zongidy, the punknunderbolt, the flipner or whatever you decide to call it. When you are no longer so serious with the problem, it ceases to be a real problem.

Now we're going to take it one step further. Imagine your zippidy, zanggidy, zonggity, whatever it is that might look like a plane or a bridge or a tall building or a snake, and incorporate some other funny things in your mind. Maybe you'd like to put a big red clown nose on it, maybe big bunny ears, or a coloured coat; you could give it big floppy clown shoes, maybe a clown's outfit; you could make it bright colours; you could even make it look like your favourite cartoon character.

Close your eyes and:
- imagine how silly it is
- notice how silly it is
- see how funny it is.

Now say, *how silly is the ... [your crazy name]? How funny is this?!* If you feel like laughing, then laugh, because this is really silly. How silly is this? You've got to admit, having that problem *is* pretty silly, having that old phobia, or whatever you're calling it now, is pretty silly, isn't it? It's pretty crazy, and it's time to let it go.

Let it go.

When you can laugh at your problem, the problem ceases to be a problem.

MIND FREE MINUTE MEDITATION

Take one minute to immerse yourself in the following power statements and affirmations as a mindful self-hypnosis practice.

Breathe in, *I am calm*
Breathe out, *I am calm*

Breathe in, *I am strong*
Breathe out, *I am strong*

Breathe in, *I am in control*
Breathe out, *I am in control*

Breathe in, *I breathe deeply and naturally*
Breathe out, *I breathe deeply and naturally*

Breathe in, *every day in every way, I grow stronger and stronger*
Breathe out, *every day in every way, I grow stronger and stronger*

I am calm and in control

THREE KEYS TO LIVING PHOBIA FREE

LESSON 1: Control your state. Tune in to feelings of strength, confidence and control as you face your fears. Change your physiology from one of fear to one of confidence.

LESSON 2: Breathe deeply and slowly as you count back from ten to one. The aim: to maintain a state of relaxation.

LESSON 3: Change the way you think. Tell yourself you are strong and in control. Come up with a funny name for your phobia that makes it seem silly. Laugh at the fear and watch it disappear.

The three decrees

I hereby decree the new me embraces strength, control, confidence and a sense of calm. I am strong, I am in control, I am confident and I am calm. Every day in every way I grow stronger and stronger. I breathe deeply as I transform fear into courage. I am safe and happy as I change my focus. I release the past and future as I return to now. I am here, I am me, I am free.

On the following scroll, copy the above in full or part, and combine with your own statements. Or, if you prefer, select your own positive emotion words, short power statements and empowering affirmations. Combine them to form your own personal decree by you, to you, for you.

Official Decree

_____

_____

_____

_____

_____

_____

_____

_____

_____

_____

_____

_____

_____

Signed

CHAPTER 10
REDUCE ANXIETY

The following exercises are not intended to replace the
advice of a medical or mental health professional.

What's wrong with me?

What's right with you?
**How many ways do you know you can change your
state from negative to positive?**

What if I can't handle it?

**What if you could handle it by learning simple
techniques to release the old feelings?**

I am strong, I am safe, I am in control.

Feeling anxious can be part of the human condition. At some time in our life most of us have experienced anxiety. Feeling anxious or having some worry shouldn't be confused with an anxiety disorder, however. It's normal to worry. Small amounts of anxiety can sometimes be a good thing, pushing us to complete projects that we may be putting off or to make changes in our life. More extreme cases of anxiety, such as the type of anxiety caused by specific traumatic events or feelings of overwhelming fear that are more long-term, may feel extremely difficult to overcome. But I want to reassure you: it is possible to break your anxiety cycle or, at the very least, reduce the intensity of your anxiety. There is help in the palms of your hands right now.

The strategies, techniques and exercises in this chapter will help with both mild or general anxiety as well as panic disorders and more extreme cases such as social anxiety.

WHAT IS ANXIETY?

Much like stress, anxiety is your body's response to some kind of threat or an imagined danger. It becomes a problem when the anxious feelings continue even after the reason, the stressor, has disappeared, or when you feel anxious most or all of the time when there's no apparent cause.

Anxiety can affect the way you think, making your negative thoughts all the more prominent. The unwanted negative thoughts in your mind are a calling card to anxiety, and can make any self-limiting beliefs spiral out of control, such as: *I'm not good enough. It's too hard. I shouldn't be here. I worry too much. I'm going to die of a heart attack.*

When your thoughts focus on what could go wrong or all the bad things in your life, your anxiety increases. The cycle of anxiety can be a negative whirlpool of thoughts and the more negative thoughts you have, the worse your anxiety gets. The feelings of anxiety or panic then increase the negative thoughts, which result in increased feelings of anxiety.

These anxious feelings can range from your own fears about yourself to worrying about others in your life or the world in general.

Often, we get stuck in a future negative thought of something going wrong – something that may never actually happen.

Left untreated for a prolonged period of time, anxiety is thought to lead to serious long-term conditions like heart disease, weakened immune system, insomnia and rapid weight changes.

OVERCOMING ANXIETY

Believe me when I say you can overcome anxiety; the exercises here will help you do just that. I have seen people who had suffered for years change their state quite rapidly, and either reduce or eliminate their anxiety. As you learn to replace negative thoughts with positive thoughts, and you learn how to change your emotional state, you discover you can reduce the feelings of anxiety, you can feel calm and in control, and you can feel happy.

The real key to success here is taking small steps and feeling good about the little wins.

Change your story

Negative thought patterns profoundly affect your anxiety. Have you ever noticed how simply thinking, *I can't do this* or *it's all too hard* makes your situation worse? Imagine instead if you said to yourself, *I can handle anything* or *I am strong* or *I've got this*. While it may take some practice, deleting negative thoughts *is* possible.

Having a mantra, an affirmation or a bank of positive thoughts you can call upon when negative thinking threatens to take over can help you stop the anxiety cycle in its tracks. You effectively replace the negative story your mind is telling you with an uplifting and positive one.

This positive affirmation or mantra helps you override repetitive negative thought patterns and excuses. It helps reprogram your limiting beliefs into limitless beliefs. When the *I can't cope* becomes *I can cope*, and *I'm not good enough* becomes *I am good enough*, you start to feel better. When you feel better, you start to act differently, and you're more inclined to feel happier and more content.

Anxiety can often be a message from your unconscious mind to focus on what you *do* want rather than what you don't want. How many times have you been strong in your life? How many times have you overcome challenges? You are still here so *you are a survivor*. You are stronger than you think.

This is the power of changing your story.

ANNA'S STORY

From a young age, Anna suffered almost daily anxiety and panic attacks.

'My heart races, I tremble uncontrollably and I get a massive lump in my throat that makes swallowing and breathing difficult,' said Anna. 'I've done so much therapy, I feel as though I could almost be a therapist myself.'

Anna's father had become increasingly violent towards Anna's mother and when Anna was about nine, she tried to protect her mother, running between the two of them and screaming STOP. Her father grabbed her by the throat and shook her until she almost passed out. Anna had been reliving this and subsequent traumatic events over and over, whenever she felt threatened or stressed.

I explained, 'We need to interrupt the pattern that has you continuing to feel these feelings. We also need to practise some simple exercises to help you take control of your state and release your fear.'

Anna explained that she was constantly fearful about having anxiety attacks. The stress connected to her expectation was actually contributing to the frequency of the anxiety attacks. Her situation was impacting all areas of her life, including her job and her relationships with her son and husband.

The first thing I did was teach Anna some simple meditation techniques to counter the feeling of anxiety. Simple breathing exercises helped reduce her stress levels. We also practised the positive breathing affirmation, *I feel at peace, I am at peace.* As each minute passed, Anna drifted into a deeper level of relaxation.

Anna listed all the limiting beliefs and fears connected to her anxiety. Writing down all your negative thoughts and fears is a wonderful exercise as it helps you take the negatives from your unconscious mind and put them onto paper. One thought at a time, we changed the old story.

The main hypnosis session involved identifying how and where Anna experienced the feelings. Because she felt a lump in her throat the size of a tennis ball, I had her imagine it was shrinking, shrinking, shrinking. The lump shrank down to the size of a ping pong ball, and then a small marble. At that moment, I had Anna breathe the feeling, like a vacuum, from her throat up into her shoulder and, as she exhaled, breathing the feeling down her arm into her hand while making a fist around the feeling. The next breath was a deep one and, as Anna exhaled, I had her open her hand and blow the feeling away. We repeated this technique a total of three times.

I asked Anna to think of three positive emotional states. She chose calm, control and happy. One state at a time, I had Anna recall times throughout her life when she felt calm, when she felt in control and when she felt happy.

Rather than simply trying to stop the anxiety or panic attacks, I felt a gentler approach was to attach the positive states to the negative states, and thereby change Anna's response. I asked her to think about something in recent days that made her feel anxious and then to bring in the feeling of calm, followed by the feeling of control, then the feeling of being happy. After repeating this exercise several times, Anna was able to experience anxiety as a calm, controlled, happy anxiety. We repeated the exercise of attaching positive emotional states to the old anxiety and guess what? The anxiety was all but gone.

'How does that feel?' I asked.

'It feels good. I feel calm, in control and happy,' said Anna.

This was followed by an *I am mindful* self-hypnosis session. I asked Anna to breathe the following suggestions as deeply as she could into herself:

Deep breath in, *I am*, breathing all the way out, *calm.*

Deep breath in, *I am*, breathing all the way out, *in control.*

Deep breath in, *I am*, breathing all the way out, *happy.*

We also did a session to release the fear from the original event all those years ago. Anna came up with a positive lesson, 'I am safe, I am okay.' Anna changed her story, changing her life.

Twelve months on, I heard from Anna who reported that her daily meditation, breathing exercises and mindful self-hypnosis affirmations were keeping any feelings of anxiety at bay.

Understand your triggers

Negative thoughts are not the only things that contribute to anxiety. Anxiety can have triggers such as lack of sleep, health issues, excessive caffeine intake, substance abuse, medication, financial stress, relationship conflicts, work disputes, social events, major life events or disruptions to your normal routine. You may find your anxiety is triggered by one or more of these factors, or you may have entirely different triggers. Do you know your triggers? You can identify your triggers by tracking your anxiety and panic attacks in a notebook or journal, documenting when you begin to experience the feelings of anxiety or start having negative thoughts.

One thing I always like to do when working with people who suffer from anxiety or panic attacks is to help them get the thoughts and triggers out of their head and down on paper, so that we can work through them one at a time. Try this yourself. You may find a pattern as to when your negative thoughts occur, based on your past experiences with anxiety. When you discover the thought or trigger, use one of the many techniques found in this book to help you change the pattern.

Breathe in, *I can't control the outside.*
Breathe out, *I control the inside.*

Remember to listen to your body when you feel the negative thoughts and anxiety creeping into your mind. A simple strategy is to interrupt the pattern and distract yourself by doing something completely different – go for a walk, have a shower, make a cup of tea, change your location, do some yoga, call a friend or do one of a million other things. Your aim is to change your focus.

Train for anxiety

In coping with anxiety, physical activity can make an enormous difference. For many people, the idea of going to their local gym or exercising in public triggers anxiety and panic attacks in itself. Ironically, however, exercise is a great way to change your anxiety cycle. When you exercise, your body produces endorphins that make you feel great, crushing those little negative thought bubbles in your head before they can spiral out of control. The more you exercise, the better you will begin to feel, and the easier you will find it to step out of your comfort zone. Even going for a walk is a great way to counter the negative feelings.

When you exercise, your heart rate increases, your breathing speeds up and, if you exercise with enough intensity, you sweat. These are the same symptoms many people experience during anxiety and panic attacks. The lesson here is if you exercise more and get your heart rate up, sweat a little, and increase the rate and depth of your breathing, then you are actually conditioning your body to cope with anxiety more effectively.

Reel the silk thread

Dr Tennyson Yiu was the most chilled-out person you could ever meet. Not only was he a highly regarded tai chi master, but he was a wonderful human being with a great sense of humour. One evening, as we were about to start practising our tai chi form, Tennyson shared a story with us.

'You wouldn't believe what happened today,' he said, smiling. 'I came out of the shopping centre to my car and discovered that somebody had taken a sharp object and completely scraped it all the way along the four panels of the passenger side. Looking at the scratch, I clenched my fists, held my breath and was really angry.' He pulled an angry face expressing how he felt. 'While holding my breath, I remembered I was a tai chi master, and so I relaxed my fists, breathed a sigh of relief, smiled and let it go. I was really angry, but only for a moment. I thought to myself, it's only a car.'

Tennyson continued with the gentle smile that always seemed to grace his face. It didn't matter if students were throwing kicks at him or attacking him with a weapon, the smile was always there. 'As you move from thinking to breathing, you can release all tension.

As you move from thinking to breathing, you can release all worries. And as you move from thinking to breathing, you begin to realise how easy it is to relax. Relax your body as you sink into your breathing. Don't even try to breathe because you'll breathe anyway. Let your breathing simply happen. If your body feels like moving or swaying, let it move,' he said. The old master continued, guiding us through a wonderful standing breathing meditation.

After a few minutes of letting the breath move in and out of the body, and letting the body move if it felt like moving, through his tai chi smile, he began to speak again. 'Let your body's energy flow like a great river, as the power of the universe pours into you. Let your breathing gently flow in and out like reeling a silk thread from a silk cocoon.'

The breathing practice of 'reeling the silk thread' allows you to slow down the pace of the world, calm your mind and heal your body. Join in with me, and let's practise this breathing meditation together.

Either standing or sitting comfortably, place your attention on your breath flowing in and out of your body. When you notice sounds or any other distractions, simply bring your awareness back to your breathing as the air gently flows in and flows out of your body. Take a pause from the world as you simply sit or stand and breathe. You may like to think *in* and *out* as you breathe. After a few breaths, begin to slow your breathing down. Think to yourself, *soft*, *smooth* and *slow* as you gently breathe in through your nose. As you exhale, slow your breathing down.

Continue to breathe slowly, as you imagine you are reeling a silk thread. Your breath is the silk thread. Your breathing is slight. Slightly and slowly, you allow the breath to gently enter your body and, equally slowly, you breathe out. Breathe all the way out until there is no more air to let out, and then slowly breathe all the way in, as you *reel the silk thread*. Continue to breathe in and out deeply, slowly and evenly. Never force the breathing. Allow your breath to be natural and gentle. When you control your breath, you control your life.

Notice how you are feeling now. Do you feel a little calmer?

With practice, you can slow your breathing down to four, or even three, breaths per minute. This puts you in a deep state of meditation very quickly.

Stay calm

With the right tools, you can easily release anxiety and control panic attacks. From this moment on, you are going to release those fears and worries, safe in the knowledge that you already have the ability to stay conscious, aware and safe in your life.

You are what you think: every thought contributes to how you feel. So, from now on, you are going to fill your mind with the thoughts that you want, so you can create the life and the future that you desire and deserve.

Try this simple exercise to calm an anxious mind and remove negative thoughts.

Take a deep breath in, as deeply as you can, as you breathe in the energy of relaxation. As you exhale, breathe out all your worries, thoughts and fears. Slowly breathe in. As you exhale, imagine you're blowing any stress away. Visualise or imagine anxious thoughts being blown off into the universe. Take two more slow, deep breaths in and, as you exhale, blow any stress away. For the next little while, there is nothing you need to do except relax. Let every part of your body relax as you continue breathing in and out. Notice if there are any areas of stress or tension in your body and instruct those areas to relax.

Feel your breath coming in through your nose and out through your mouth, filling your lungs with fresh oxygen and breathing out 'release'. With every breath, become more relaxed and realise what a wonderful mind you have, even when there are times your thoughts have felt out of control.

As you continue to breathe calmly in and out, repeat to yourself: *I am in charge. I am enough. I feel safe, calm and at peace. I am centred and grounded. I am doing the best I can. I am in control of my body. I am growing stronger every day. My life is what I make it. I am not anxiety; it is simply an experience. I am as good as anyone else. Change is normal. I embrace change. I control my destiny. I continue to improve myself every day. I look forward to each new day. Every day in every way I grow stronger and stronger.* Notice how those few deep breaths and repeating those positive thoughts to yourself make you feel.

Sometimes, when we're in the middle of an anxious moment, it can feel impossible to stay calm. Try this quick exercise to calm your mind and body.

Recall a time when you felt really calm or happy. When the time comes to you, close your eyes for three breaths and allow in the good feelings of calm or happy. Allow these feelings to radiate through your body. Do this now with a gentle smile on your face. Notice how you are feeling. My guess is you feel a little happier or calmer. When you change your focus, you change how you feel.

As you learn these and other techniques, you'll begin to discover that you can easily cope.

Breathe in, *I easily cope.*
Breathe out, *I easily cope.*

Change your state

You can change your state in an instant. A great way to do this is by learning how to use a positive resource anchor, a physical gesture connecting you unconsciously with a positive state. If you want to feel anxious, think thoughts that increase your anxiety, or imagine bad things happening. If you want to feel calm, think calming thoughts that will generate calm feelings.

Once you have created a positive resource anchor, use it as a switch whenever you're feeling anxious or stressed. Making the physical gesture of the anchor will quickly take you back into a positive state.

We all have times in our past when we have felt strong, in control, calm and happy. This exercise will help you tap into those past positive experiences so you can override any negative states. Politicians, business leaders and elite athletes use this positive anchoring technique to rapidly change their state and stay strong, positive, calm and in control. Now it's your turn.

POSITIVE ANCHOR EXERCISE

STEP 1

With your non-dominant hand, I want you to make a firm but not overly tight fist. Alternatively, you may like to form a circle with your thumb and index finger. Notice which feels more comfortable. This action will be your switch. Now relax your hand. This is the unconscious switch that will help you get into a positive state.

STEP 2

Recall a time when you felt really strong. If you are unable to recall a time, imagine how you would feel if you *were* strong, or think of a scenario in which you could be strong. Maybe you were mentally strong, maybe you were physically strong or maybe you were emotionally strong. Maybe you remember a time from recently or one from years ago, or an imagined time. Imagine you are floating back to that time and float down into your own body.

Make your fist or circle with your index finger and thumb as you see what you saw and hear what you heard, as you feel the good feelings of being strong. Notice what thoughts run through your mind when you are feeling strong: *I am strong.* The moment the memory begins to fade, relax your hand and let go of the anchor.

STEP 3

Recall a time when you felt in control. It could have been any time at all recently, or a time from years ago. If you are unable to recall a time, imagine how you would feel if you were in control.

Imagine you are floating back to that time and float down into your own body. Apply your anchor by making a fist or circle with your index finger and thumb as you see what you saw and hear what you heard, as you feel the good feelings of being in control. Notice what thoughts run through your mind when you are feeling in control: *I've got this, I am in control.* The moment the memory begins to fade, relax your hand and let go of the anchor.

STEP 4

Recall a time when you felt really calm. You may remember a time from recently, a time from years ago or an imagined time. Visualise or think about drifting back to that time and float down into your own body. Apply your anchor as you see what you saw and hear what you heard, as you feel the good feelings of being calm all over again. Notice what thoughts run through your mind when you are feeling calm: *I am calm, I feel at peace.* The moment the memory begins to fade, relax your hand and let go of the anchor.

STEP 5

Recall a time when you felt really happy. You may remember a time from recently or one from years ago, or imagine how you would feel if you were really happy. Recall that time when you felt really happy, one of those really happy moments of life. Imagine you are floating back to that time and float down into your own body. Apply your anchor as you see what you saw and hear what you heard, as you feel the good feelings of being happy all over again. Notice what thoughts run through your mind when you are feeling happy: *I am really happy.* The moment the memory begins to fade, relax your hand and let go of the anchor.

You can continue to build up and strengthen your positive resource anchor by repeating steps two to five. Or you may like to apply your anchor at any time you are feeling one of those states – for example, if somebody says something that makes you happy or you see something that makes you happy, hold your anchor for five to 15 seconds. Whenever you experience a positive state take a few seconds to strengthen your anchor.

When the need arises apply your anchor and think positive thoughts like *I am strong, I am in control, I am calm* and *I am happy*. You may just surprise yourself at how quickly you can change your state from negative to positive.

MIND FREE MINUTE MEDITATION

Take one minute to immerse yourself in the following power statements and affirmations as a mindful self-hypnosis practice.

Breathe in, *I breathe through it*
Breathe out, *I am in control*

Breathe in, *I release all fear*
Breathe out, *I am safe*

Breathe in, *I am stronger every minute*
Breathe out, *I stay strong*

Breathe in, *I change my focus*
Breathe out, *I stay calm*

Breathe in, *I feel at peace*
Breathe out, *I am at peace*

Breathe in, *peace*
Breathe out, *release*

THREE KEYS TO COUNTER ANXIETY

LESSON 1: Rather than focusing on the worst, bring your attention back to the present moment with one of the many meditations or mindful self-hypnosis scripts in this book. Start focusing on positives.

LESSON 2: Notice where you feel anxiety in your body. Breathe into the feeling as you imagine it shrinking. Then breathe the feeling up into one of your shoulders like a vacuum. Exhale it down your arm into your hand. Take another deep breath in and blow away the feeling.

LESSON 3: You can change your state in an instant. Create a positive anchor so you can change your state whenever you need to. In an instant you can change from anxiety to a feeling of control, calm or strength.

DISCOVER MORE MIND FREE

For more mindful self-hypnosis to help you deal with anxiety, go to p. 302 of the Mind Manual. You can also listen to recorded sessions on anxiety via the Mind Free app and website mindfreeapp.com.

The three decrees

I hereby decree my mental, emotional and physical state is one of strength, safety and calm. I am strong, I am calm, I am safe. As I breathe in strength and breathe out fear, I embrace change. I easily handle life's challenges; they make me stronger. I step outside my comfort zone as I move from surviving to thriving. I give myself permission to be strong and in control.

On the following scroll, copy the above in full or part, and combine with your own statements. Or, if you prefer, select your own positive emotion words, short power statements and empowering affirmations. Combine them to form your own personal decree by you, to you, for you.

Official Decree

_____

_____

_____

_____

_____

_____

_____

_____

_____

_____

_____

_____

_____

_____

Signed _____

CHAPTER 11
THE 21 STATES

In *Mind Free* we've explored how changing your thoughts can transform your life. You've seen how this approach can work with everything from stress and anxiety to weight loss and sleep. Now I want to take you through a holistic approach to your life beyond any specific issues you may be facing. This is a way of living; these are the 21 States.

Change your thoughts, change your state.
Change your state, change your life.

As we ride the rollercoaster of life, we realise that not every day will go to plan, and our positive state may change to a negative one, and vice versa. One minute we may be feeling happy, content, calm, energetic or excited and then something happens to change our state. We end up feeling stressed, frustrated, angry, sad or any one of a hundred other states. This is pretty normal.

This is life.

How much time you spend in the negative state, however, is entirely up to you. Along with changing your thoughts, changing your state – how you feel – is a key to overcoming a great many challenges. The following list of 21 States covers the main positive states we can keep returning to. By reading – and rereading – the following declaration affirmations you will continually reinforce the positive messages to your mind and body, allowing you to change your state whenever the need arises. These positive beliefs will also help to keep you in a positive state for longer periods of time. When you start and end each day with a strong statement and the expression of a positive state, such as appreciation, compassion or love, negative feelings will fade away.

Instructions

1. Select one positive state for the day.
2. Recite the declaration out loud or quietly in your mind first thing in the morning and last thing at night. Breathe each statement into your mind and body, turning the reading of each state into a meditation.
3. Recite the declaration at any time of the day or night when you feel the need to reinforce your positive state and positive thoughts. Meditate on the words.
4. Turbocharge your positive feelings by reading several or all of the 21 States first thing in the morning and last thing at night.
5. Take your favourite affirmations from all 21 States and combine them with any positive thoughts that appeal to you to create your own customised super state (use the space on p. 226 or your favourite journal).

THE 21 STATES

1. **Acceptance**
2. **Appreciation**
3. **Calm**
4. **Compassion**
5. **Confidence**
6. **Control**
7. **Determination**
8. **Energy**
9. **Enthusiasm**
10. **Focus**
11. **Forgiveness**
12. **Happiness**
13. **Health**
14. **Laughter**
15. **Love**
16. **Mindfulness**
17. **Motivation**
18. **Optimism**
19. **Strength**
20. **Success**
21. **Wisdom**

ACCEPTANCE

Today I breathe in *acceptance*.

I approach today with an attitude of acceptance. I approve of myself and accept who I am unconditionally. I accept others for who they are, for we are all different. I am accepting. Pictures, thoughts and feelings about myself and others that do not nourish me, I now release. I accept there is no other person quite like me. I am unique. I am amazing.

Today I breathe in acceptance.

I accept that change will happen with or without my consent, therefore I embrace change: it is a part of life. I change the things I have the power to change and accept there are some things I cannot change. As I acknowledge and accept my past, I am free to embrace the present and move into the future. I remind myself: I am here now and I'm okay. As I accept myself completely, I create the opportunity for positive change in my life.

Today I breathe in acceptance.

I recognise I make mistakes, from which I learn. I release all thoughts of judgment as I accept that everyone is different and has their own story. We all have our own joy and our own suffering. As I am more accepting, I feel the good feelings of acceptance and self-approval. No longer do I need to prove myself to others: my opinion is the one that matters most. I realise I matter and what I do matters.

Today I breathe in acceptance.

As I think thoughts of acceptance and speak these words into the world, acceptance flows back to me and the cycle of good continues. I accept today, for every day is a precious gift. I am loved and accepted by the most important person in the world: myself. I accept me, I approve of me, I am free.

Today I breathe in *acceptance*.

APPRECIATION

Today I breathe in *appreciation*.

I allow appreciation and gratitude to flow to every cell of my being. I give thanks for all things great and small. I appreciate both the seen and the unseen in this world. I appreciate the warmth of the sun as it shines upon the earth. I appreciate the moon and all the stars as they light the night sky. I appreciate the wind and the rain and the air that I breathe. I live my life with an attitude of gratitude.

Today I breathe in appreciation.

I appreciate all of nature in its magnificent beauty. From the animals of the land and the sea, to the birds in the sky and every tree, I am grateful. I appreciate the perfect colours of nature. I appreciate every wonderful plant the land provides for sustenance and strength. I am grateful for the farmers who provide food to eat and those who work hard to prepare these foods. From every drop of water I drink to every grain of rice I eat, I am grateful.

Today I breathe in appreciation.

I appreciate my community, my friends, my family and my closest loved ones. I appreciate the smile of a stranger. I appreciate the roof over my head, and these walls around me that protect me from the elements. I appreciate my bed and my pillow, which give me a place to rest. I appreciate every organ, every muscle and every bone in my body. I think to myself, how lucky am I, I have so much to be grateful for. Today I am appreciative and appreciated. I appreciate today. I appreciate my life, and for that I am grateful. Thank you.

Today I breathe in *appreciation*.

CALM

Today I breathe in *calm*.

I allow peace to flow through every cell of my being. I am calm, I stay calm. As I think calming thoughts, I feel calm. When the ocean of my mind is churned up by the wind of thought, I take a slow, long breath in and return to the place of deep calm within me. I now release from my body and mind all pictures, thoughts and feelings that cause stress in my life. I realise some stress is inevitable, but it does not control me.

Today I breathe in calm.

I feel at peace, I am at peace. All is well, I am well. I breathe in peace; I breathe out release. I easily let go of stress, tension or worries as I blow it all away. I feel at peace with myself and the world around me. I am surrounded by the energy of peace and serenity. As I think calming thoughts, I begin to feel calm. Before reacting to the energy of others or events around me, I take a slow deep breath of peace and maintain a calm energy.

Today I breathe in calm.

I am not my thoughts, my emotions and the events in my life. I easily relax and breathe through every situation. I find a peaceful, calm resting place in my breath. I let go of past worries and future worries as I maintain a state of calm by returning to now. In letting go of the past and the future, I find peace. I give no energy to the negativity of others. I feel calm about my past, my present and my future.

Today I breathe in *calm*.

COMPASSION

Today I breathe in *compassion*.

I demonstrate compassion to myself and to all I meet. May I learn to look at myself and others with understanding, compassion and love. Today I act with kindness to those who need it the most. I replace criticism of others with compassion, as I put myself in their shoes. If I have the opportunity to help another and show kind-heartedness, I do. Compassion is the rising tide that lifts all ships.

Today I breathe in compassion.

My compassion and kindness will melt the coldest of hearts. When others care less, I will care more. I give myself permission to be kind to me. I take care of myself mentally, emotionally and physically. Every day is a new opportunity to show compassion, kindness and understanding to every person whose path I cross. Rather than judging others for their mistakes, I offer understanding and bring relief to their suffering. I am caring. I am compassionate.

Today I breathe in compassion.

As I imagine every person on the planet, I send loving thoughts as I think to myself, *may you be free of suffering, may your life be healthy, happy and safe*. When I find myself stuck in a difficult state or challenging times, I use this as an opportunity to generate compassion by reminding myself that many others may also be suffering. My compassion has no limit. May my heart be filled with kindness and compassion, allowing me to extend my heart and goodwill to others.

Today I breathe in *compassion*.

CONFIDENCE

Today I breathe in *confidence*.

I believe in me. My thoughts and feelings are unique to me. I release all thoughts, pictures and feelings that do not support my self-esteem. My mind overflows with thoughts of I can, I am capable, I am worth it. I deserve to be here as much as the next person – the world is my home. As I breathe the good feelings of confidence into every cell of my being, my confidence grows stronger and stronger. I see my future self as confident. I roll my shoulders back, I look up, I stand tall as I walk and talk with confidence.

Today I breathe in confidence.

Confidence and self-esteem are what I say to myself. No longer will I wallow in thoughts of not being good enough, because I am good enough, I am more than good enough. The negative thoughts of others will not determine who I am. I replace all self-doubt with self-belief. I am worthy. I am enough. Some days I will need to stand up for myself. There will be times when I need to say no. I will say no with confidence. When I say no I mean no.

Today I breathe in confidence.

I reaffirm that I truly am enough and I am perfect just the way I am. Today is a great day to be me. I outweigh each negative thought with ten positive thoughts. I am talented, I am smart, I am learning, I am great, I am evolving, I am valuable, I am aware, I am wonderful, I am me and I am confident. I stand by my own beliefs. I have complete confidence and trust in myself and my choices. My feelings of self-confidence grow stronger by the day, stronger by the hour and stronger by the minute.

Today I breathe in *confidence*.

CONTROL

Today I breathe in *control*.

I am in control of my thoughts and my feelings. I am in control of my life. From the deepest part of my mind to the tips of my fingers and toes, I feel a sense of control. I am in charge, I am decisive. I have the power to change my thoughts and change how I feel. Therefore, I change my actions and how I behave. Under pressure I stay calm and in control.

Today I breathe in control.

As I control my breath, I create a positive anchor in my life. I control my breathing. I am in control; I stay in control. I am in control of my reactions to what others say and do. I am in control of my thoughts and what I say. I pump my fist as I anchor myself into the feeling of being in control; as I breathe and think the thought: *I am in control*. I easily reject thoughts, habits and actions that do not bring me health and happiness.

Today I breathe in control.

I control what I allow to enter my mind and body. Only nourishing thoughts will enter my mind. Only nourishing foods will enter my body. I control my stress by relaxing, I control anger with peace, I control sadness with joy, I control fear with courage and I control hurt with forgiveness. I have no desire to control others, although I may gently guide. I choose to control me.

Today I breathe in *control*.

DETERMINATION

Today I breathe in *determination*.

I am persistent, I am resilient and I am determined. If life knocks me down 100 times, I will always get up one more time. My mistakes are not failures. Mistakes merely teach me what doesn't work. I do not understand quitting. I learn life's lessons and move forward. I will never give in; I will never give up. I know that persistence and perseverance conquer resistance. Every day I will take one more step towards my goals. My goals are achievable. I never give up.

Today I breathe in determination.

Once I make up my mind, I stay determined until I succeed. I have the fortitude to keep going. I dig deep, I give it my all, and then I give a little more. As I push on, my determination grows stronger. I see myself as determined, I think thoughts of determination and feel the good feelings of being determined. To climb a mountain, I must take one step at a time. To read a book I must read one page at a time. Whatever I set out to do I complete it. I just keep going, one thought, one action, one step at a time.

Today I breathe in determination.

I welcome challenges for they strengthen my willpower. With determination, I move over, around or through obstacles. Nothing will stand in my way. Nothing will stop me. The trials and tribulations of life may slow me at times, but they will not stop me. I am resolute. My internal compass guides me in the right direction. I move forward as I live each day with purpose. Every day in every way my determination grows stronger. I have a burning desire to reach my goals and nothing will stop me.

Today I breathe in *determination*.

ENERGY

Today I breathe in *energy*.

I am energetic. My source of energy comes from how I think. I am a get-up-and-go person with boundless energy. As I think energising thoughts, my energy increases. When others look at me, they wonder where all my energy comes from. My secret weapon is my energising thoughts.

Today I breathe in energy.

A positive energy flows through every muscle, every organ and every bone of my body. Nutritious foods give me energy. Water gives me energy. Positive people give me energy. Inspiring ideas give me energy. Positive thoughts charge my life with an uplifting energy. I breathe energy in from the tips of my toes to the top of my head and down through my body again. Each breath I take fills me with vigour. Movement gives me energy.

Today I breathe in energy.

If anyone projects negative energy in my direction, I project positive energy. And in the same way that we plug a power cable into a wall, I will only give energy to positive thoughts, positive feelings and positive people. When it comes to negative people, I give them no energy. I counter all negative energies with a calm, confident positive energy.

Today I breathe in energy.

At certain times my energy is dynamic, at other times I maintain a calm energy, and at other times I am filled with and radiate a healing energy. Energy fills the universe and I draw this energy into every cell of my being. Every part of me is filled with a wonderful positive energy.

Today I breathe in *energy*.

ENTHUSIASM

Today I breathe in *enthusiasm*.

When I think enthusiastic thoughts, my body is filled with feelings of enthusiasm. Enthusiasm is the fuel that drives me beyond setbacks and towards success. I live each day with enthusiasm and excitement. My potential and life's possibilities fill me with anticipation. I program my mind and body with thoughts of enthusiasm. I am enthusiastic.

Today I breathe in enthusiasm.

As I expect great things to happen, great things do happen. Enthusiasm is my greatest asset, helping me overcome negativity and doubt. Enthusiasm keeps me young, filling me with exhilaration. I nourish my enthusiasm with new projects and goals. My new projects and goals nourish my life with enthusiasm. The speed of my actions and the excitement in my voice matches the level of my enthusiasm. I delete negative thoughts from others with thoughts of enthusiasm.

Today I breathe in enthusiasm.

I realise that spring follows winter, and the sun comes out after every storm. In the same way, if I have feelings of indifference or apathy, I quickly replace them with feelings of passion and enthusiasm. The more enthusiastically I think, the more enthusiastic I feel. When I reach each fork in the road, I don't take the low road, I take the high road. Every day in every way my enthusiasm grows stronger and stronger.

Today I breathe in enthusiasm.

Like an old friend, enthusiasm lifts me when I need it most and encourages me to keep going. When life throws me a curveball I keep moving forward with enthusiasm. When I face setbacks, I start again and keep moving forward with enthusiasm. When I feel rejected, I pick myself up and keep moving forward with enthusiasm. I live my life with an abundance of excitement and enthusiasm.

Today I breathe in *enthusiasm*.

FOCUS

Today I breathe in *focus*.

My actions are focused, my thoughts are focused, I am focused. I give my attention completely and wholeheartedly to every action I undertake. I avoid distraction, as I keep my mind fully focused in the moment. My power of concentration is growing stronger every day. My mind can focus like a laser.

Today I breathe in focus.

Thoughts may come and go, but I return to the task at hand with undivided attention. As I focus, I get in the zone and stay in the zone. I find it easy to finish what I start. My time and my energy are valuable, therefore I don't waste them. I stay focused on what I am doing.

Today I breathe in focus.

I override indecision with decisiveness. I make a decision and I stick with it. I organise my thoughts and the space around me. All of my energy is focused on my goal. I am a person of action and I do what needs doing. A relaxed mind is a clear mind and a clear mind is a focused mind. My mind is relaxed, my mind is clear, my mind is focused. I complete what needs completing.

Today I breathe in focus.

As I breathe the thought of focus and the feeling of focus into every cell of my being, I have a sense of purpose. I stick with my goals to fruition. While I may have many tasks that need completing, I focus on one at a time and get the job done. I know where to start, I know what to do, I get into it and get it done.

Today I breathe in *focus*.

FORGIVENESS

Today I breathe in *forgiveness*.

I am forgiving. I release resentment towards others and myself. If I had my time over, I would do things differently. I forgive myself for the wrongs of the past. Equally, I forgive others who have wronged me – they too may carry feelings of guilt. I release all thoughts and feelings of regret – they no longer serve me.

Today I breathe in forgiveness.

Today I forgive, releasing myself and others from the prison of guilt. I embrace empowering thoughts that will heal the old wounds of anger, guilt and hurt. These new thoughts will lead me in the right direction. I live in the present, I am moving forward, I am healing, I am a survivor, I am evolving, I am sincere, I am here.

Today I breathe in forgiveness.

None of us are perfect, we all make mistakes. I release all negativity from my past. The past is over; it is done, finished, gone. I choose to live in the present. As I learn from my own mistakes, my hope is that others may also learn from their mistakes. If I am unable to forgive another for *them*, I forgive them for *me*. The power of forgiveness sets me free. I choose to live in the now.

Today I breathe in forgiveness.

I have my own life to live, I have the power to forgive. I forgive unconditionally. The past has passed and I let it go. Today is a new day and a new beginning. I have the rest of my life to live, and live it I will. I am ready to move on as I tell myself: *I forgive you, I forgive me, I am free*.

Today I breathe in *forgiveness*.

HAPPINESS

Today I breathe in *happiness*.

Whether I am happy or not is my choice. When I think happy thoughts, I feel happy. Today I choose to feel happy. I choose to feel happy for no reason at all. I choose to be happy. I am happy. Happiness flows through my mind and body. As I give myself permission to be happy, my happiness radiates out to all those I come in contact with.

Today I breathe in happiness.

A smile goes a long way and costs nothing. Today I will give away many smiles. Happiness is a gift and costs nothing. Today I give away happiness. I focus on the small and simple things in life that bring me joy. In this way my day will be filled with joy and happiness. I find happiness in the present moment. I find happiness in the kind words of a friend or loved one. I find happiness in acts of kindness. Though happiness may seem elusive, it is everywhere. Happiness is my state of mind.

Today I breathe in happiness.

Happiness is not found in material things. True happiness is found in peace of mind. Happiness is not found in money. True happiness is found when someone is kind. Happiness is being true to myself. Happiness is not caring what others think. Happiness is helping another or being helped. Happiness is a star in the sky, a bird flying by. Happiness is a beautiful piece of music or the laughter of a child. Happiness is generosity, kindness, compassion, awareness and love. Happiness can be found everywhere.

Today I breathe in *happiness*.

HEALTH

Today I breathe in *health*.

I deserve to be healthy and full of vitality. As I think healthy thoughts and eat healthy foods, I nourish my mind and body. My body, my mind and my emotions are a blueprint for perfect health. I choose to be healthy and to stay healthy. I say *yes* to health.

Today I breathe in health.

My body is meant to move. I love to move. The more active I am the better I look. The more active I am the better I feel. Whether it's a walk or a swim or a sport I play, I aim to be active twice every day. As I move more, I radiate health and vitality. Movement creates strong muscles, strong bones and a healthy heart, therefore I move more. I am inspired when I move. I move in any way I can.

Today I breathe in health.

I treat my body with love and respect. Only goodness enters my body. I nourish my body with healing foods. I eat what nature intended: from the land, from the sea, from the ground, from a tree. My body craves water. If I am thirsty, I drink more water. I realise I need to drink more water, drink more water, drink more water. I am tomorrow what I eat today, before each meal that's what I say. I make healthy choices.

Today I breathe in health.

Every day in every way the new me chooses health. I choose to drink more water, be more active, eat small healthy portions. Every day my lifestyle moves me towards health and healing. I am healthy. Today, my health is my number one priority. I make time for my health. I recognise my health is my wealth.

Today I breathe in *health*.

LAUGHTER

Today I breathe in *laughter*.

 With a light heart I laugh at myself, I laugh with others and I laugh at the world. And how can I add more laughter into my life? I find the funny side of things and share a laugh with friends and strangers alike. Laughter is endearing and connects me to others. I laugh out loud; I love to laugh. As I laugh, I am bursting with bliss.

 Today I breathe in laughter.

 When I laugh at my problems, they cease to have power over me. Laughter releases powerful feel-good chemicals. The more I laugh, the better I feel. My laughter is effortless and heals my body. I choose to laugh. While there is a time to be serious, there is also a time to laugh. I counter anger and stress with a good laugh. When I laugh at my fears, their power disappears. I laugh with childlike abandon.

 Today I breathe in laughter.

 The gift of laughter is contagious. Laughter is free, yet I realise its value. As I laugh, others laugh with me and, as they laugh, I laugh more. Laughter truly is the best medicine. I am fun-loving and I am playful. Laughter improves my mental, emotional and physical well-being. Laughter is great therapy. I make the time to laugh. I spread laughter and happiness wherever I go. As I harness the power of laughter and comedy, I lighten the load of life for myself and those around me.

 Today I breathe in *laughter*.

LOVE

Today I breathe in *love*.

Love is the most powerful force in the universe. As I bathe myself in the healing power of love, I realise I am lovable, I am loving and I am loved. I am love. As I breathe love in, I also breathe it back into the world. The light of love expands beyond my body to the space I am in, beyond the space I am in to fill the entire region, the country and the planet. The light of love expands infinitely to fill the entire universe.

Today I breathe in love.

While I hold onto love, it is impossible to feel negative feelings and to think negative thoughts. I choose love over anger, I choose love over sadness and I choose love over hurt. Love is the power and the key. Love is what sets me free. Love is everywhere and everything. Every day in every way my love grows stronger and stronger.

Today I breathe in love.

I will approach today with love in my heart and radiate that love to every person I meet. I think loving thoughts, I feel love and act with love. Love shines from my eyes. Like a river that gives endlessly and is constantly replenished, the more love I give, the more love flows into me. Like a flower opening to the morning sun, I radiate love to myself, to the world and to everyone. Love is in my heart.

Today I breathe in love.

As love flows through me, I send thoughts of self-love to every part of my being. I love my heart and my ears, my laughter and my tears. I love every bone in my body. I love me for who I am and how I am. I step into love as I become love. My love will bring healing to those who are suffering. I will do the little things that express love to myself, to my closest loved ones and to all I meet.

Today I breathe in *love*.

MINDFULNESS

Today I breathe in *mindfulness*.

I ground myself in the present moment by connecting my body with my breath. When my mind gets lost in the past or future, I connect my thoughts with the present moment. I do this by grounding myself in the present moment with my breath and my actions. I connect my mind with my actions. I am awake, I am aware, I am here. My power and calm are in the present moment.

Today I breathe in mindfulness.

Like a boat drifting with the current or being blown around by the wind of thought, I anchor myself to the moment. My body, breath, activity and positive thoughts combine to create the anchor of mindfulness. I watch my thoughts, let them go and clear my mind. I breathe into each moment as I am mindful of my own actions. I am mindful of what I do, of what I say, and of those around me. Today is the day and now is the time. I always remember that time is precious and the time is now. When I am mindful, every moment is special, every moment is precious.

Today I breathe in mindfulness.

As I am mindful, the mundane things in life become magical and meaningful. My senses are tuned into the present moment. As I eat an apple, drink a glass of water or walk, I tune into the moment and become more mindful. Awareness in mindfulness now becomes a part of my everyday life. When my mind drifts away, I return to now with a single breath as I repeat: *body and mind together as one*. I live in the present moment with joy. Every day in every way my awareness grows stronger and stronger.

Today I breathe in *mindfulness*.

MOTIVATION

Today I breathe in *motivation*.

Today I am feeling motivated. I am feeling motivated to achieve my goals. I will take the first step, and then another as my motivation mounts. I will celebrate each step, and my motivation will grow. I make things happen. I am determined and focused, and nothing will stop me. Every positive thought I generate motivates me. My motivation makes me unstoppable.

Today I breathe in motivation.

I am highly motivated. I am inspired to give it a go, inspired to give my best. Motivation is a powerful force – recognition is the switch that ignites it. I recognise my strength, my focus, my ability, my enthusiasm, my optimism, my energy and my drive. These things give me motivation – motivation drives me forward. I do not tire easily; I do not give in – my motivation defeats everything in its path.

Today I breathe in motivation.

I am motivated. I tell myself, *if it is to be, it is up to me.* If others have done it then I can do it. If no one has done it then I will find a way. I will start, and I will not stop. Motivation is my secret weapon; it fuels everything else. My motivation is not to prove to others what I can do, but to prove to myself what I already know. I am driven, I am motivated. I can do anything I set my mind to. Today is a building block for tomorrow – for me, and for my world.

Today I breathe in *motivation*.

OPTIMISM

Today I breathe in *optimism*.

I am optimistic. I have reason to be optimistic today and every day. I am healthy, I am happy, I am intelligent, I am loved. I see beauty in all things. I appreciate the world I live in. I am optimistic about my life in this world. I am an important part of it. I am me, and I am optimistic. I use my optimism and inspire others to be optimistic. I expect the best.

Today I breathe in optimism.

I am full of hope. Not all things are perfect. I choose to see the glass half-full; I see the potential; I am hopeful for the future. I believe in it, I believe in me, I believe in the value of my part in the world and the future. I am optimistic. Not all roads are smooth, but all roads lead somewhere. I overcome the bumps of life with motivation, a positive attitude and perseverance.

Today I breathe in optimism.

I am an optimist. I see the beauty in people, I see the beauty in things. I expect good things to happen and good things happen. When things don't go according to plan, I think to myself, *next*, and then I move forward. Optimism is a magnet for happiness and achievement.

Today I breathe in optimism.

I face the sun, and the shadows are always behind me. My optimism acts as a protective shield and guards me from all negativity. I choose optimistic thoughts like: *I can, I will, it's possible*. I radiate optimism to my family, to my friends and to the world. I can play my part. I share my optimism; I share my hope. The future is bright; I will make it so. The world is a miracle, I am a miracle. Every day in every way my optimism grows stronger and stronger.

Today I breathe in *optimism*.

STRENGTH

Today I breathe in *strength*.

I am strong today. I am physically strong. I am mentally strong. I am emotionally strong. Every day in every way I become stronger and stronger. I am stronger than my thoughts. I am stronger than my emotions. I have unlimited power. I have unlimited potential. My strength comes not from what I can do, but from doing the things I thought I couldn't do. I can do anything, because I am strong.

Today I breathe in strength.

I am strong. I am stronger than I ever thought possible. I continue to get stronger. I am stronger than the challenges I face. I confront obstacles. I make mistakes, but I learn from them – they make me stronger. I believe in myself. I have high self-esteem. That gives me strength. I am happy, I am healthy, I am loved. These things make me strong.

Today I breathe in strength.

My strength gives me resilience. My strength gives me determination. My persistent efforts bring me growth. My persistent efforts bring me success. My strength of purpose motivates and inspires me. I feel in control of my life. This feeds my strength. Storms cause trees to have deeper roots – adversity only makes me stronger. I can overcome anything life throws at me. I can cope, I can thrive, because I am powerful and I am strong.

Today I breathe in strength.

I overcome obstacles, I overcome fears, I overcome doubt. I can do these things because I am strong. I deal with the pressures of life. I find my inner strength. I harness the inner power that is truly me. I have this power within me. It gives me strength. Nothing defeats me. I am strong today – I will be stronger tomorrow.

Today I breathe in *strength*.

SUCCESS

Today I breathe in *success*.

Success does not lie with money or fame, success lies within. Success is a mindset. It is not only in the end result, but also in the journey. Success is in having the courage to begin, the determination to overcome the hard road, the conviction to see it to the end. Success travels with me. I put a label on myself and it reads: *success*. I have all the resources needed to succeed. I deserve to succeed, I am succeeding.

Today I breathe in success.

Every task I tackle, every doubt I dispel, every fear I face down: there is my success. I am the creator of my own success. As my mind stays focused on thoughts of success I continue to succeed. While I play to win, I do not have to win to succeed. If I play better than last time, if I never give in, never give up, if I give my best, I will hold my head high; I am proud of my success. I measure my success by my effort and how I feel. I was born to succeed.

Today I breathe in success.

Success is my happiness, my belief in myself, my gratitude, my peace. I do not have to pursue success; I realise that I already have it. I am success. Failure does not exist, only lessons. When I expect to succeed I will. Every small win I have is another step towards greater achievements. And my greatest success is when I inspire and help others to succeed.

Today I breathe in *success*.

WISDOM

Today I breathe in *wisdom*.

I breathe deeply and I relax, and release from my mind any negative thoughts. With a calm and uncluttered mind, I see things more clearly. I take time to express my thoughts from a place of wisdom and understanding. Wisdom is my friend, wisdom provides me with comfort, wisdom reinforces my self-worth. Others can be wise. I can be wise. What would a wise person say? I ask myself the question and I receive the wise answer. I choose to learn wisdom. I choose to show wisdom. I choose to live wisely.

Today I breathe in wisdom.

I see wisdom in others. I value their wisdom. I learn from their wisdom. Wisdom is more than knowledge. Wisdom grows by the determination to acquire it, and the sense to use it properly. Wisdom is a process. Wisdom is a journey. The journey begins by knowing myself. Wisdom comes from experience and doing what you have learned. Today I choose wisdom. Wisdom travels with me and is me. I am wise.

Today I breathe in wisdom.

I now see wisdom in myself: in my thoughts, in my words, in my actions. Wisdom in others gives me comfort. My wisdom gives others comfort. My wisdom is a friend. I rely on my wisdom. My wisdom is a tree: to be nurtured and appreciated. Wisdom provides me with strength. It protects me from storms. The tree of my wisdom grows over time. My wisdom is rooted in the earth, and reaches for the sky. Every day in every way I grow wiser and wiser.

Today I breathe in *wisdom*.

MY SUPER STATE

Take your favourite affirmations from all 21 States and combine them with any positive thoughts that appeal to you to create your own customised super state here.

_____

_____

_____

_____

_____

_____

_____

_____

_____

_____

_____

_____

_____

_____

_____

_____

_____

_____

_____

_____

_____

_____

_____

CONCLUSION
THE BEGINNING

After eight years of training, with more than a few bumps and bruises along the way, the day finally arrived to sit for my black belt grading. More than 3000 classes had prepared me for this day.

To pass, I would have to demonstrate the ability to proficiently handle full-speed attacks with weapons from all directions. Those weapons included knives, chains, baseball bats and chairs. Part of the grading included unarmed mob attacks, which meant five people circled you and all charged at once as fast as they could with kicks and punches. We had to handle attacks from lying on the ground, against a wall and standing in a corner. And then there were the 72 judo throws, numerous ground-fighting locks and positions, as well as demonstrating any defensive move from the seven grades below black belt. We had to demonstrate an understanding of the principles and philosophy of jujutsu if asked, as well as know the names of the throws in Japanese. We would also have to handle surprise attacks, meaning anyone at any moment could simply attack. This was a test of both skill and knowledge.

There were four of us going for our black belt that day: George, Dave, Greg and myself. We had trained for thousands of hours in preparation for what was before us. I was the most junior, with George,

Dave and Greg all having trained for at least five years longer than I had. Just before the grading started, Brian, who was now a sixth dan, informed us the grading would go all day and well into the night.

'This is the closest you will get to real combat without being on the street or on the battlefield. Your attackers will be going at full speed to try to take you down and stop you from being graded. We have a first aid kit on hand, and Sutherland Hospital is only five minutes away if needed,' he said in a deadly serious tone.

Until that moment, I'd felt relatively calm and in control. All of a sudden, I could feel my breathing starting to become more rapid. I started getting butterflies in my stomach. And as quickly as those feelings snuck up on me, they disappeared. I took some slow deep breaths thinking, *just breathe, I've got this*. All the stress dissolved almost instantly.

After hour upon hour of being attacked with every kick, punch and weapon from every direction you could imagine, the grading was over. There *were* bumps and bruises, black eyes and lacerations. Fortunately, the first aid kit with its butterfly stitches and bandages did the trick. The four of us, soaking in sweat, with bloodied uniforms and ready to fall over from exhaustion, lined up in front of Brian when instructed to do so. Did we all pass? Did I do enough to get my black belt? *Just breathe, I've got this.*

After a short yet inspiring speech, Brian congratulated each of us for doing so well. He said that our demonstration of focus and control was inspiring. He said that our ability to handle the attacks and our accurate use of weapons were deserving of a black belt.

'You have all passed with a comfortable margin,' he said.

Brian then proceeded to pass each of us our black belt and congratulate us individually with a bow and a handshake.

'Congratulations, gentlemen, you have achieved the rank of Sho Dan, first-degree black belt. This means you have achieved your first step. Now we can start training,' he said, with a fraction of a smile and a nod.

First step, I thought to myself. *Eight years of training and **now** we can start?*

Life is truly precious. If you've been putting yourself last and suffering, I hope that immersing yourself in these teachings will help you make the time to put yourself first – to make time for healing. When I had cancer in 1990, I realised how precious life, and the time we have, really is. I appreciated that health had to become the highest value and priority in my life or I would have no life.

It may be one minute to midnight, yet so many of us live our lives as though our time here is unlimited.

It's not.

My purpose in writing this book was to provide you with some simple tools for change and to help you achieve peace of mind and healing. My hope is that, through these writings and through your applying what you learn, you move on from your old story – you will stop clinging to whatever thoughts and emotions have been holding you back and you will overcome your biggest challenges.

As you return to the chapters, the 21 States and the Mind Manual scripts again and again, taking a few minutes each time to meditate on and visualise yourself feeling the good feelings of each experience, you will continue to change for the better. Always remember, where your mind goes your energy flows. When you continue to combine the power of your thoughts with the power of your chosen positive states you will move forward on a path of unlimited possibilities. You will have set your mind free.

Find someone to share these lessons and daily rituals with. Imagine if your newfound peace and what you've learned in *Mind Free* rippled out to impact family members and friends. Their lives would also change for the better and they may in turn impact others in a profound and uplifting way.

Now that you have reached the end of this book, let the transformation continue. It only takes a minute to meditate or repeat an affirmation. From the bottom of my heart, I wish you well.

Always remember, make time for yourself. You are worthy.

And keep breathing – you've got this.

THE BEGINNING

MIND MANUAL

In the pages that follow you will find a carefully selected library of meditation techniques and mindful self-hypnosis scripts that link to the chapters you've already read in *Mind Free*. These are to further help you overcome the challenges you may be facing.

Some of these scripts are from my private collection and are the same ones I use when running retreats or doing private breakthrough sessions. Many scripts were created specifically for this book and some are techniques I learned more than 50 years ago.

Feel free to experiment with the scripts and create your own methods of meditation to bring about the changes you wish to make. Remember: all hypnosis is self-hypnosis and all meditation is personal to you. As you harness the power of your unconscious mind, you'll shift your thoughts from negative to positive and take control of your mind and, with that, your life. *You* are the hypnotist.

As you scan every word in the following scripts, and breathe them into your life and thus into existence, you'll discover how easy it is to let the old thoughts and negative emotions fade away. You'll find yourself thinking new thoughts, as you set your mind free. The more you allow your mind to absorb each and every word, the more your life will change.

Most importantly, you will take on board the words, declarations and affirmations that resonate with you. Eventually the new way of thinking will become second nature, as you recite any or all of the following scripts and practices in addition to the ones you've tried in the chapters. Whenever you feel the onset of negative thoughts and negative emotions, simply open the book and read a script that feels relevant to you at that moment. With each breath you take and each word you read, you'll continue to discover that change is possible.

If you have not already visited the Mind Free website to listen to the relevant audio sessions and videos that support this book, you can do that now. Visit mindfreeapp.com, click on the picture of the book and then enter the code: mindfreebook (all one word and lower case).

To get the best out of this bonus material, here are instructions on how to practise the meditations, self-hypnosis, affirmations and mandala exercises in the Mind Manual. Remember, the following scripts will change how you feel and how you act and react in life. The more you read and practise the following techniques and exercises, the greater your results.

MEDITATION INSTRUCTIONS

If only meditation were easy; I'd like to do it but my brain is just too busy; I can't concentrate. These are the comments I often hear at the beginning of seminars and retreats.

Wow! I really felt myself relax. I can't believe how easy it was to meditate; I found it easy to focus. These are the comments I hear at the end of seminars and retreats.

To begin meditating, you might like to turn on some relaxing background music and burn a scented candle or some incense. You may like to sit near a window, in your yard or at a park. The reality is you can pretty much meditate anytime and anywhere.

Most sessions start with you sitting, lying or standing in a comfortable position and concentrating on your breath flowing in and out of your body. By taking a few slow, deep breaths at the start of each meditation practice or script, you'll allow your body and mind to relax and absorb every important word.

For the best results, practise a meditation session first thing in the morning as you are waking up and last thing at night just before going to sleep. These are the times when your mind and brain are most receptive. Even if you begin with just one or two minutes a day, it's a great start and you can build your meditation practice from there.

MINDFUL SELF-HYPNOSIS INSTRUCTIONS

Follow these steps to practise mindful self-hypnosis at home.

1. Find a quiet place where you can sit back or lie down and won't be disturbed for five to 15 minutes.
2. As you sit or lie down and breathe, listen to the sounds around you without labelling them. Move from the sounds you can hear to your thoughts. Notice your thoughts and how you are feeling without judging or attaching a story to them.
3. Feel your breath flow in and out of your body. Don't force your breath at all, just watch, feel or listen to your breath falling naturally in and out of your body in its own rhythm. Focus your awareness on your breathing.
4. Add an affirmation. As you slowly breathe in, repeat the first half of the affirmation and, as you breathe out, repeat the second half of the affirmation. Powerful affirmations become even stronger when you're in a state of mindful self-hypnosis. Consider including affirmations such as: *I feel at peace. I am at peace. My body is healing. I am strong. I am in control. If it is to be, it is up to me. I am open and honest. I deserve to be happy. I am worthy. I am grateful. I am good enough. I am a survivor.*
5. Once you feel yourself sinking into a deep relaxation, begin reading your chosen Mind Manual script as you use the power of your imagination to see and feel yourself overcoming challenges, mentally rehearsing the achievement of goals and

making positive changes in your life. You may find it helps to visualise yourself in a beautiful natural setting, such as a beach, rainforest or mountaintop, as you feel stress and anxiety floating out of your body.

6. When you have completed your mindful self-hypnosis session, bring your awareness back into the space you're in, with several deep breaths or by slowly counting from one to five as you feel the energy re-enter your body.

As you read the mindful self-hypnosis scripts, take your time and feel your breath flowing in and out just before you start. As you read, see each word, think each word in your mind and feel the feelings of each word. Imagine or feel the words flowing on your breath. Feel your breath and the words becoming one. It's as if your breath is drawing the word or words into you, and breathing those words back out into the world or into your body. For example, you would read the script like this:

Breathing in, *love* – breathing out, *heals all.*

Breathing in, *I now release* – breathing out, *all negative beliefs.*

AFFIRMATION INSTRUCTIONS

When you read the affirmations in each section, think about and feel each word, allow the words to float with your breath as you breathe in, and to flow from your conscious mind into the deepest part of your unconscious mind. As you exhale, allow those words to float back again from the back of your mind to the front of your mind, and then breathe these words into every muscle and every cell of your body. You may also like, as you exhale, to speak these words either aloud or in a whisper and breathe them into the world.

You'll begin to notice these words will float with you each and every day and you'll begin to live these words. They will become a part of your everyday thinking. When you read these thoughts daily, you'll fill your mind with uplifting positive thoughts. Here are two ways to practise the affirmations:

Method 1: Breathe in and recite the entire affirmation in your mind and, as you breathe out, recite the entire affirmation again.

Method 2: Breathe the first half of the affirmation as you inhale in and the second half of the affirmation as you exhale.

MANDALA INSTRUCTIONS

At the end of each section in the Mind Manual you'll find a mandala. I've drawn these for you to colour in as a meditation. As well as colouring in the mandala, I encourage you to fill up the page with as many positive power words, declarations, affirmations, symbols or pictures that will support you in overcoming your challenges and reaching your goals.

Once you complete each mandala exercise and fill the page, spend a few minutes each morning and night staring at the mandala and meditate on the thoughts you feel you need that day. You may like to repeat one of the affirmations you've written on the page or all of them. Allow these thoughts, feelings and words to sink into your wonderful unconscious mind, and every part of your being.

Mind free guide

In the first chapter of the book (see p. 19) I explained the power of meditation and self-hypnosis to create change and healing. The practices in this section of the Mind Manual will support and prepare you before you do any of the meditation and self-hypnosis scripts in the Mind Manual.

FIVE STEPS TO TRANQUILLITY THROUGH BREATHING

Follow the five steps in this exercise to achieve a tranquil, peaceful state.

Step 1: Feel the breath

Allow yourself to be open to relaxing through feeling your breath flow in and out.

With your eyes either open or closed, quietly feel your breath fall into and out of your body. As you do, simply notice the sound the air makes as it passes your nostrils as you inhale, and notice the sound of the air as you exhale, either through your nose or your mouth. Can you feel your body moving with every breath? Focus on the air moving in and out of your lungs as you relax your chest and shoulders. All cares and worries are easily released simply by feeling your abdomen rise and fall.

Make no effort to breathe, just be breathed, let the universe breathe into you, as the air flows in and out.

Your breathing is naturally happening anyway. Just notice your breath.

Place your attention on the air flowing in and out.

Clear your mind as you focus on the natural rhythm of your breath.

You may like to set a timer and practise this now for one minute. Alternatively, you may like to count each breath. Depending on the speed of your breathing, one minute will take between six and 12 breaths.

Step 2: Slow the breath

Take a few slow, relaxing breaths. Slow your breathing down a little more. Whisper in your mind the word *relax* as you breathe in and *release* as you breathe out. Concentrate on the words *relax* and *release* with every breath for the next six to 12 breaths. Feel each breath becoming a little slower as any tension just melts away. Practise this for one minute.

Step 3: Focused breathing

Again, experience a few slow relaxing breaths. Allow yourself to completely relax all the muscles of your body. Pick one area of your body to focus on and direct your awareness to that part of your body. You may like to focus on your navel or on the bottom centre of your feet. You may like to put your attention on your hands or your heart. You may like to focus on that point in the centre of your forehead just between your eyebrows. Without force, you inhale and exhale slowly and evenly as you imagine or feel the breath flowing to that point. Maintain your focus on this point for the next six to 12 breaths. Practise this for one minute.

Step 4: Affirmation breathing

Your inner mind knows exactly what to do as you pick a word or phrase and repeat the word or phrase as you inhale and exhale. Breathe the word or phrase in, and breathe the same word or phrase out. Alternatively, you may like to breathe half of the phrase in and the other half out. If your mind drifts off to a different thought, allow that thought to float away, like a cloud drifting off in the sky, and simply bring your awareness back to the word or phrase you are focusing on. Starting now, repeat the word or phrase for one minute or as long as you'd like.

Method 1: Breathe in: *I am calm*. Breathe out: *I am calm*. Repeat.

Method 2: Breathe in: *I am*. Breathe out: *calm*. Repeat.

Choose a word or phrase from the following list or use a positive word or phrase of your own that has meaning to you. Ask your unconscious to select the words or phrases you most need to hear.

I am calm

I am well

All is well

Love and harmony
Light and free
I am the light
I choose to be happy
I am strong
Calm and relax
Peace release
Appreciation
Compassion
Joy
Love
Strength
Energy
Determination

Step 5: Energy breathing
Either sitting or standing with good posture, take a slow deep breath all the way in as far as you can, and then breathe a little deeper. As you exhale, blow out four fast breaths as if you are blowing out four candles with one breath. 1, 2, 3, 4. Repeat the exercise five times and notice how invigorated you feel. Practise this for one minute.

STANDING MEDITATION - THE ENERGY FIELD

Energy flows through everything in the universe. From solar energy and the energy of the moon to wind energy and the energy of the foods we eat, we both absorb and generate energy day and night. The pictures and movies we hold in our minds along with our emotions and thoughts are powerful energy in themselves. In this meditation you will tune into drawing energy from the field around you and then radiating a positive energy back out to the universe.

Step 1
Stand where you are standing as you take a few slow, relaxing breaths and allow your mind and body to soften and relax. Allow your awareness

to expand as far as it is able, all the way out in front of you, as far as your imagination will go. Imagine all that energy from the field in front of you radiating into your body as you breathe slowly and deeply. Imagine the field of energy as far behind you as your imagination will go. Relax and breathe that energy in from the field behind you. You may like to imagine the energy pouring into you like a stream of light or beams of light. Now imagine the field of energy all the way out to your left as far as your mind will go, as you allow that energy to flow back into you and radiating into every cell of your body. Now shift your awareness to the right. Allow your mind to float out as far as it can to the right and feel the energy flowing into you from that direction. Allow your body to breathe all that energy in from the field in front of you, from behind you and from your left and your right. You may like to close your eyes for a few breaths and really feel that energy pouring into you. Allow yourself to be filled with light. Allow every cell of your being to be coated with pure energy, pure light.

Step 2

In the same way, imagine the energy field beneath you. Allow your mind to drift through the ground, through layers of Earth all the way to the centre of the planet. Feel all the Earth energy flowing up through your feet into your body. With each breath you draw that energy in and feel the power of the Earth, the strength surging through you. Mentally tell yourself *I am strong*.

Step 3

Focus on your breathing flowing in and out, and empty your mind of any thoughts as you shift your awareness and your attention to the energy field above you. Allow your awareness to expand through the atmosphere above you, beyond the sky, beyond the ozone layer, deeper into the stratosphere and even further out into space. Feel, visualise or imagine all that energy pouring into you from above. You may like to think of it as beams of light radiating down from the entire solar system, the galaxy and the universe. You may like to close your eyes for a few breaths and really feel that energy pouring into you.

Step 4

As you allow every cell of your being to be bathed in the light, imagine your every muscle, every bone, every organ and even every thought and emotion transforming into pure light. Take a moment to close your eyes and feel the feelings of the light penetrating every cell of your being. At the same time, the light begins to pour out of you in all directions. Allow the light to radiate to the energy field directly around you, to the energy field around the entire planet, to the energy field in the solar system, to the energy field in the galaxy, and to the energy field that fills the universe. Take a few breaths to allow the light of you to fill the entire universe.

Step 5

With each breath, you absorb. With each breath, you radiate. Keep breathing.

MINDFUL WALKING MEDITATION

Normally we walk without thinking about our walking. Our mind wanders off to a thousand different things while we miss the moment. With mindful walking you become consciously aware that this meditation starts the moment you begin walking. As you walk, tune into the feeling of your feet touching the ground, your legs moving, your arms swinging and your breath flowing in and out. When your mind wanders, return your attention back to the senses of feeling and movement as you breathe and walk.

As you walk, you may like to open up your senses to take in what you see, what you smell and what you hear.

LOVING SMILE MEDITATION

When you smile, your brain releases happiness hormones such as endorphins, dopamine and serotonin. These feel-good chemicals reduce stress, strengthen your immune system, reduce pain and make you feel better. While it's great to share your smile with others, it's time now to smile to the one person who needs it most – you.

Begin by sitting or lying down. Relax your entire body, from head to toe, as you feel each breath flowing in and out of your body. Focus on the air moving in and out of your body as you completely relax. As you inhale gently and quietly, repeat in your mind the word *calm*. As you slowly exhale, quietly repeat the word *relax*. Feel yourself let go of any tension.

Allow every muscle in your body to go loose and soft, soft and loose. Relax everything. Slowly breathing in and out, feel yourself gently smiling.

Let your thoughts imagine or remember a place that is beautiful and special to you. It could be in a forest, on a beach, by a river, in a field or in a beautiful garden – any peaceful place special to you. Imagine you are there in your special place now ... Remember the smell in the air ... the sounds you can hear ... What images can you see around you? How does it make you feel to be in this special place? Allow yourself to gently smile.

Recall something or someone that makes you smile, and feel the corners of your mouth beginning to lift as your cheeks rise. You may like to imagine the universe itself is smiling pure, loving energy into your eyes and your smile.

Imagine a beam of light flowing with your smile as you direct your smiling energy down through your body. Continue to breathe in and out calmly as you smile down to every organ in your body. Imagine the light flowing through your heart, your lungs, your stomach, your liver, your kidneys, your colon, your bladder, your bowel and every other organ inside of you. You may like to thank these organs one at a time or all together. You love your organs. You thank your organs. Feel yourself gently smiling.

Thank you, organs, thank you.

Bring your awareness back to your smile and now radiate that light and smiling energy through every muscle of your body. As you do this, you release any tension in your neck, shoulders, back, arms, chest, glutes and legs. Feel the smiling energy, feeling every muscle in your body. You love your muscles. You thank your muscles.

Thank you, muscles, thank you.

Let your inner mind bring your awareness back to your smile as the light fills you once again. Allow the light and your smile to flow to every bone in your body. Imagine now it's as if your entire skeleton is becoming a skeleton of beautiful shining light. You may like to imagine every other part of you dissolving away as you focus on yourself as a skeleton of pure light. You love every bone in your body. You thank your bones. Feel yourself gently smiling.

Thank you, bones, thank you.

Imagine now every single part of you is filled with light. Every organ, every muscle, every bone is filled with a wonderful smiling energy. Allow the light and smiling energy to now flow into your mind, your thoughts and your emotions. You love every part of yourself and you give thanks.

Thank you, thank you.

AFFIRMATION FOR TODAY

Start breathing:
Today I will live in the now
I release the past
I embrace the future
Today is the day and now is the time

Reset your mind guide

If you haven't yet read Chapter 2 (p. 34), head there now as it gives you the tools and techniques to reset your mind. This lets you move from negative to positive thoughts, from negative self-talk to nurturing self-talk, and is a vital step before working on issue-specific healing. Here are more techniques to help you reset your mind.

MINDFUL SELF-HYPNOSIS SCRIPTS

Every day in every way

Focus on your normal breathing rhythm flowing in and out. Either sitting comfortably or lying down, allow your body to completely relax.

Each word you read will sink deeply into your unconscious. As you slowly breathe in and out, notice if there is any stress or tension in any part of your body. Imagine that part of your body completely relaxing as you slowly breathe into the area with the thought *relax* and, as you exhale, think to yourself *release*.

Continue thinking *relax* and *release* for the next few breaths.

Breathe in *relax*, breathe out *release*.

Slow deep breath in *relax*, breathing out *release*.

Breathe in *relax*, breathe out *release*.

As you start to feel relaxed, imagine a whiteboard in front of you. You are holding your favourite-coloured marker. In a moment I'll ask you to draw numbers from five down to one. After you draw each number, you will wipe it away. As you wipe away each number, you can allow yourself to be even more relaxed.

Imagine you are drawing a large number 5 in the middle of the board.

Now imagine you are wiping the number 5 away with the whiteboard eraser.

You feel yourself or see yourself writing the number 4.

Once you imagine the number 4, you can wipe the 4 away.

Imagine you are drawing the number 3 in the middle of the board. Once you think about the 3 or you can see the 3, wipe the number 3 away.

Now you draw the number 2 in the middle of the board, a large number 2. And then, as you rub the number 2 away, you watch the number disappear.

Imagine you are drawing the number 1 right there in the middle of the board. Then wipe the number 1 away until the board is completely clean.

You may begin to feel your mind and body relaxing slowly and quietly. Read to yourself the following thoughts, and then close your eyes for a few moments as you repeat a second time those thoughts that feel right to you.

Breathe in, *every day in every way*, breathe out, *I am growing stronger and stronger.*

Breathe in, *I accept myself*, breathe out, *for who I am.*

Breathe in, *I deserve*, breathe out, *to feel good.*

Breathe in, *I embrace*, breathe out, *change.*

Breathe in, *I stay*, breathe out, *positive.*

Breathe in, *anything*, breathe out, *is possible.*

Breathe in, *I stay*, breathe out, *calm.*

Breathe in, *I easily*, breathe out, *overcome challenges.*

Breathe in, *I believe*, breathe out, *in myself wholeheartedly.*

Breathe in, *anything I put my mind to*, breathe out, *I can achieve.*

Breathe in, *I treat myself*, breathe out, *with love and respect.*

Breathe in, *I am*, breathe out, *enough.*

Breathe in, *I am unstoppable*, breathe out, *I am unstoppable.*

Breathe in, *I am*, breathe out, *determined to be my best.*

Breathe in, *my life is valuable*, breathe out, *I am valuable.*

Breathe in, *I am the master*, breathe out, *of my own destiny.*

Breathe in, *if it is to be*, breathe out, *it is up to me.*

Breathe in, *every day in every way*, breathe out, *I am growing stronger and stronger.*

All of these thoughts are now part of my everyday thinking. Whenever a negative thought arises, I replace it with an empowering, positive and uplifting thought. As I repeat each positive thought throughout the day, I am generating positive emotions and feelings. My positive thoughts and positive emotions will generate positive actions and behaviours.

Breathe in, *every day in every way*, breathe out, *I am growing stronger and stronger*.

Bringing all of these positive thoughts back with you now to full awareness, count each breath up from one to five.

One, take a slow deep breath all the way in and then expel every little bit of air in your lungs.

Two, as you take another slow deep breath in, you may like to wiggle your fingertips or move your feet around, and again, as you exhale, expel every little bit of air from your lungs.

Three, begin to roll your shoulders around or stretch your arms as you take another deep breath in, and simply let the breath fall out of your body as you begin to feel very aware and present.

Four, breathing even more deeply, you begin to feel invigorated and energised.

Five, breathing naturally and normally, you are now ready to allow all of these positive thoughts to work for you in your everyday life.

I am good enough

Let yourself become aware of your breathing as you relax your entire body. Either lying down or sitting comfortably, enjoy the feeling of nobody needing you or wanting anything from you for the next little while. With each slow deep breath in, feel yourself relaxing even more. If your mind wanders off from the breathing, simply bring it back to the feeling of your breath flowing in and out.

With your eyes either open or closed, feel your breath flowing in and out for the count of three breaths.

As you begin to read the following words, they will sink into the deepest part of your mind and be there for you whenever you need.

You have made a decision. From now on you will replace negative thoughts with positive thoughts.

Breathe in and out comfortably and easily.

You now think of what you can do rather than what you can't do. You think of what is possible rather than what is impossible. You think of what you can be grateful for rather than what you don't have.

Breathe in and out comfortably and easily.

No longer do you let setbacks slow you down. You have a can-do attitude. And because you begin to think more positive thoughts, more positive things begin to happen in your life.

Breathe in and out comfortably and easily.

From now on, if a negative thought pops into your mind, or somebody says something negative, you simply think to yourself, *delete*. In the same way you would delete junk emails, you now find it easy to delete negative thoughts from your mind. You realise the old thoughts were nothing more than a waste of energy. Whenever you feel the onset of a negative thought your automatic delete button causes it to vanish. And all you have to do is think *delete*.

Breathe in and out comfortably and easily.

You can enjoy the good feelings that positive thoughts generate. You begin to see yourself in a new light. You hear yourself saying things like, *I can, I will, I'll do it now, I am strong, I am good enough.*

Breathe in and out comfortably and easily.

Now concentrate your mind on the words that follow as you continue to breathe in and out with each affirmation. Allow each word to sink deeply into every part of your being. *I find it easy to turn negative thoughts into positive thoughts. I have the power to control my thoughts. I can do it. I stay positive. I choose to be happy. I am strong. I care about me. I have courage and confidence. Every day in every way I'm getting better and better. I do good things for myself. My best is good enough. I value my health. What I set my mind to I can achieve. I am in charge of my thinking. I am in charge of my results. Today is a new day and a new beginning. I breathe in strength and exhale fear. I breathe in compassion and exhale judgment. I breathe in calm and exhale anger. I train my mind to see things in a new light and think differently. I allow myself to be my best me. What I think matters, what I do matters, I matter. I am good enough.*

In your own time, allow yourself to come up with as many positive thoughts as you can. As you breathe those thoughts into your mind you feel everything beginning to change. Go ahead and do that for the next few minutes now.

When you're ready, bring your awareness back to your body. Maybe you can feel the air against your skin and hear the sounds around where you are, and you feel your breathing flowing in and out. You are fully alert as your body and mind return to total awareness.

AFFIRMATIONS TO RESET YOUR MIND

Love heals all

When practising this affirmation meditation, slowly breathe in and out, and let the words float on your breath.

Method 1

Breathe in	Breathe out
Love	*heals all*
Every day in every way	*I grow stronger and stronger*
I now release	*all negative beliefs*
I now release	*all negative feelings*
I now release	*all negative memories*
Love	*heals all*
I now allow	*myself to heal*
I am	*strong physically*
I am	*strong mentally*
I am	*strong emotionally*
Love	*heals all*

Method 2

Alternatively, repeat the entire affirmation as you breathe in and repeat it again as you breathe out.

I am

I am are two of the most powerful words you can say to yourself. Change your *I am* and you will change your life. Repeat each of the following affirmations twice. Read it first as you breathe in and out and then repeat the affirmation with your eyes closed.

Start breathing.

courageous appreciated inspired

confident amazing healthy loving kind

happy calm strong

open-minded relaxed

determined

dynamic *I am* powerful

good enough

empowered enthusiastic content

genuine positive worthy joyful

grateful

fantastic valuable

energetic optimistic satisfied

Stress less guide

Right now, all your stress begins to drift away. The more you allow your mind to absorb the following methods and suggestions, the more you realise how easy it is to relax and let stress go. And it only takes a minute to switch stress off. You'll surprise yourself how easy it is to stress less and let it go. There are thousands of ways to let go of stress, and thousands of ways to meditate. Following are a few of my favourite methods. If you haven't yet read Chapter 3 on stressing less (see p. 66), please read that now as it will help you prepare for the following meditations and mindful self-hypnosis scripts.

BREATHING EXERCISES

The countdown breath
In a minute or two your body and mind will become so relaxed that all tension will dissolve away. Either sitting or lying down, count each breath in reverse from 100 down, or from ten to one. You can count the numbers on inhalation and silently say to yourself the word *relax* as you breathe out. Feel your body relaxing as you exhale. For example, *breathe in 100, breathe out relax, breathe in 99, breathe out relax, breathe in 98, breathe out relax.*

    If you lose concentration, start again. Keep practising until you can comfortably count all the way to the end. If you find it too difficult, start at 50, 20 or even five, and count backwards from there.

The even breath
Each time you breathe into your abdomen, count slowly throughout the breath to five. Then as you exhale, count to five at the same speed. Time

your breathing so that each inward and outward breath are complete as you reach five. Keep your chest relaxed and feel yourself breathing the way you do when you are asleep. Let your abdomen rise and fall with every breath.

This practice allows your breathing to be smooth and even. As you learn to slow the breath, gradually increase the length of each breath to eight or ten. This method of breathing is a good one to use while practising qigong and tai chi. It helps to create a rhythm and evenness as your breathing and movement become one.

Holding the breath

Repeat the even breath method and then, when you have completely inhaled, hold for the count of one. As you practise over a period of weeks or months, gradually increase the hold to three or four.

For example, breathe in: 1, 2, 3, 4, 5. Hold: 1. Breathe out: 1, 2, 3, 4, 5.

You can alternate by holding the breath after exhaling.

Example: Out: 1, 2, 3, 4, 5. Hold: 1. In: 1, 2, 3, 4, 5.

The next level is to hold at the end of both inhaling and exhaling.

Example: In: 1, 2, 3, 4, 5. Hold: 1. Out: 1, 2, 3, 4, 5. Hold: 1.

Expelling stale air

Sit comfortably and upright, either in a chair or cross-legged on a cushion, or stand if that's more comfortable for you. Form light fists with both hands and begin by taking a deep breath in through your nose while raising your hands up to the front of your chest.

Breathe out as you open your hands and push forward with the hands reaching out as you lean forward. Exhale through your mouth as much as you can, making the sound *haaa* or *paaa*. Stretch your arms forward and extend your body leaning a little further forward as you exhale even more and expel all the stale oxygen from your lungs.

Feel yourself squeezing out any remaining air. Form a light fist and inhale as you draw your hands back to front of the chest.

As you inhale slowly and as deeply as you can, resume your upright position.

Repeat the movement from three to ten times.

Energy breathing

This exercise can be performed any time you feel as though you need an energy lift. It's best to stand up and change your physiology; however, the exercise can be performed from a lying down or seated position with no physical movement at all. You can also practise this breathing meditation with its movements while sitting.

Take a few moments to listen to your breathing. Think of yourself as a tall tree standing upright. Take a deep breath in through your nose as you reach for the stars. Stretch your arms up as you breathe in energy. Repeat the word *energy* in your mind as you stretch up. As you exhale and draw your hands back to your shoulders, say the word *power* in a breathy tone of conviction or think the word *power* in your mind.

On your second breath, stretch up and breathe in *energy*. As you draw your hands back and exhale, repeat the word *power* in your mind or aloud. Feel your thoughts moving with your breath as you fill your body and mind with energy.

On your third breath in, inhale as deeply as you can, stretch up and draw in even more energy as you think *energy*. Exhale and blow the word *power* out into the world and throughout your body, as you bring the hands and the power back to your body.

One set of three breaths should be enough to charge you up. However, if you do not feel energised enough after these three breaths, repeat the sequence until you do.

PROGRESSIVE MUSCLE RELAXATION

Do you recall a time when you were so deeply relaxed that every muscle in your body felt as though it was just flopping? An extremely effective way to relax very quickly is to perform a progressive muscle relaxation. You will surprise yourself at how quickly you master these exercises. Progressive muscle relaxation can be used as a stand-alone relaxation technique or at the beginning of a meditation. This is a great exercise to do at the end of the work or school day or just before going to bed.

Following are my favourite progressive muscle relaxation methods to try. As you relax every muscle in your body, deeply and completely, you will be training your unconscious mind to relax automatically.

Lift and flop

Begin by lying in a comfortable position either on a bed or on the floor, or outside on the ground. Close your eyes and begin to focus on your breathing. Tell yourself that there is nowhere to go and nothing you need to do right now; this is your time to relax. Feel your breath falling in and out of your body.

As you inhale, raise your left leg a few centimetres off the ground. Hold your breath and the position for a moment ... Now exhale and let it flop down like a rag doll.

Inhale as you raise your right leg just a little. Feel the weight ... Hold it ... Exhale and flop.

Breathe in as you raise your left arm a few centimetres off the ground. Hold it ... Exhale and let it drop.

Lift your right arm as you breathe in ... Hold it ... Feel the weight ... Exhale and drop.

Be very careful now, and raise your head about half a centimetre as you inhale. Hold your head up ... Feel it getting heavier ... Exhale and gently let it drop.

Let every muscle in your body completely flop like a rag doll.

Focus on your breathing. Feel what you're feeling now as you become more and more relaxed.

With each inward breath, count down from five to zero.

With every outward breath, quietly repeat in your mind the word r–e–l–a–x.

Letting go

Find a comfortable position to sit or lie down. In the next two minutes you are going to feel so relaxed you will ... float away ... This is your time to relax and just completely let go.

Allow your eyelids to become heavy but not closed ... as you read the words that follow, focus on your feet ... Maybe even wiggle your toes a little. Now, tense the muscles of your feet as you breathe in. Feel that tension for a moment and, as you exhale, let the tension go. Feel the relaxation flowing through your feet. Take a slow deep breath in and out.

Now move your awareness to your calves ... Quickly contract the muscles of your calves as you inhale ... and let them go as you exhale ... Completely relax, as you feel the freedom in your calves.

As you inhale, tighten your thighs by pushing the backs of your knees towards the ground ... Hold the tension for a moment ... and now as you exhale, just let them go. Your thighs become soft and loose. Imagine your legs are like a bag full of loose rubber bands ... Feel the letting go ...

Feel the relaxation flowing through your legs as you completely let go and move deeper and deeper into relaxation.

Focus on your buttocks ... Inhale as you squeeze your cheeks together ... Hold the tension ... and relax as you exhale ... Experience the sensation of letting go, as you free yourself ... Completely relaxed.

Imagine someone is about to drop a large medicine ball on your abdomen. Take a quick breath in and contract your abdomen ... Hold the tension ... and now relax as you exhale ... Feel the letting go ... Feel the relaxation.

Breathe in deeply and form a barrel with your chest ... Tighten your chest muscles ... Hold the tension for a moment then, as you exhale, completely let go ... Notice how you feel more and more relaxed as your mind and body drift deeper into relaxation.

Push your shoulders backwards as you take a deep breath in and tighten all the muscles of your back ... Feel the tension ... Hold it for a moment ... and exhale all the way out as you let every bit of tension go. Feel any tight muscles softening ... relaxing ... letting go ... more deeply relaxed than ever before.

Focus on your arms ... Clench your fists tightly as you take a deep breath in, tense the muscles of your arms as much as you can ... Flex your arms ... Hold the tension ... and now exhale and just let them go ... Relaxed ... soft and loose ... just like a bag full of loose rubber bands ... totally letting go ... Letting go.

Tighten your throat and neck as you inhale, clench your jaw and purse your lips ... Feel the tension ... and now breathe out slowly and deeply as you let it go ... Feel your jaw and neck softening ... relaxing ... notice how good it feels to let go.

Imagine someone shining a bright torch into your eyes ... Take a deep breath in as you close your eyes as tightly as you can ... Hold the tension for a moment ... and completely let go as you breathe all the way out ... Feel your eyes softening.

Push your eyebrows up and tighten your forehead like a drum, as you breathe all the way in ... Feel it ... Hold it ... and now completely let go as you exhale ... That's right, feel the brow smoothing out.

Let yourself become more and more aware of how relaxed your body is as you continue to breathe and relax even more deeply.

Feel the deep relaxation flowing through your body as you completely let go. Take a minute to focus on your breathing. With every outward breath, quietly and softly repeat in your mind ... L-e-t-t-i-n-g ... g-o.

In your own time, have a stretch and open your eyes.

AFFIRMATIONS TO REDUCE STRESS

Breathe in and out with each affirmation.

I am calm

I feel at peace, I am at peace

I release all tension

I am calm and in control

I release stress easily and naturally

I am peaceful and centred

This too shall pass

I let it go

Inhale energy, exhale calm

I embrace my stress

I am in control

Stress is a challenge I can grow from

I am relaxed and calm

I am safe and calm

Breathing is my power

All is well, I am well

Stop procrastinating guide

Think about everything you've been putting off and what you want to achieve in your life. The more you keep reading the positive words, declarations and affirmations that follow, the easier it will be to feel motivated, take action and reach your goals. If you haven't read the procrastination chapter yet (see p. 83), please read that first so you can get the most benefit from the following scripts. As you create an AM and PM daily ritual of reading these scripts, you'll notice these suggestions sinking into your unconscious mind and becoming part of your everyday life.

MINDFUL SELF-HYPNOSIS SCRIPTS

Stop procrastinating

As your unconscious mind records the following script, you'll discover taking action is easy.

Begin by sitting or lying down comfortably and allow yourself to focus on your breathing. With each breath you become more and more relaxed.

For the next few minutes, nobody needs anything from you, nobody wants anything from you, this is your time to completely relax.

Maybe you can notice the sounds around you. You can feel and hear the sound of your own breath flowing in and out. It's possible you can hear the sound of traffic or people talking in the distance, or maybe you hear the sound of birds or wind through the trees. Simply notice those sounds without judging them or attaching any story to the sound. Notice the sounds simply come and go. Keeping your eyes open (or closing your eyes if you've memorised the steps), take three slow deep breaths and then read the words that follow. Allow the words to float into your unconscious mind and from there into every cell of your body and mind.

You realise you have 1440 minutes every day. And every minute is precious.

You realise it's time to do what you want to do. It's time to take action.
I take action. Every minute is precious.

Focus on one goal you have in mind. Allow that idea or thought to float to the top of your mind. And reflect for a moment on what achieving this or reaching this outcome will do for you. Why is this important to you and what will it do for you? How good will you feel when you achieve your goal? With each passing day you find it easier to avoid distractions.

You are now aware that continued inaction is the old you, and the new you is a person of action.

The thought *I am a person of action* begins to run through your mind over and over.

I am a person of action. I avoid distraction. I am a person of action.

With each and every idea that follows – the ones that feel right to you – allow that thought to float off the page and into your mind as you breathe in and then, as you exhale, you breathe it out into every cell of your being. For any thoughts that really resonate with you, take the time to close your eyes and repeat the thought quietly in your mind several times. Allow these thoughts and ideas to sink into the deepest part of your unconscious. Breathe the following words into your mind and body.

You make the time.
I make the time.
Your goals are important.
My goals are important.
You now realise the time for talking is over and it's time for action.
I am a doer.
I stay focused on my goals.
I have an abundance of energy.
Every day in every way these ideas and thoughts grow stronger and stronger.

Allow all of these thoughts to sink into the deepest part of your wonderful unconscious mind.

In your own time, when you're ready, bring your awareness back to the present moment. As you count up from one to five, with each number you feel more motivated. Begin to take deeper breaths as you feel every word of the count up.

One, deep breath in, *my goal is important*, breathing out, *I am important*.

Two, another deep breath in, *I have an abundance*, breathing out, *of energy*.

Three, breathing in, *I stay focused*, breathing out, *on my goals*.

Four, breathing in, *I am a doer*, breathing out, *and a person of action*.

Five, breathing in, *I make the time*, breathing out, *for my goals*.

Take a deep breath in and stretch as you prepare to take one action step towards your goal.

Get things done

In this script, whenever you read the words, *I now allow myself to _____*, you should finish the sentence with the goal you have in mind and the action step you are going to take.

Sit back or lie down and allow yourself to feel really, really comfortable.

Take a slow deep breath all the way in, and hold your breath for a moment.

As you exhale slowly, let all stress just drift away, as you think the thought *relax*.

Take another deep breath all the way in and, as you exhale, *relax*. Continue to breathe in and out naturally as you let all tension drift away from your body. You could imagine any tension drifting away like steam from the top of the teapot. Simply be aware of the breath falling in and out of your body.

As you continue to breathe in and out naturally and easily, take a moment to pause at the end of each breath in. Repeat these three more times as you continue to relax.

Slowly breathing in, pause, and relax your breath all the way out.

Slowly breathing in, pause, and relax your breath all the way out.

Slowly breathing in, pause, and relax your breath all the way out.

Continue to slowly breathe in as you take a moment to reflect on what you would like to have achieved by now. Bring to mind one goal you will take an action step towards today. Think about, visualise or imagine yourself taking action on your goal.

I now allow myself to ___

If it is to be, it is up to me.

Allow this thought to run through your mind over and over, *if it is to be, it is up to me.*

If it is to be, it is up to me.

When it comes to distractions or bad habits you simply think to yourself, *I don't need it, I don't want it, I won't do it.*

I don't need it, I don't want it, I won't do it.

You realise you are a person of action. The more action you take, the happier you feel.

I am a person of action.

Remember what it feels like when you complete a project. You feel a sense of achievement.

I now allow myself to ___

I feel good when I complete a project or task.

And with every action step you take, you are making progress. As you make progress you feel a sense of achievement.

I make progress.

Every day in every way you feel more motivated to take action on your goals. You make your goals an important priority.

My goals are important.

And while you'll never find the time, you can certainly make the time, because your goals are important.

You hear yourself think, *I make the time, my goals are important.*

I make the time, my goals are important.

All thoughts of doing it later are instantly transformed into *do it now, do it now, do it now.*

I now allow myself to ___

With each passing day and each passing week, you find yourself becoming more motivated to take action on your goals. No one else will do it for you. It's up to you.

I take action on my goals. If it is to be, it is up to me.

You realise you have an abundance of energy, and the more you do, the better you feel. The more you do, the more energy you have.

I have an abundance of energy.

You find yourself every day doing what you need to do as well as doing the things that are important to you.

I now allow myself to ___

Every day you look at your action plan and you feel inspired and happy that you are doing things for you.

I do things for me. I make progress. I take action on my goals.

The thought runs through your mind: *I make a plan and stick to it. I get things done.*

I make a plan and stick to it. I get things done. If it is to be, it is up to me.

No longer will you sit around wasting time, because you are a person of action. The thought runs through your mind over and over: *I am a person of action, I am a person of action, I am a person of action.*

You find it easy to get up and go.

I get up and go. I am a doer. I am a person of action.

I now allow myself to ___

If the best time to plant a tree was 20 years ago and the second-best time to plant a tree is today, you realise today is the day, now is the time. With every project you get it started, get into it, get it done.

Today is the day, now is the time.

I get it started, I get into it, I get it done.

All of these suggestions are now embedded in the deepest part of your unconscious mind. Armed with these thoughts, you will become unstoppable in the pursuit of your goals.

Each day you remind yourself to make the time and that your goals are important. You find it easy to get things done, as you just do it. You are a person of action.

I am a person of action.

In your own time, count yourself up from one to five and take one action step towards achieving your goals.

AFFIRMATIONS TO SMASH PROCRASTINATION

Start breathing.

Inhale:　　　*I get it started, get into it, get it done*

Exhale:　　　*Today is the day, now is the time*

Close your eyes and repeat.

Inhale:　　　*3, 2, 1 get it done*

Exhale:　　　*I'll do it now*

Close your eyes and repeat.

Inhale:　　　*I make the time*

Exhale:　　　*My goals are important*

Close your eyes and repeat.

Inhale:　　　*I make a plan and stick to it*

Exhale:　　　*I get things done*

Close your eyes and repeat.

Inhale:　　　*I get up and go*

Exhale:　　　*I just do it*

Close your eyes and repeat.

Inhale:　　　*I am on a mission*

Exhale:　　　*I am a person of action*

Close your eyes and repeat.

Break your bad habits guide

Please read the chapter on breaking bad habits (see p. 103) before using these scripts. As you create an AM and PM daily ritual of reading these scripts, you'll begin to realise how powerful your unconscious mind is.

MINDFUL SELF-HYPNOSIS SCRIPTS

Break a food or drink habit

Sitting or lying down comfortably, take a slow deep breath all the way in. As you exhale, let your eyes close and relax your body. For the next minute or so, feel your breath flow in and out. You may hear sounds around you fading off into the distance. Let those sounds come and go in the same way that your breath flows in and out. If any thoughts enter your mind, simply notice them as you let them come and go.

Take a minute or so to slow everything down.

You feel your breathing slowing down, becoming calmer.

With each and every breath, you become more and more relaxed. Count backwards from three down to one as you let go of all tension.

Three, allow yourself to feel more and more relaxed.

Two, relax your entire body as you simply think, *letting go*.

One, deeper and deeper down, you become more and more relaxed.

Your wonderful unconscious mind now listens very carefully to the conscious instructions you will give yourself. You are in control. You have an old habit you wish to change. What is it? Name it. Your desire to do this old habit is diminishing.

You hear this thought run through your mind: *I don't need it, I don't want it, I won't have it.*

Think about the new you. Imagine seeing yourself in this picture being the person you want to become. Feel yourself being drawn towards **the new you**. This is the you that no longer has the old limitation, who no longer has the old problem, who no longer has the old habit. You see the new you happy and content with more options and new choices. When it comes to anything unhealthy, *you don't need it, you don't want it, you won't have it.*

I don't need it, I don't want it, I won't have it.

Ask your unconscious mind if it's okay for you to make healthy choices. If it is okay with your unconscious mind to make healthy choices, repeat the following thought three times:

I make healthy choices.

I make healthy choices.

I make healthy choices.

You are now mindful and aware of what you put into your body. You develop new healthy eating habits. Every day you make small healthy changes. You have no desire to put anything unhealthy into your body.

Continue to imagine, picture or think about yourself making new choices. You have made a decision; you have what it takes to become the new you. You really want this. It's important to you.

Notice how you look and how it will make you feel being **the new you**. Close your eyes for ten to 20 seconds as you think about or visualise the new you, the you who is content and happy, the you who is in control.

Bring that picture and those good feelings back to now as you count up to three.

One, breathing deeply as energy fills your body.

Two, you realise you can replace the old habit with good healthy habits.

Three, you are now free from the old habit.

You have unlimited options, you now make healthy choices, you are in control.

Break a behaviour habit

Sit back or lie down as you close your eyes and let your body relax. Imagine you are walking down a set of three steps. Counting each step down, you feel yourself becoming more and more deeply relaxed.

Three, breathing slowly and deeply.

Two, release all and any tension.

One, deeply and comfortably relaxed.

As you think about it, you realise you have an old habit you wish to change. Imagine you are looking through your own eyes and you can see the picture of you about to do the bad habit or behaviour. As soon as you bring that picture to mind, you tell yourself, *I don't need it, I don't want it, I won't do it,* and the picture disappears.

How would you like to feel or act instead? Imagine seeing yourself as the new you. You see yourself *in* this picture, *being* the person you want to become. Feel yourself being drawn towards the new you.

You see the new you happy and content with more options and new choices. When it comes to the old habit you realise you don't need it, you don't want it, you won't do it.

I don't need it, I don't want it, I won't do it.

You are in control.

I am in control.

Your unconscious mind now realises ... there's always something better to do.

There's always something better to do.

You have unlimited options and new choices now.

I have unlimited options and new choices.

Take a moment to picture or think about yourself making those new choices. Notice how you look and how it will make you feel being **the new you**. How will things in your life be different? You really want this. It's important to you. You have no interest in the old habit or behaviour. Your desire to be the new you grows stronger and stronger as you feel yourself drawn towards this picture. This is the new you, the you who is calm and content and happy.

You realise there's always something better to do. You tell yourself, *I don't need it, I don't want it, I won't do it.* You think to yourself, *I don't need it, I don't want it, I won't do it.* You feel this thought flowing through every part of you, *I don't need it, I don't want it, I won't do it.* You are content and happy. This is the new you. Bring up the picture of the new you, the positive thoughts and those good feelings as you count up to three.

One, breathing deeply as energy fills your body.

Two, you realise you can replace the old habit with new healthy habits.

Three, you easily make new choices now. You can do it, you know you can.

AFFIRMATIONS FOR CHANGING A HABIT

Breathe in and out with each affirmation.

I don't need it, I don't want it, I won't do it

I don't need it, I don't want it, I won't have it

There's always something better to do

I am in control

I am content and happy

I grow stronger every day

I make healthy choices

Change is good

I develop new healthy habits

I choose

My choices matter

I am stronger than my excuses

I control my habits

I say yes to good health

I believe I can

Every day I develop new habits

I am in charge of my actions

I am strong

I am determined

I take control

There is always something better to do

I can do it. I know I can

Sleep deeply guide

Sleep is vital to our wellbeing and the techniques in this book will help you achieve deep, restful sleep. Read the chapter on sleeping deeply (see p. 118) and then incorporate some of the following additional practices into your day and your bedtime ritual.

MINDFUL SELF-HYPNOSIS SCRIPTS

Blackboard countdown

Lie down in bed. As you become more and more relaxed and settle back, you let go of any tension, any stress, any worries.

Imagine in front of you there is a whiteboard or an old-fashioned school blackboard. You pick up a marker or a piece of chalk in your favourite colour, and in the middle of the board you write the number 100. Either feel yourself drawing a number 100, see a number 100 or simply think about a number 100.

Then in your own time – there's no hurry at all – pick up the eraser or duster and rub the number out. Rub it all the way out until the board is clear. Think of the word *relax*. Think of each letter of the word relax: the R, the E, the L, the A and the X. You feel your body completely and deeply relax.

As you become even more relaxed and you feel your entire body going soft and loose, you draw a large number 99 in the middle of the board. You see the two 9s, or you feel yourself drawing the two 9s, or you simply think about the two 9s.

And then you take the eraser and rub the 99 all the way out, until the board is totally clear and clean.

Take three slow in-breaths and each time you exhale, you think to yourself *relax*.

Then in the middle of the board, you draw the number 98, as you sink even deeper and deeper into relaxation. And maybe your mind begins to wander or drift away from time to time and that's okay because this is your time to completely and deeply relax. This is your time to soften and relax. It's okay to let go. See or think about the number 98. As you become more and more relaxed, you pick up the eraser and you rub the 98 out until it's gone. You now relax deeply and let go. *Letting go, letting go, letting go.*

This is your time to sink into a wonderful deep sleep: a healing sleep, a rejuvenating sleep.

You can continue to slowly count down each number as you write it on the board followed by rubbing it out and then thinking the word *relax*. If you lose count start again at number 100 and keep counting down.

Soften and relax

The key to a deep, quality sleep is switching off your internal dialogue and releasing any stress you've been carrying around during the day. By reading this next script and following the instructions, you'll learn how to let go of any tension and completely relax your body in order to bring on a good night's sleep. You'll surprise yourself at how easy it is to completely relax and let go of all thoughts about not sleeping.

When you're ready, lie down and make yourself really comfortable. Wiggle around until you find a position where you feel completely relaxed.

Either feel your breath flow in and out of your body or listen carefully to your breathing. With every breath, quietly repeat in your mind the words *soften* and *relax*. Breathe in as you think *soften*. As you breathe out, think *relax*. Allow your entire body to soften and relax. As you breathe in, feel your body soften and, as you exhale, feel your body relaxing.

There are many ways to completely relax and enter a deep, natural sleep. Sometimes, you're awake, and you feel very, very sleepy. Other times, you may be asleep and dream that you're awake. And sometimes when you're awake, you dream. Continue to breathe in and out without even trying. Just notice the breaths falling in and out of your body. Your breathing is natural and effortless. This is your time to just let go.

Think for a moment what *let go* means to you. Imagine letting go of every bit of tension in your body.

I get all the sleep I need
My body clock naturally sends me to sleep at night
I wake up in the morning feeling refreshed
I am happy to be able to sleep
Sleep rejuvenates me
I always sleep well
My mind feels calm and serene
I deserve this rest
I can sleep whenever I choose
My head feels heavy on my pillow
I sleep all through the night

Live pain free guide

If you're living with pain, I encourage you to try these different self-hypnosis and meditation techniques. Do them at a quiet time, with no distractions, and pay attention to which ones work best for you. As you create an AM and PM daily ritual of reading these scripts, you'll begin to realise how powerful your unconscious mind is. Remember, pain often creates stress, anxiety and sleep problems, which in turn boomerang back and create more pain. Be sure to immerse yourself in the chapters on stress (p. 66), sleep (p. 118) and anxiety (p. 185) as well as reading the chapter on living pain free (see p. 130).

PAIN-DISAPPEARING MEDITATION

Pain creates stress, which in turn creates even more pain. It often feels like a never-ending cycle. The following meditation was taught to me by a German psychologist in 1980. The psychologist had travelled to Tibet to study Buddhism for three months; she didn't leave the monastery for ten years. The psychologist-turned-monk explained that the purpose of this meditation is to become one with the feeling of pain rather than rejecting it, thus turning the negative energy into a positive energy, and turning the loathing of the pain into self-love. When you become one with the feeling of pain, it often reduces substantially, or completely disappears.

Before beginning the meditation, make a mental note of where your pain is on a scale of zero to ten, with ten being the most intense. Once you have registered the number, set it aside in your mind. Turn your attention to the thought *feeling*, as you replace the word *pain* with the word *feeling*.

Following are questions designed to help you become one with the feeling. It helps to close your eyes between each question so you can really tune into the answer.

For the next few minutes notice your breath flowing in and out. Simply watch your breath or feel your breath flowing in and out, as you allow yourself to relax as much as possible. Notice your breath falling in and out of your body without effort.

Bring your attention to the area of the feeling or sensation in your body that you had labelled as pain. There is no longer a need to label this feeling as *pain*. Simply think of it as a *feeling*. Notice how far in from the surface of the skin in centimetres or millimetres or inches is the feeling. Take a mental note of the distance you feel the feeling from the surface of your skin. Take a slow deep breath in and out and, as you do, notice the shape of the feeling. Give it a shape. What shape is the feeling? What size is the feeling? Now, notice the texture of the feeling. Is it bubbly, smooth, rough, sharp, rocky, fluffy or any other texture? Be aware of the texture of the feeling. Take a slow deep breath in and out as you notice the colour of the feeling. What colour is it? If the feeling has an energy in or around it that is moving in a certain direction, notice the direction that energy is moving in. Now notice on a scale of ten down to zero, with zero being no feeling at all, where is the feeling now?

Repeat the meditation.

How far from the surface of the skin is your feeling now? You may notice it has moved. Maybe it's in the same place or maybe it's moved closer to the surface of your skin. As you slowly breathe in and out, allow healing energy to flow through to that part of you and notice the texture of the feeling. Has the texture changed? What is the texture now? And if you could give the feeling a colour, what colour is it now? Notice which direction the energy is moving in. Would it be okay to move that energy and have it turn in the opposite direction? If that's okay, reverse the direction of the flow of energy. As all the energy in your body flows through to this part of you, notice on a scale of ten down to zero, with zero being no feeling at all, where is the feeling now?

Continue to ask these questions:

1   How far in from the surface of the skin is the feeling?
2   What shape is the feeling?
3   What is the texture?
4   What colour is the feeling now?

5   Which direction is the energy moving in and, if you want to, can you reverse the flow?
6   On a scale of ten to zero with zero being no feeling at all, where is the feeling now?

Repeat steps 1–5 between three and ten times.

GLOVE ANAESTHESIA SELF-HYPNOSIS SCRIPT

Self-hypnosis is a powerful tool to help you manage pain. One of the methods is glove anaesthesia, which is a self-hypnosis technique that helps you create a feeling of numbness in a specific part (or parts) of your body. This technique can help you reduce challenging feelings or eliminate them altogether. When you combine the power of hypnotic suggestion with imagination and visualisation, you have the power to change the sensation of what you are experiencing.

In some cases, this technique has relieved and reduced intense and challenging feelings temporarily. In other cases, chronic conditions that existed for years completely disappear and never return.

Before starting this self-hypnosis script, take a moment to notice on a scale of zero to ten, with ten being extreme sensation, where is your feeling now? Take a mental note of the number. Now use your imagination to absorb yourself as fully as possible in the following story. Find a comfortable place to sit or lie back and relax. Feel your body relaxing more and more with each and every breath. Imagine any tension or stress drifting away like steam from the top of a teapot or steam drifting off the road on a hot day after rain.

Take five slow deep breaths as you count down from five to zero. With each breath, allow yourself to be more and more relaxed.

Five, take a slow deep breath in and out as you feel every part of your body relaxing.

Four, slowly breathe in and out as you become more and more relaxed.

Three, take another deep breath in and, as you exhale, feel yourself completely letting go.

Two, breathe in and out as you allow your whole body to go loose and soft.

One, take another slow deep breath all the way in, hold your breath for a moment and, as you exhale completely and totally, let go of all tension and relax.

Zero, imagine you're inside a log cabin on the side of a snow-covered mountain.

Take a moment to paint this picture in your mind's eye. The walls are made from logs with each log laid horizontally one upon another. There may be a large fluffy rug in the middle of the room in front of a comfortable sofa piled high with soft cushions. On one side of the room there is a kitchen bench. The sink and open cupboards are filled with cups, plates and bowls. A sturdy timber table sits in the kitchen surrounded by chairs. There is a stone fireplace set into the wall. In the middle of the fireplace, small timber logs are burning and crackling. A cosy glow radiates out from the fireplace as yellow and orange flames hypnotically dance around the burning pile of wood. You feel very warm and comfortable inside. Outside, it's cold and snowy. Snow gently drifts down from the bluish-grey clouds that fill the sky. As you look out the window, you notice everything is white. The trees and shrubs are covered in snow. Everything is covered in a blanket of pure, white snow. You watch as fine, fluffy white snowflakes gently fall to the earth. Some snowflakes drift over, resting gently on the window ledge. Slowly, the pile of sparkling crystals builds higher and higher. You know at some point the crisp white snow will become too heavy on the window ledge and will drop to the ground. Maybe you can remember a time when you played in the snow, making snowballs or creating a snow angel on the ground, or if you've never been in the snow, you could imagine what this would be like.

You decide to go outside into the snow. You pull on your snow pants and your snow boots, along with your jacket, a beanie and your gloves. As you open the door, you feel the cool crisp air blowing on your face. Brrr it's cold ... Closing the door behind, you step out into this magical place of pure, white peace. The snow is approximately 30 centimetres deep. As you walk along, making footprints in the snow, you feel at peace in this cool white, wintry paradise.

Let yourself notice if one of your hands feels a little different to the other one. Maybe the hand feels lighter or maybe it feels warm or buzzy or tingly. Close your eyes for just a moment and take note of which hand feels a little different. Imagine now that you are taking the glove off that hand. As soon as you do, you feel the cool crisp air against your skin. Imagine now that you are reaching into the snow. As you hold your hand in the snow for a few moments, it begins to feel icy and cool, cool and icy. Close your eyes for a few moments and imagine your hand in the snow while repeating in your mind, *icy and cool, cool and icy*. You pick up a handful of snow. As you hold the cold, white snow in your hand, your entire hand and fingers start to feel numb. You know the feeling of numb. The same feeling you feel when you're at the dentist and you get a needle. The entire area becomes numb. *Numb, numb, numb.* Your hand feels so cold. *Icy and cold, cold and icy, numb, numb, numb.*

As you keep yourself focused on the thoughts of numb, icy and cold, bring your awareness to the feeling, and either physically move your hand to the area of that sensation or imagine your hand is touching that area. Let the icy, numb feeling flow into that area. Imagine that part of your body is now becoming icy and cold, cold and icy, numb, numb, numb. You know the feeling when you're at a dentist and you get that needle, and the entire area goes numb, numb, numb, just like an anaesthetic, everything goes numb, numb, numb. You may like to take a moment to close your eyes and think to yourself *cold and icy, icy and cold, numb, numb, numb.* Imagine you feel the entire area of your body covered in snow. This part of you is becoming cold and icy, icy and cold, numb, numb, numb.

As you continue to think the thought, *icy and cold, cold and icy, numb, numb, numb*, notice what's happening to that area of your body.

Slowly bring awareness back to your body and your breath as you gently wiggle your fingers and toes.

On a scale of ten down to zero, where is the feeling now?

EMOTION RELEASE – LET THE PAIN GO

There are times when pain results from not paying attention to our emotions. A simple and effective way to help reduce pain messages from your brain and connect with your emotions is to pay attention to what you are feeling emotionally. Ask yourself: what emotion are you feeling right now? Accept that this is how you are feeling. Is the physical sensation gone? If not, ask yourself, what emotion am I feeling now? Keep repeating the question, what am I feeling now?

Rather than ignoring or hiding from your feelings, pay attention to them. The key here is not to describe the feeling of pain, where that physical pain is, or to even say that you are feeling pain. You want to notice what emotion you are currently feeling, and then describe that emotion. You are shifting your focus from your physical experience to your emotional experience.

Some examples of positive emotions that we all experience are happiness, compassion, love, security, contentment, acceptance, playfulness, awareness, hopefulness, fulfillment, gratitude, calmness, completion, strength, confidence, invincibility, high energy and so on.

Some examples of negative emotions that we all experience at times are complacency, resentment, jealousy, anger, frustration, upset, irritation, anxiety, fear, loss, hurt, guilt, sadness, helplessness, pessimism, inadequacy, loneliness, shame, disappointment, rejection and so on.

The exercise is not to analyse or intellectualise how you should be feeling, but to simply recognise *what* you are feeling. Bear in mind that your emotions and the way you feel can change from minute to minute, or even second to second, with most of us experiencing a wide range of emotions every day.

Sit back or lie down and get very comfortable. Keep your eyes open or closed, it doesn't matter. As you tune into what you are feeling, ask the question: What emotion am I feeling now? Notice the emotion you are feeling at the present moment. What emotion are you feeling now? As you pay attention to your emotions, notice how that affects the feeling of discomfort in your body. Come back to the emotion you are presently feeling. Has it changed? What emotion are you feeling now? And as you feel that feeling and tune into your emotions, what emotion are you feeling now? Keep paying attention to your emotions and notice how easily you can transform what you are feeling.

If you find you are overwhelmed with negative feelings, immerse yourself in the 21 States on p. 202 to reinforce your positive feelings.

AFFIRMATIONS TO RELEASE PAIN

Breathe in and out with each affirmation.

I become one with the feeling

I acknowledge my emotions

I stay calm

I release negative thoughts

My sensations do not define me

My body is healing

This won't last, this will pass

I feel at peace, I am at peace

I can get through this

Release excess weight guide

The keys to successfully releasing excess weight are choosing healthy portions, controlling emotional eating and increasing activity. Once you've read the chapter on weight loss (see p. 144), explore the following self-hypnosis techniques to help with your weight loss. You can read these scripts in sequence or choose the one that you want to work with first.

MINDFUL SELF-HYPNOSIS SCRIPTS

Portions and food choices

Sit or lie down in a comfortable position as you feel the natural rhythm of your breathing. For the next little while, this is your time to reset your mind and change your relationship with how much you eat. Maybe you've been overeating; it's possible you have been binge eating. And sometimes it just feels like you don't know when to stop.

Take a few slow, deep, relaxing breaths all the way in and, as you exhale, simply think the thought *relax*. You may like to close your eyes for the next three breaths and when you open your eyes, allow the following words to sink into the deepest part of your mind.

I choose to eat small healthy portions. I listen to my body and know when to stop. I find when I eat slowly, I am more satisfied. I eat slowly. I make healthy choices. No longer do I need to overload my body with unhealthy foods. I choose to eat small healthy portions. I find when I eat light at night, I have a better sleep and wake up with more energy. I eat light at night. I prepare smaller amounts, I serve smaller amounts, and I eat smaller amounts. I eat light at night. I find it easy to eat less food. I choose to eat small healthy portions.

I'm now in control of how much food I put into my body. Nobody forces me to eat, I am in control. I make healthy choices and eat small healthy meals. What I put into my body matters. How much I eat matters. This is about being kind to myself. I form a wonderful new relationship with food. I find it easy to eat less food. I choose to eat small healthy portions.

Before I set the table, I set my mind. I eat mindfully and am aware of the amount of food going into my body. I now know when enough is enough. When I eat small healthy meals, I have an abundance of energy. I eat small healthy meals. I don't need more of anything; I eat small healthy meals. It's my choice to eat light at night. I only eat when physically hungry. I find it easy to eat less food. I choose to eat small healthy portions.

How I eat is as important as what I eat. I take my time and eat slowly as I savour the flavour. I give every bite of food my full attention. My food is my fuel and nutrition. I am in control of how much I eat and I choose to eat small healthy meals. I find it easy to eat less food. I choose to eat small healthy portions.

I eat what nature intended,
From the land, from the sea,
From the ground, from a tree.

In your own time bring your awareness back to your breathing and the feeling of your body. As you count up from one up to five, you are going to become more energised and more focused on making healthy choices.

One, feeling more in control.

Two, ready to make healthy choices.

Three, committed to eating light at night.

Four, remembering food is for fuel and nutrition.

Five, you only eat when you are physically hungry.

Emotional eating

Pay attention to the next few relaxing breaths as they effortlessly float in and out of your body. Relax and allow any thoughts of eating or food to disappear from your mind. Allow your mind and body to relax as you continue to breathe in and out slowly and comfortably.

You may find it easy to forget to eat for any other reason than nutrition and fuel. In the past, you may have eaten when you were sad, bored, lonely or feeling hurt. But you no longer need to eat for any of these reasons. Your unconscious mind records each idea and thought that is right for you. With each passing day, you will find it easier and easier to forget to eat for emotional reasons. You realise that no amount of food ever fixes the problem. You will only eat when physically hungry.

It's easy to forget. Can you recall what you had a few weeks ago, for lunch, on that rainy Wednesday? It doesn't matter, so you just forget all about it. Maybe you walked into a room and couldn't remember why you were there, you just forgot all about it. It doesn't matter now; you can simply forget. You forget, in the same way that when that person told you their name, and a few moments later you couldn't remember their name – what was their name? You just forget all about it; it doesn't really matter. From now on you will easily forget to eat for emotional reasons. You no longer need to overeat.

Close your eyes for three slow deep breaths. Pay attention to the relaxing feeling of the breath flowing in and out of your body. When you open your eyes, begin to read the following script and, as you do, allow the words to float off the page and into your mind and body.

My health is number one. No longer do I eat for emotional reasons. No longer do I sweep my feelings under the rug of emotional eating. My health is number one. Every bite of food and every sip of water turns me into a healthy, slim, happy me. I respect my body. I treat my body with the care and the respect it deserves. I say goodbye to unhealthy, toxic, fattening junk food.

Those foods are no longer for me.

Those foods are for the other people.

I choose quality over quantity and I choose quality over convenience. My health is number one. I choose to eat natural healthy foods. I only eat when I am physically hungry.

I eat what nature intended: from the land, from the sea, from the ground, from a tree. I eat what nature intended. I only eat when physically hungry.

I say yes to health.

From this day forward I will drink more water, be more active and eat small healthy portions. Throughout the day, this thought floats to the surface of my mind. Drink more water, be more active, eat small healthy portions. I only eat when I am physically hungry. I realise the more water I drink the more I shrink. The more I drink the more I shrink, the more I drink the more I shrink. Much of the time I am not hungry, I am thirsty, so I drink more water, drink more water, drink more water. The more I drink the more I shrink.

High-calorie foods, high-sugar foods, fatty foods are no longer for me. Those foods are for the other people. My health is number one. My food is my fuel.

I say yes to health.

I eat small regular meals and make healthy choices. Overeating doesn't solve any problems. No longer do I eat my emotions. I realise it's not what I'm eating that is the problem, but what's eating me. I easily overcome the challenges of life. I take action and resolve all challenges. I do other things to feel good. I phone a friend, go for a walk or do some other type of activity. I find I have more energy when I eat small regular meals. I eat when I am physically hungry. Small regular meals help balance out my blood-sugar levels and my mood. I am happy to eat less and make healthy choices.

I say yes to health.

If I have a setback, I don't give up, I get up and start again, I find it easy to eat what nature intended: from the land, from the sea, from the ground, from a tree. Unhealthy fatty foods are no longer for me, those foods are for the other people. My health is number one, I am number one. I only eat when I am physically hungry.

My food is my fuel. I give myself permission to make healthy choices.

I say yes to health, and I mean yes.

In your own time, bring your awareness back to your breathing. Notice the sounds around you, the feeling of air close against your skin, the temperature of the room, and feel your breathing flowing in and out of your body. You realise from this moment forward you only eat when physically hungry. As a result of reading these scripts you'll find that with each passing day you will outweigh any negative thoughts and negative emotions with positive thoughts and positive emotions. There is only one way to go from here, forward.

Exercise motivation

Allow yourself to sink into a really comfortable position, as you either sit back or lie down and totally relax. As you read every word that follows, you will be resetting your mind in relation to movement and activity. You realise your body is functional and your body is meant to move. Allow every word to float into your mind and into your body. Take three slow deep breaths in your own time and feel yourself relaxing as you keep your breathing with you. You may like to close your eyes for those three breaths and, when you begin to read, allow the words to float off the page and sink into the deepest part of your mind and body.

With every day of exercise, I feel more energetic. Exercise strengthens my body, tones my muscles and keeps my heart healthy. My body is meant to move and I love to move. The more I move the better I feel. The more active I am the more fat I burn. I love to move. Exercise improves my mood and lifts my spirit. Exercise energises me and helps me focus. Each day I get up with an energy I didn't know I had. With each passing day I feel more motivated to move.

I love to move.

Whether I go for a walk, go to the gym, go for a swim or ride a bike, it matters not. What matters is, I am moving. If I am able to go to a gym and I enjoy the gym, great, I do that. If not, I remember the most important thing: my body is a gym. The moment I begin to move I am exercising and I love to move. My body is a gym. Anywhere, anytime I can do some simple exercises, I can do incidental activity because I love to move. The most important thing is, I am moving. Every day in every way, I am getting stronger and stronger.

I love to move.

Every day I look forward to getting up and moving. I realise my body is meant to move. The more I move, the stronger I become. The more I move, the more energy I have. The more I move, the happier I am. Every day in every way, I am getting stronger and stronger.

I love to move.

With each passing day I grow stronger and stronger. I feel fitter and stronger than ever before. I now realise activity helps me turn back the hands of time. I feel younger and I look younger. My body is not meant to be sitting around all the time, my body is meant to move.

I love to move.

As you breathe deeply, you feel energy entering your body. As we count up from one to five, you'll feel more focused on your goal and more committed to your health.

One, breathe deeply as energy fills your body.

Two, you realise how much you love to move.

Three, and how much energy you have when you do move.

Four, you always remember: your body is a gym.

Five, it's time to get up and move.

AFFIRMATIONS TO RELEASE EXCESS WEIGHT

Breathe in and out with each affirmation.

I keep moving

My body is meant to move

I love to move

I have the power to change

I make time every day

I make time for my health

I have an abundance of energy

I am creating a strong body

I make healthy choices

I am what I eat

I eat natural healthy foods

I stop eating when satisfied

I control what I eat

I eat light at night

I eat for nutrition and energy

I find healthy alternatives

I eat slowly

I eat mindfully

I choose healthy rewards

I tune in to what my body needs

I only eat when physically hungry

I know when to stop eating

My health is number one
It's okay to leave food on my plate
I earn it and burn it
Unhealthy foods are for the other people
My body craves water
I am not hungry
I'm thirsty, drink more water, drink more water, drink more water
The more I drink the more I shrink

Live phobia free guide

Please read the chapter on fixing phobias (see p. 167) before practising the techniques in this section. Because phobias can involve extreme fear, I recommend you also read the first chapter (p. 19) and the chapters on resetting your mind (p. 34) and managing stress (p. 66) if you haven't yet done so.

MINDFUL SELF-HYPNOSIS SCRIPTS

Phobia free

Pay attention to your breathing as it effortlessly flows in and out of your body. This is now your time to let go. Find a comfortable place to either sit back and relax or lie down and get really, really comfortable. This is a time for you to learn new things and to unlearn unwanted behaviours, unwanted patterns, unwanted thoughts. And you will learn easily and effortlessly.

Start to get comfortable as you let your imagination focus on these words. Maybe you could drift all the way back to a time when you first began to learn. Remember when you learned to walk and you learned to talk. You learned many things to help you survive. You know you have a conscious mind and you have an unconscious mind. And your unconscious learns and stores many things.

Focus on your natural breathing rhythm. You effortlessly breathe in and out. Slowly count three breaths before you read on.

Imagine now a blank sheet of paper in front of you. You are going to write a manual for survival, a manual filled with strategies, techniques and ways of putting you in control. It's possible that your fear or phobia started from one single traumatic incident, or maybe you had taken on board another person's fear. It's possible you even took on a fear from watching a movie or even while dreaming of a traumatic event. It's also possible the fear slowly built up inside you over time. Because you weren't born with this fear or this problem, it was a learned experience. Therefore, you can easily learn another new experience. You can easily unlearn the old behaviour because it's time to let it go.

Take a few slow relaxing breaths as you prepare to continue.

As you lie there now, so calm, so deeply relaxed, count very slowly from ten down to zero. And with every number, you will feel yourself going even deeper, deeper down until you reach zero, and you are completely tranquil, you feel serene, completely relaxed.

Going down from ten all the way down, down to nine.

Letting go, further and further down, eight.

Completely relaxing, seven.

Everything becoming heavy as you sink deeper down, more deeply and deeply relaxed.

Six, all the way down.

Five, deeper and deeper.

Four, more deeply relaxed.

Three, completely letting go.

Two, all the way down.

One, and totally calm, totally relaxed.

Zero.

The thought runs through your mind, as you breathe deeply, *I am calm and in control.*

I am calm and in control. You are aware of your breath flowing in and out.

Problems of the past become just that, the past, nothing more than a distant memory, fading away, fading away, and disappearing for all time.

The new you is a strong, in-control and confident person.

I am strong, in control and confident.

And maybe you recall the paper in front of you, and you see yourself writing, *I am calm. I am confident. I am in control of my thoughts and my feelings.*

You think to yourself: *Every day in every way, I am growing stronger and stronger.*

You have found a new inner strength and all things from the past, all worries, all problems no longer have control over you. They no longer have power because they don't deserve to have power. You are strong, in control and confident.

I am strong, in control and confident.

You don't need those old problems, you don't want them, and you won't have them in your life. The new you is a strong, in-control and confident person.

I am strong, in control and confident.

The old feelings disappear for all time as you continue to become stronger and more confident with each passing day. From this moment forward, you'll greet each day with confidence and enthusiasm. The thought runs through your mind, as you breathe deeply, *I am calm and in control.*

I am calm and in control.

And you see yourself writing again: *I will live each day with confidence and enthusiasm. Each day I grow stronger and stronger. Each day I am in charge of my life.*

You will no longer allow external influences to affect you in any way. You will take control of your thoughts, your feelings and your emotions. The new you is a strong, in-control and confident person.

I am strong, in control and confident.

You realise you can be relaxed whenever you choose to be relaxed. All you need to do is breathe slowly and deeply, and repeat in your mind a phrase that is important to you. It may be, *I am strong and in control*, or *Nothing worries me. I have no fear. Nothing worries me.*

And you feel your confidence growing each day. You feel your stress diminishing with each passing moment. You replace thoughts of doubt with thoughts of confidence. The area in your mind where the old memory was stored just drifts away. Maybe it drifts away out into space and disappears. Maybe it just drifts away and melts out through your body, all the way down your legs, out through your toes, onto the floor, and melts down through a crack in the floor, through a hole in the ground and just disappears and melts down. Or maybe it melts down and disappears into the ground and vanishes for all time. But you find that place and you let it disappear. You let the old feeling go, the old memory vanishes because you have chosen to let it go. The old feelings are leaving you. There is no worry, no fear, no anxiety. Nothing to worry about any longer. The new you is a strong, in-control and confident person.

I am strong, in control and confident.

You are calm and in control.

I am calm and in control.

And your confidence grows with each passing day. Deep, deep down within you, you know what you need to do to be in control. Each and every day the suggestions you think now and the confident voice within you grows stronger and stronger. And you feel more confident, you feel happier, you feel more at peace.

You are aware of your breath flowing in and out. Take a few slow deep breaths and continue.

Imagine a situation in the future where you may have had those old, negative feelings. But this time you feel calm and in control. Paint that picture in your mind's eye or think about the situation with you in total control. You remain calm and easily overcome all fear. You are now in total control. You breathe slowly and deeply, staying calm. The thought runs through your mind, as you breathe deeply, *I am calm and in control.*

You will remember all you have learned. You will recall the right thing to do, the right answers easily and effortlessly come to you, because you are now prepared. You know what to do. You easily and effortlessly control your life and your emotions. You are now in control. You replace all negative thoughts and feelings with positive thoughts and feelings.

Take everything you have learned with you, slowly count up from one to ten. And with each number, you will become calmer and more in control. You will be more relaxed, more confident and stronger than ever before. And any time you need to use these resources, they will be there for you.

Counting up from one to two, become aware of your breathing. From two to three, maybe wiggle your fingertips and your toes. Up to four, becoming more aware, maybe you begin to roll your shoulders. Five, become aware of the feeling of your clothes against your skin. Six, you may like to roll your body from left to right or begin to twist your body and move a little bit and stretch. Seven, bringing your awareness all the way back, all the way back. Eight, maybe you want to stretch all the way up and take a deep breath in and even if you feel like yawning, you can do that. Nine, in your own time, whenever you're ready. Ten, you are now a strong, in-control person. You are now calm and in control.

I am calm and in control.

You know how to do whatever it is you need to do to be in control. You have the strength. You have the confidence. You have the control and the power within you. You are calm and in control.

This is your new life, confident and phobia free. You realise how silly the old worry was. You have learned to tap into those memories: those powerful, strong, in-control, confident, relaxed, successful, laughing, happy memories. You remember how good it feels and how at any time you can take deep breaths and count backwards to feel more relaxed. You can choose to feel happy by focusing your thoughts. You know how to stand up tall and roll your shoulders back. You know how to take a deep breath in, smile and look up. You are filled with strength and confidence, as you let every waking thought be one of confidence, of strength, of control. Any negative emotions are now in the past. Every day is a fresh beginning. Every day you begin the world anew. There is no need to live in the past. The past has passed. And you choose now to let it go because that was yesterday.

Perhaps you see yourself writing on your manual, on your page: *I choose to let go of the past because that was yesterday. I stand tall and roll my shoulders back as I breathe deeply. I am strong and confident. I release the past and embrace the present. Every day is a fresh beginning. Every day is a new day.*

Change your state

With each of the following positive statements you are going to learn how to create an unconscious *switch*, a positive anchor, that will allow you to reinforce a positive feeling and change your state.

Recall a happy memory, something you hadn't thought of for a long time. As the memory comes to mind, make a fist with your non-dominant hand. Maybe you were young and playing with friends or family, maybe you were at a party. Recall that happy time as you make that fist. In the same way you would adjust the controls on a TV set, turn up the brightness to make the image really bright. Turn up the sounds or the colour and relive that moment. Imagine you are looking through your own eyes as you re-experience the event. Let those feelings, those happy feelings, flow through every part of your being as you relive that time. Continue to hold that feeling throughout your body and in your fist as you see what you saw, hear what you heard and feel those good feelings of being happy. Maybe you begin to recall other happy times, other happy events. And allow those happy, good feelings to flow through your entire body. Allow those memories to fill you with happiness.

When the memory begins to fade away, relax your fist and open your hand. You realise there is no room for fear, that you can overcome all challenges, all obstacles. You can choose to feel happy any time you want to feel happy.

Now, recall a time when you were completely calm and totally relaxed. Make the fist again with your non-dominant hand as you see what you saw, hear what you heard and feel the good feelings of being calm all over again. As you relax the fist, allow that relaxation to flow through your body and join with the feelings of happiness. Now you feel happy and relaxed. Allow those feelings to flow through every part of your being, to fill every cell. Allow that feeling of happiness and relaxation to expand and grow. Double the feelings of happiness, double the feelings of relaxation.

Recall a time when you felt strong. As you recall that time when you felt really strong, go ahead and make a fist with your non-dominant hand. Maybe you were opening a jar or lifting something, or just talking to somebody in a strong, confident way. Allow that strength to flow through every part of you. It's possible you felt physically strong, mentally strong or emotionally strong. Make that image as real as possible. As you relive that strong moment, what were you thinking to yourself? What were you feeling? How were you breathing when you were filled with strength? How was your posture? And allow that strong feeling to now join in with the feelings of happiness and relaxation. And now every part of your being is filled with strength, relaxation and happiness. Open your hand and relax your fist for just a moment.

Now recall a time when you felt totally safe and secure. You may have been very young or it may have only been recently. Make your fist as you see what you saw, hear what you heard and feel the good feelings of being safe and secure all over again. Drift all the way back to that time when you felt very safe. It may have felt like you were wrapped in a cocoon of safety, very safe, very secure, very comfortable. And allow that feeling of safety and security to flow through you. As you relive that event, turn the brightness up. Make the image, the memory, as real as possible. And allow that feeling to flow through every part of you. And then join the feeling of safety and security with your feelings of strength, with your feelings of relaxation and with your feelings of happiness. And let that flow all the way through every part of your being. Relax your fist for just a moment as you open your hand.

Recall a time when you felt confident. Bring back that image, that thought, that feeling. Make the fist as you see what you saw, hear what you heard and feel those good feelings of being confident. Make that picture bigger and brighter. Make the sounds louder. Make the picture as real as possible. And as you do, feel that confidence flowing through every part of you, every muscle, every bone, every organ. And your thoughts are filled with confidence, as you relive that time. Relax the fist the moment the memory begins to fade.

And now allow that confidence to join in and become one with the feeling of safety and security, with the feelings of strength, relaxation and happiness. Allow these feelings to join together and become one as they flow through your body. And your mind is filled with thoughts of confidence, with thoughts of strength, with thoughts of safety, with thoughts of happiness. And allow that to expand beyond your body until you are radiating those feelings of being confident, safe, strong, relaxed and happy. When it comes to the old problem, you choose to let it go. You choose to let it go because those problems are in the past. That was yesterday. Today is a new day.

That was yesterday and today is a new day.

That was yesterday and it no longer worries you because you are worry free. You are fearless. That was then, this is now and you're okay now.

That was then, this is now and I'm okay now.

Any time you need to change your state, make that fist and remember the positive feelings of being confident, strong, calm, safe and happy.

AFFIRMATIONS TO FIX YOUR PHOBIA

Breathe in and out with each affirmation.

I am calm
I am in control
I am strong
I am safe
I am confident
I'm okay now
I release all fear
I embrace change
I am safe and happy

Reduce anxiety guide

Regardless of whether you feel anxious occasionally or you feel like you are suffering from anxiety and panic attacks 24/7, you will be able to increase moments of feeling calm and happiness as you train your brain to feel better. The more you practise, the more your feelings of calm and happiness grow. The following techniques are each powerful when used individually, but, when combined, the results are astounding. Learn them well and discover which scripts give you the best results. Each time you read the chapter on reducing anxiety (see p. 185) and these scripts you are a step closer to being anxiety-free.

BLOW ANXIETY AWAY BREATHING TECHNIQUE

Find a comfortable place where you won't be disturbed for a few minutes and then sit back or lie down and relax. Close your eyes and simply feel your breathing flowing in and out. Slowly breathing in and out for the next little while, you realise this is your time to simply relax, and for the next little while nobody needs anything from you. Slowly breathing in and out, become more and more relaxed.

To help you reduce your anxiety or totally let go of the feeling of anxiety, you're going to learn a very simple technique where, with several slow deep breaths, you can blow away and throw away anxiety.

As your breathing begins to deepen, be aware of where the feeling of anxiety exists within your body. Is it in your solar plexus, your chest, your throat? Maybe the feeling of anxiety is in some other place. Simply be aware of where that feeling usually is and, as you breathe in and out, imagine the feeling shrinking down. Imagine the feeling shrinking to half its size and half again, and half again. As you breathe into the feeling, keep thinking to yourself, *shrinking, shrinking, shrinking*. Imagine the feeling is the size of a golf ball or a marble. As you focus your attention on the feeling shrinking, continue to think the thought, *shrinking, shrinking, shrinking.*

As you focus your attention on the feeling continuing to shrink down to a small size, I want you to imagine with the next breath, like a vacuum, you breathe that feeling up into one of your shoulders. Once the feeling is in your shoulder, breathe the feeling all the way down your arm and let it flow into your hand. Allow the feeling to rest in the palm of your hand and make a fist around that feeling. Then, when you're ready, take another slow deep breath in and, as you exhale, open your hand and you blow away the anxiety, you throw away the anxiety. Blow it away and throw it away. You don't need to hold on anymore. It's okay to let it go. You can repeat this technique over and over until the feeling is completely gone.

MEDITATIONS TO OVERCOME ANXIETY

Change your state

The more you repeat positive thoughts, the better you will feel. Allow yourself to feel really comfortable. The only thing you need to do in the next little while is relax. Maybe you can feel your breath flowing in and flowing out and, if you can feel your breath flowing in and out, why don't you allow yourself to become twice as relaxed with each and every breath. You realise you have a wonderful unconscious mind and even though there are times when your thoughts may feel out of control or you may feel a certain way that you think you have no control over, the fact is you can change your state, and you're going to learn how to do that right now. The simple act of thinking a different thought allows you to feel differently. And when you feel differently, you behave differently. We become that which we think about most. Therefore, it makes good sense to think positive, uplifting, relaxing thoughts. As you relax, you can take on board all the positive thoughts and ideas that feel right to you.

Now concentrate your mind on the following words. Allow your thoughts to drift away as you feel your breathing flowing in and flowing out. Notice the calming rhythm of each breath you take. With each breath, allow a wave of calm to gently wash over you. Close your eyes for three slow breaths before slowly opening your eyes to absorb every word that follows.

Three breaths, eyes closed.

With every passing minute you have control over your thoughts. Your thoughts are wonderful and powerful tools. Your positive thoughts are uplifting and the simple act of thinking a different thought can make you feel better. Your inner mind knows exactly how to think of positive thoughts to nourish your mind.

What you believe about yourself is very important. As you sit back and relax, take on board all the positive suggestions or thoughts that feel right to you. With every breath you breathe in, you feel stronger and more positive. Every day you grow stronger and stronger. You are in charge of how you feel. You choose how you feel. Feel happy, breathe in peace and breathe out release. You know that you have the ability to change your thoughts and release the negativity. Welcome calm into your mind. The past has passed and you have the power to let it go. Today will be a good day. You are always so much more than you think. You are allowed to feel relaxed. You deserve to feel at peace. You are worthy and deserving. You are strong and can overcome any challenge.

If you feel negative thoughts trying to creep into your mind, you know that you can overcome any challenges. You can turn your thoughts around and return calm thoughts to your mind. Welcome the positivity back into your mind. Release the anxiety as you breathe out. You have survived before and you will survive again. This feeling is passing and you breathe in strength and calm. The way you feel does not define you. You are strong and you grow stronger every day.

Slowly breathing in and out, repeat the following in your mind:

Every day in every way I grow stronger and stronger. I am in charge of how I feel and I choose to feel happy. I breathe in peace, I breathe out release. All is well. I have the ability to overcome any negative feelings. I remain calm and positive. I have the power to change my thoughts. I release my inner power. The past has passed so I let it go. Today will be a good day. I am always so much more than I think myself to be. I am relaxed and calm. I am worthy and deserving. I choose to think positive thoughts and feel positive feelings. I can overcome any challenge. I can do this. I know I can. I am strong. If it is to be, it is up to me. This feeling is only temporary. I can overcome any challenge. I accept myself and release all anxiety. I am good. This feeling is passing. I take things one step at a time.

I have survived before, I will survive again. Anxiety and the way I feel does not define me. I am stronger and growing stronger all the time. I am in charge. I am enough. I feel safe, calm and at peace. I am centred and grounded. I am doing the best I can. I am in control of my body. I am growing stronger every day. My life is what I make it. I am not anxiety, it is simply an experience. I am as good as anyone else. Change is normal, I embrace change. I control my destiny. I continue to improve every day. I look forward to each new day. Every day in every way I grow stronger and stronger.

Appreciation

Expressing gratitude or appreciation as a meditation allows you to reflect on the people or things in life that you are grateful for. When you fill your mind with thoughts of appreciation and gratitude it's impossible to hold a negative thought consciously at the same time. This type of meditation is wonderful for reducing stress and anxiety while increasing feelings of happiness. I personally like to start my evening pre-bed ritual with an appreciation meditation. The Tibetan monks will include appreciation of everything from the universe to the smallest thing in their life. You may like to simply list three or four things or people you appreciate.

It's important you appreciate and express gratitude for those things in life that you are grateful for and you appreciate. My appreciation list sometimes starts with the stars, the sun, the moon, the clouds and rain, the atmosphere and air we breathe, the wind, the forests, the oceans, the animals of nature, my community, my car, friends, home, bed, blankets, pillow, pyjamas, my legs, arms, eyes and other parts of my body. I always include Linda in the appreciation meditation and that makes me smile.

You may like to appreciate the doctors, nurses and all people working in the services at this time. You may like to appreciate your neighbours or anything else at all that comes to mind. The most important thing is, this is personal to you. When you smile as you think of each thing or person you appreciate, the meditation is even more powerful.

You start the meditation by simply saying, I appreciate, or I am grateful for _____ and insert your list. Below is a sample:

I appreciate the wind and the rain

I appreciate the sun that warms me

I appreciate the farmers who grow the food I eat

I appreciate my loved ones

I appreciate this roof over my head that protects me from the elements

I appreciate my bed

I appreciate my life.

In the following space, take a few moments to write down what you appreciate. Then take a few moments to read through it as you turn it into a meditation. Or simply close your eyes and run through in your mind what you can express appreciation for.

Start each line with either: *I'm grateful for* or *I appreciate.*

_____

_____

_____

_____

_____

_____

_____

_____

MINDFUL SELF-HYPNOSIS SCRIPT

Clear your mind as you relax and get comfortable. Wiggle around if you need to and settle where you are most comfortable. Relax your eyes and begin to relax your body from head to toe. Sentence by sentence you notice yourself relaxing more and more.

Just let the breath ... flow in ... and out. Breathing in *peace* ... Breathing out ... *release.*

In *peace* ... out ... *release.*

Breathing in *peace* ... Breathing out ... *release*.

Feel each breath ... as you sink ... deeper and deeper ...
more ... and more relaxed.

Each breath relaxes you ... even more deeply ... than the breath before.

Feel your entire body relaxing, feeling comfortable and calm.

From the top of your head to the tips of your toes ... any tension just ...
drains away.

You feel ... sooo relaxed ... You find it easy to ... relax deeper and deeper.

At this moment ... it's as though you haven't a care in the world.

Nobody needs anything from you right now, relax ... deeper and deeper.

Letting stress go ... Notice how good it feels.

You are very aware of how relaxed you feel.

Your mind and body are becoming more and more relaxed.

You feel at peace ... your body resting ... relaxing.

Every part of you ... now relaxed ...

Every muscle ... every bone ... deeply deeply relaxed ... your body is
healing ...

Every cell ... every fibre of your being is deeply and completely relaxed ...
and even your thoughts ... relax ... drifting away like clouds ... high in the
sky.

Let any old worries, any old problems ... dissolve away ... like steam
dissolving ... disappearing. Tension ... melts ... away.

Any old doubts ... any old anxieties ... they just drift away. They are no
longer a part of you ... They are dissolving and drifting away.

You feel safe ... You feel calm ... You feel a sense of ... peace. And you
can hold onto this peace ... it is now a part of you ...

Everything is ... slowing down ...

You are growing more and more relaxed ... deeper and deeper. And
maybe your body is feeling warm and relaxed.

You don't need to feel stressed any more ... You feel so comfortable, so
deeply ... deeply ... relaxed.

In a moment you can count backwards from ten down to zero ... You
may find yourself relaxing even more with every number.

Ten, allow yourself to relax even more deeply.

Nine, letting go ...

Eight, deeper and deeper ... more ... and more relaxed.

Seven, you feeeel ... sooo comfortable ... sooo calm ...

Six, have you ever been asleep and knew you were asleep ...

Five, or dreaming ... and you knew you were dreaming ...

Four, or have you ever been so relaxed you wanted that feeling to go on and on?

Three, and it really is a wonderful feeling to relax ... and let go ...

Two, and maybe your mind is wandering ... just let it wander ... it's okay ...

One, this is your time ... to let your body heal ...

Zero, so deeply ... relaxed ...

And if you want to let your conscious mind sleep, that's okay ... because your wonderful unconscious mind ... can listen at a deeper level ...

Sometimes you're awake ... and you feel sooo sleepy ... and other times you're asleep ... but you're dreaming ... and you feel ... as though you're ... awake ... and that's neither here nor there ... but the interesting thing is ... your unconscious ... never sleeps ... so your unconscious can take on board any positive suggestions that you feel ... or think ... are right for you. Breathe the following thoughts into every part of your being.

All is well ... I am well ... My body is healing.

I respect myself ... I respect my body.

Every day in every way I am getting better and better.

I release the past ... and live in the now.

I embrace change ... change is good.

I accept myself and love myself.

I matter ... I really do.

What I do matters.

I breathe in strength and breathe out fear.

I am here ... I am me ... I am free.

As you bring your awareness back to the present moment slowly count yourself up from one to five.

One, breathe deeply in and out as you feel your lungs expanding and relaxing.

Two, continue breathing in and out as you feel energy flowing through your body.

Three, you're feeling calm and in control.
Four, stretch your arms and legs.
Five, bring your awareness back to the present moment.

AFFIRMATIONS TO RELEASE ANXIETY

Breathe in and out with each affirmation.
I handle life's challenges
I stop and breathe
I am present
I am here, I am me, I am free
I am calm. I am in control
I stay calm, I am calm
I feel at peace, I am at peace
This too shall pass
I am a survivor and I am strong
I can do anything
I step outside my comfort zones
I am enough
I have unlimited potential
I allow my inner compass to guide me
I give myself permission to release the past
Challenges only make me stronger
I am grateful
I release the past
To change my life, I change my thinking

WHAT'S NEXT

If you're ready to increase calm, reduce stress, control pain, sleep better and feel happier, I've created the Mind Free app to help you 24 hours a day, seven days a week. You will have your own meditation teacher, hypnotherapist and motivation coach with you at all times to help you overcome life's biggest challenges. And the best part is all you have to do is sit back, close your eyes and listen. It's that simple.

In the Mind Free app you'll find:

- more than 400 audio and video sessions to help you transform your life
- a lifetime subscription for a mindset of health and happiness
- every Think Slim audio and video session ever published
- every pain control hypnosis session we have ever created
- the entire range of Phobia Free, Think Calm, Think Sleep and Think Quit audio and video sessions
- new sessions added regularly.

Visit mindfreeapp.com, check out Mind Free app on the App Store or Google Play store, or call (+61) 1300 760 073.

You can also join myself and the Mind Free team at one of our Innermakeover retreats, seminars or virtual weekends. When you attend a retreat, you learn to let go of what has been holding you back and you can reset and recharge.

At every retreat you learn to:

- break bad habits and transform your life
- control pain and enhance your quality of life
- eliminate cravings and learn to eat mindfully
- harness your mind power to reduce stress
- relieve anxiety and improve sleep.

Visit innermakeover.com.au for the retreat schedule, more information and to be inspired by some of our amazing transformations and success stories.

ACKNOWLEDGMENTS

Generation after generation, the master teaches the student and the student proceeds to become the teacher. Spring returns and the cycle continues.

This book is dedicated to those teachers who for thousands of years have devoted their lives to learning, and to passing on their lessons for healthier, happier and more peaceful living.

I express my gratitude to *my* teachers, for without your lessons and years of training this book would not exist. I offer my heartfelt thanks to Brian Watts – jujutsu, John Harbor – jujutsu, Pat Halloran – tai chi, Dr Tennyson Yiu – tai chi and qigong, Run Yang Wu – tai chi, Samson Quan – qigong, Gita Bellin – Tibetan meditation, Ben Adcock – Tibetan meditation, and Tad James – hypnotherapy.

To Brady Halls: a thousand thanks for introducing me to people whose personal challenges and ultimate bravery helped shape this book. Thank you for believing in my work enough to share a few of these stories to inspire others.

I acknowledge and give thanks to the fabulous team at Murdoch Books for believing in this project, and without whose support and patience we would have a very different book: to the wonderful Lou Johnson, thank you for backing *Mind Free* from day one; much appreciation to my ever-enthusiastic publisher Corinne Roberts; and thank you to both Justin Wolfers, my encouraging editorial manager, and Megan Pigott, the head of creative for your enthusiasm and flexibility. Special thanks to Alexandra Payne, my editor extraordinaire, who worked with me every step of the way to ensure my rambling and writing was on point and readable.

Completing this book has been a 23-year project. To my mother, Lynnie, who will tell you she taught me everything I know: your obsessive reviewing of my drafts was invaluable. Your constant encouragement, support and positive belief is in my DNA – thank you.

To my mother in-law, Valli Kneale: every minute with you was a lesson in love, acceptance and gratitude. You lived the 21 States and inspired this chapter. If ever there was an angel on Earth, you are it. Thank you.

To my soul mate and beautiful wife, Linda: every coach needs a coach – you are my life coach, my nutrition coach and my happiness coach. Your unending support, encouragement and inspiration lift me to do more and to be more. For your patience, limitless love and always positive energy, I thank you from the bottom of my heart. If not for you, my undertakings and realities, including this book, would still be dreams.

To the thousands who have attended retreats or private sessions, your questions, your feedback and your strength to rise above your challenges has inspired every page of this book. You have my eternal gratitude and respect.

Importantly, I thank *you*, my reader, for putting your faith in these writings to help transform your life. I wish you empowerment and joy. This book is for you.

ABOUT THE AUTHOR

From the age of eight, Mark Stephens began learning yoga breathing and meditation to help counter the effects of chronic asthma. Trained by traditional Japanese masters, Tibetan monks and Chinese teachers, he is a Master Practitioner of Hypnosis, jujutsu black belt and tai chi teacher and is dedicated to sharing his many years of experience with meditation and self-hypnosis to improve the lives of others.

In a career spanning several decades, Mark has transformed many lives. He's worked with a world number one tennis player and elite sporting teams to turn around bad seasons through to war survivors, CEOs and thousands of everyday people.

Mark created the ground-breaking Think Slim, Think Calm, Think Sleep and Think Quit programs and the Mind Free app (mindfreeapp. com). When he is not running sessions at his Little Forest Health Retreat, he is a regular guest media expert and conference keynote speaker.